STREET FIGHTER®
WORLD WARRIOR ENCYCLOPEDIA

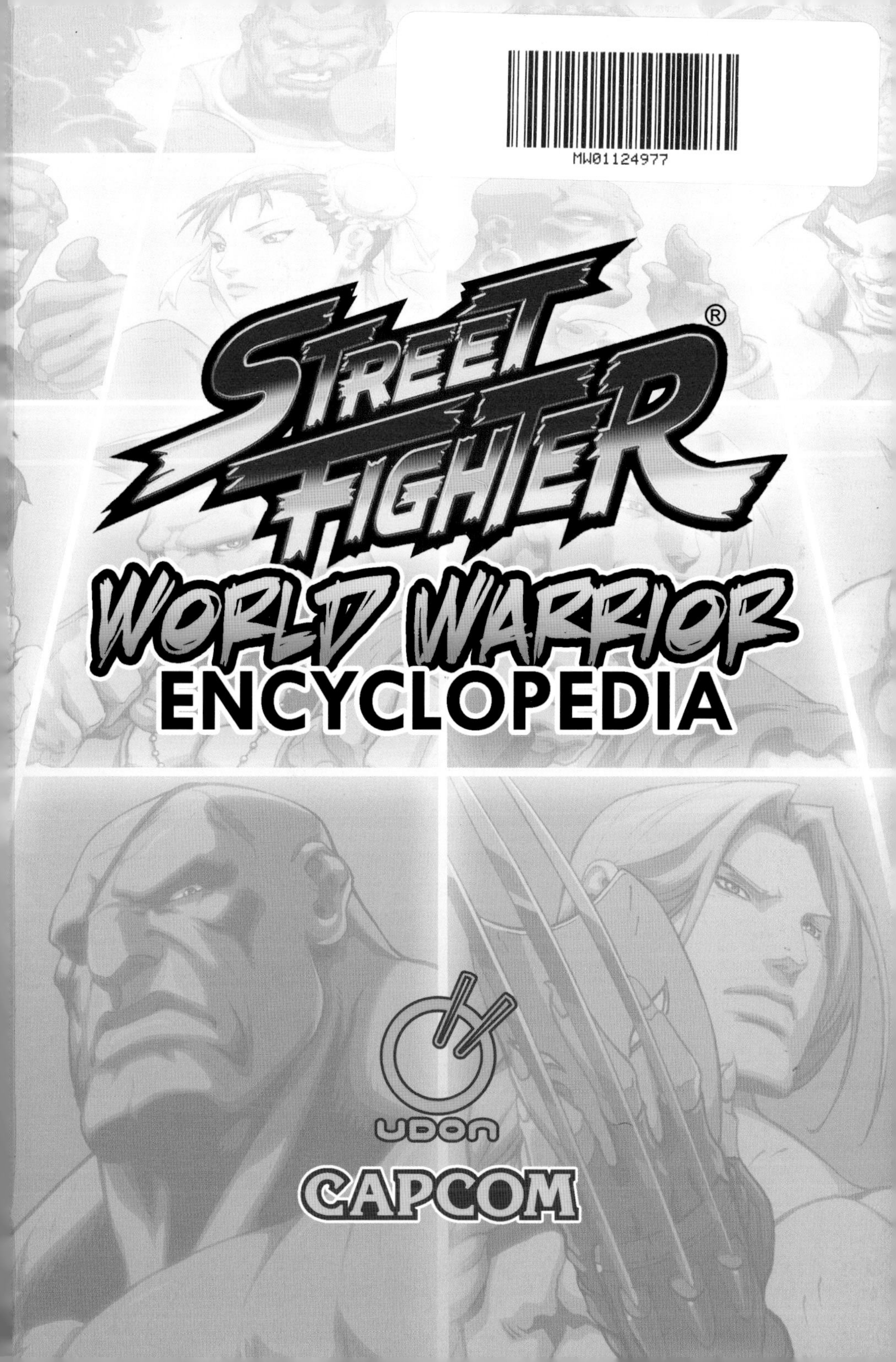

UDON

CAPCOM

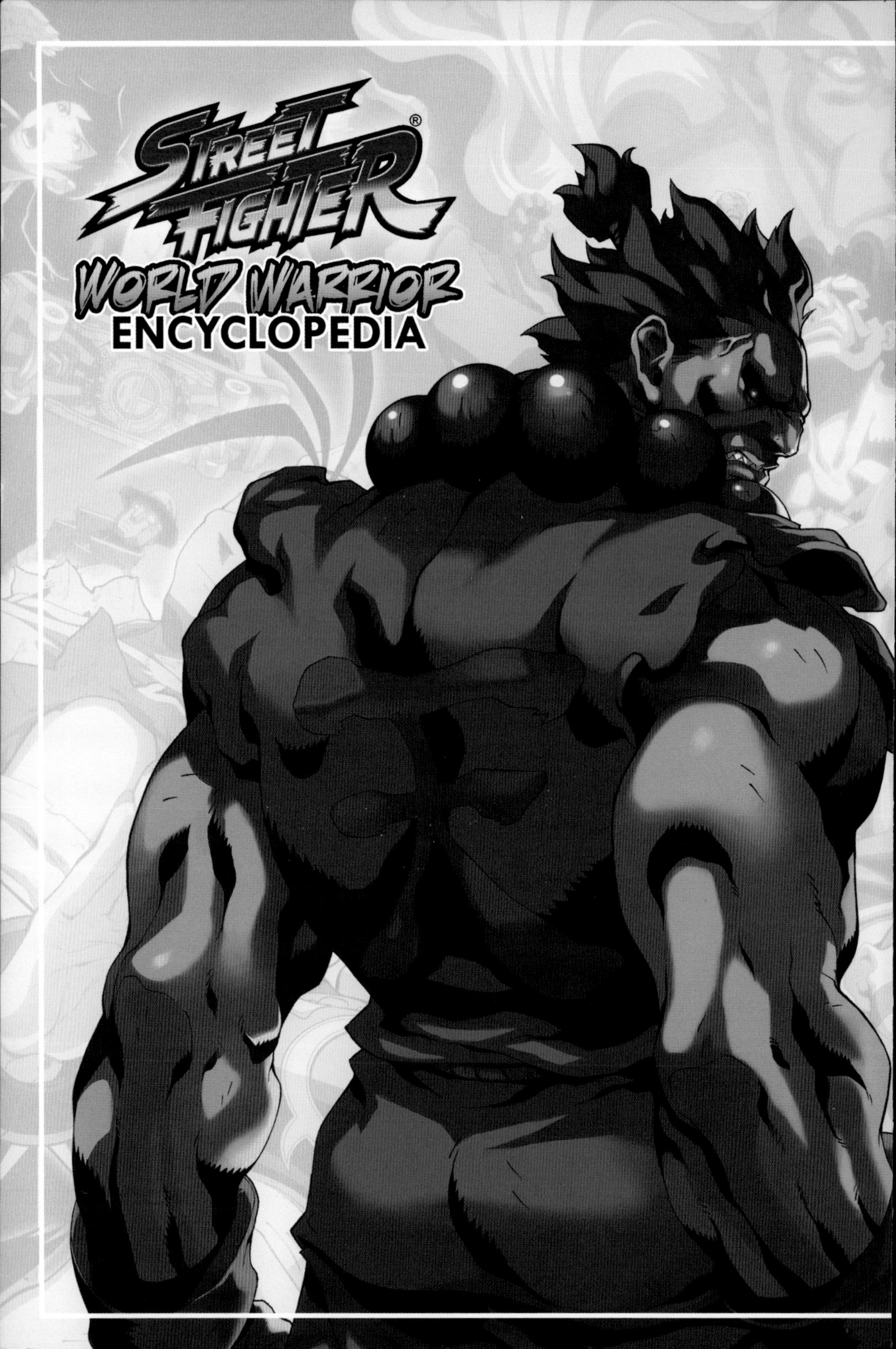
STREET FIGHTER®
WORLD WARRIOR
ENCYCLOPEDIA

FOREWORD

I'll admit it — I'm not that great of a *Street Fighter* player. I don't know anything about frame data, hit priority, or how to pull off a Shun Goku Satsu. I pretty much always choose Ryu or, on an especially adventurous day, Ken. So I'm not going to be winning any tournaments any time soon… but I still love the *Street Fighter* universe.

It's been revealed only piece by piece over the years - a game ending here, some character dialogue there. But in the twenty-plus years since the first game, the world of *Street Fighter* has grown into a rich one full of unique characters, each with their own drives, goals, and relationships. *Street Fighter* history is filled with bitter rivalries, life-long friendships, grave injustices, and hard fought victories. Old heroes fall from grace, while enemies become allies. Wrestlers, ninjas, and martial artists fight alongside cyborgs, school girls and even an electric green man-beast. *Street Fighter* has it all.

This book is meant to be your ultimate guide to the *Street Fighter* universe. The information within was researched through a variety of official sources — game endings, game documentation, discussions with the *Street Fighter* producers, and Japanese source books such as *Street Fighter: Eternal Challenge* and *All About Street Fighter*. I had a lot of fun putting this together and hope all you *Street Fighter* fans out there enjoy it as well.

The whole *Street Fighter* universe is now at your finger tips, and you didn't even have to defeat Sheng Long!

~MATT MOYLAN
Managing Editor
UDON Entertainment

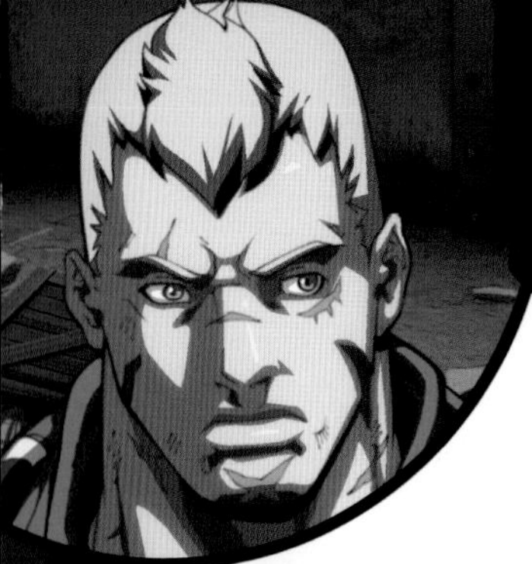

ABEL

The Man Without a Past

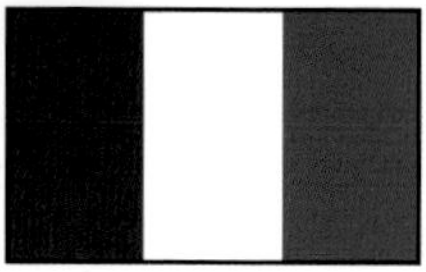

BIRTHDAY: November 5
COUNTRY OF ORIGIN: France
FIGHTING STYLE: Mixed martial arts based in Judo
HEIGHT: 198 cm **WEIGHT:** 85 kg
MEASUREMENTS: B130/W85/H89
BLOOD TYPE: A
LIKES: Dogs
DISLIKES: Oysters (once gave him food poisoning)
SPECIAL ABILITIES: Sewing

Abel is a former mercenary who is searching for clues about his true origins. He utilizes a mixed martial arts fighting style that he picked up from his mercenary training.

Abel can only recall the past five years of his life. His first memory is of a mysterious figure rescuing him from a burning building. After the fire, Abel awoke in a hospital bed under the care of a French mercenary, but his mysterious savior had vanished. The French mercenary took Abel into his freelance military unit, teaching Abel everything he knew about combat . The mercenary quickly became a surrogate father to the young amnesiac. His new father gave him only one rule: no matter what, Abel was to stay away from S.I.N. and Shadaloo.

After this father figure was killed in a car crash, Abel decided he must seek out the truth about his past. Shadaloo was the only place he could get those answers. He would eventually learn that the man who had saved his life five years ago was named Charlie Nash. Abel's father and Charlie had met during maneuvers with the USAF, and he was the only person Charlie could trust to care for Abel after the fire.

Abel did not learn the full story of his connections to Shadaloo until an encounter with Seth. Both Seth and Abel were early products of M.Bison's "Living Incubator" program, a plan developed alongside the "Doll" program with the goal of creating an endless line of replacement bodies for Bison's consciousness. Considered defective, Abel was discarded and meant to be destroyed until a military operative, Charlie Nash, discovered his unconscious body while infiltrating a Shadaloo base. Viewing Abel as an innocent, Charlie decided to rescue him shortly before destroying the facility.

Because he is so polite and proper, some people get the impression that Abel is not very friendly. Charlie was the one who named Abel, just before returning to his mission against Shadaloo. Abel has a pet dog, which he rescued from the street during a stormy day. He has also become quite skilled at sewing, after having to repair his own clothes so many times in his mercenary days.

FIGHTING STYLE

Abel is a mixed martial artist who uses grapples and throws to confuse and wear down his opponents. He's also quite aggressive, and isn't afraid to get right in another fighter's face. He's fond of rolls, which allow him to both avoid enemy strikes and get in close to perform a devastating attack.

SIGNATURE MOVES: Marseilles Roll, Tornado Throw, Wheel Kick

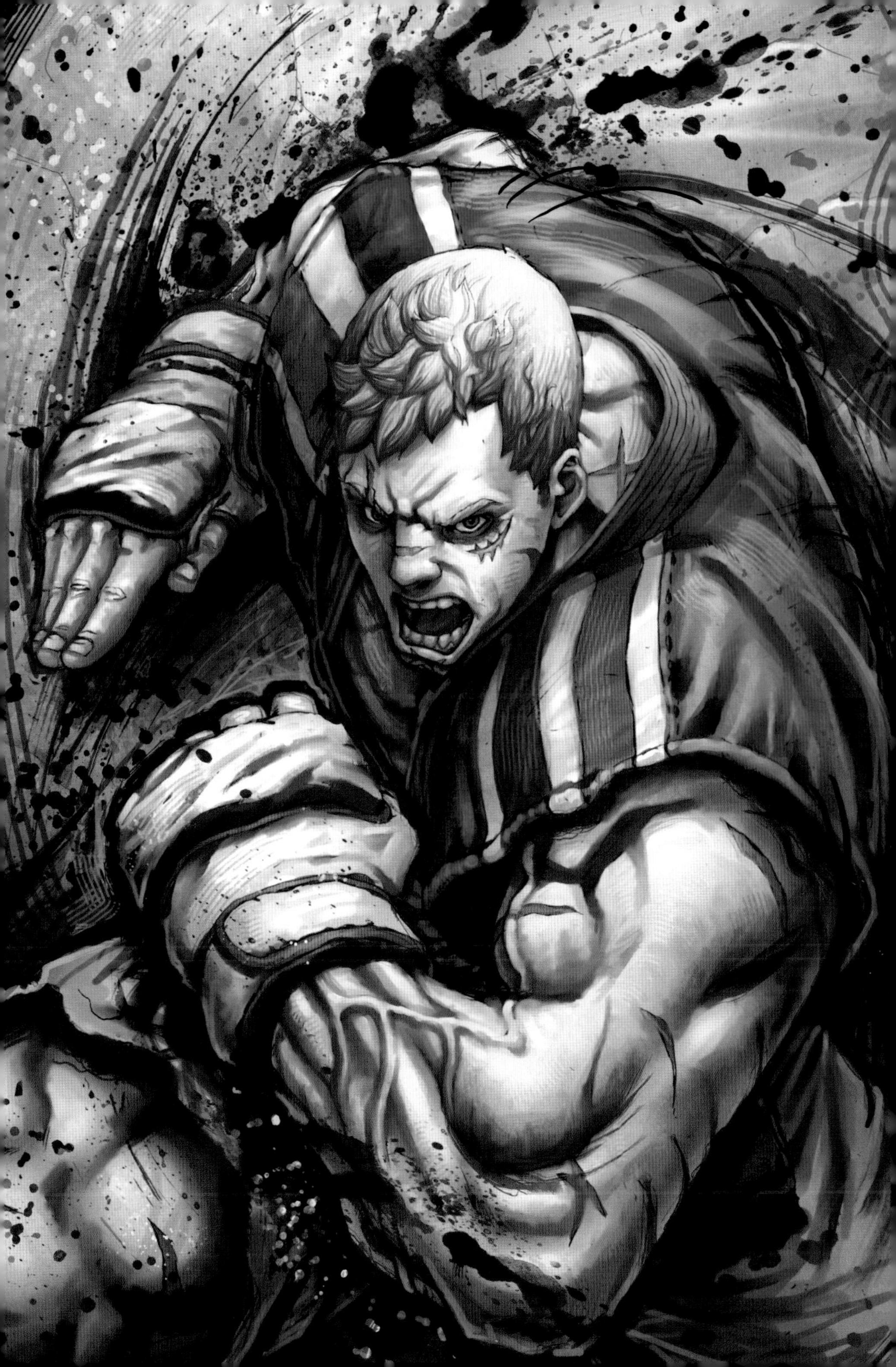

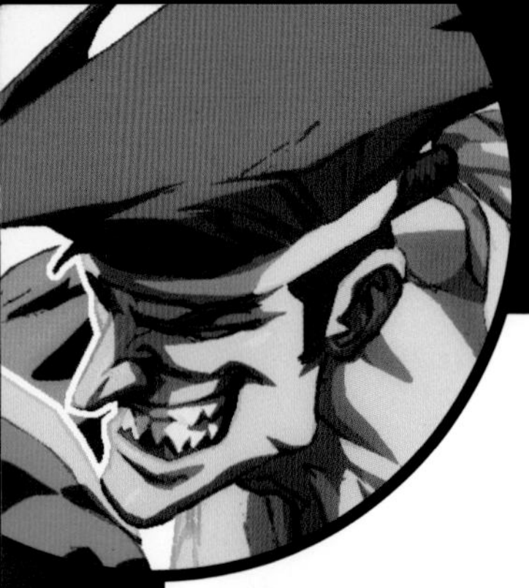

ADON

The Wild Jaguar

BIRTHDAY: ---------
COUNTRY OF ORIGIN: Thailand
FIGHTING STYLE: Muay Thai
HEIGHT: 182 cm **WEIGHT:** 73 kg
MEASUREMENTS: B112/W80/H85
BLOOD TYPE: B
LIKES: Muay Thai
DISLIKES: Sagat, people who talk big
SPECIAL ABILITIES: Waiku (a dance of Muay Thai)

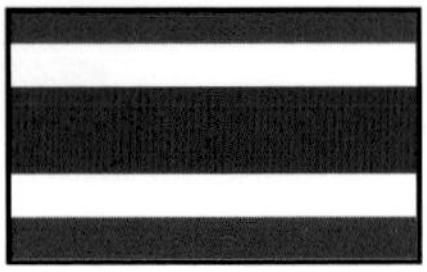

Adon is a Muay Thai expert who favors quick, speedy attacks. He studied under Sagat, the Emperor of Muay Thai. Adon was Sagat's best student, and can actually move faster than his master.

Infuriated by the news that his master, whom he believed to be invincible, was defeated by an unknown Japanese fighter (Ryu), Adon rejected Sagat as his mentor. He embarked on a quest to prove that he and the style of Muay Thai are destined to be the greatest in the world.

Having learned that Ryu's use of the Satsui no Hado allowed him to defeat Sagat, Adon became interested in the dark art, wishing to bring its power into Muay Thai. Adon began searching the world for Akuma, the ultimate practitioner of the Satsui no Hado, in order to learn the secret of this deadly power.

Although Adon acts quite youthful, he is actually very close in age to Sagat. He was also once offered a position in Shadaloo by M. Bison, but turned it down.

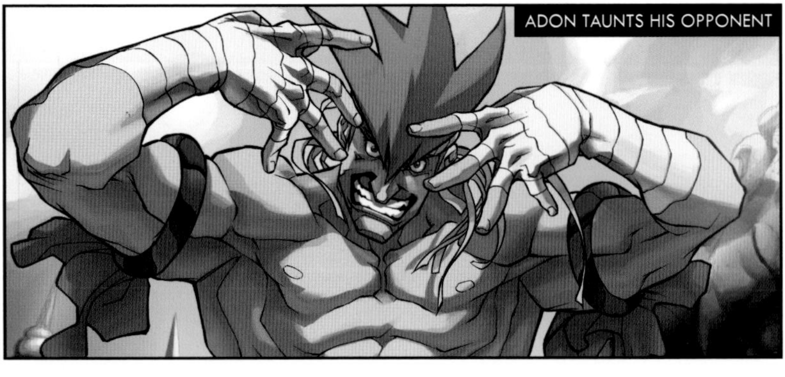
ADON TAUNTS HIS OPPONENT

FIGHTING STYLE

Adon's fighting style grew from Sagat's own and is built upon heavy special attacks mixed with light footwork and the potential for repetitive strikes to batter his foes into defeat. The persistent speed of his acrobatic movements is punctuated with the deep determination to succeed at any cost.

SIGNATURE MOVES: Rising Jaguar, Jaguar Kick, Jaguar Tooth

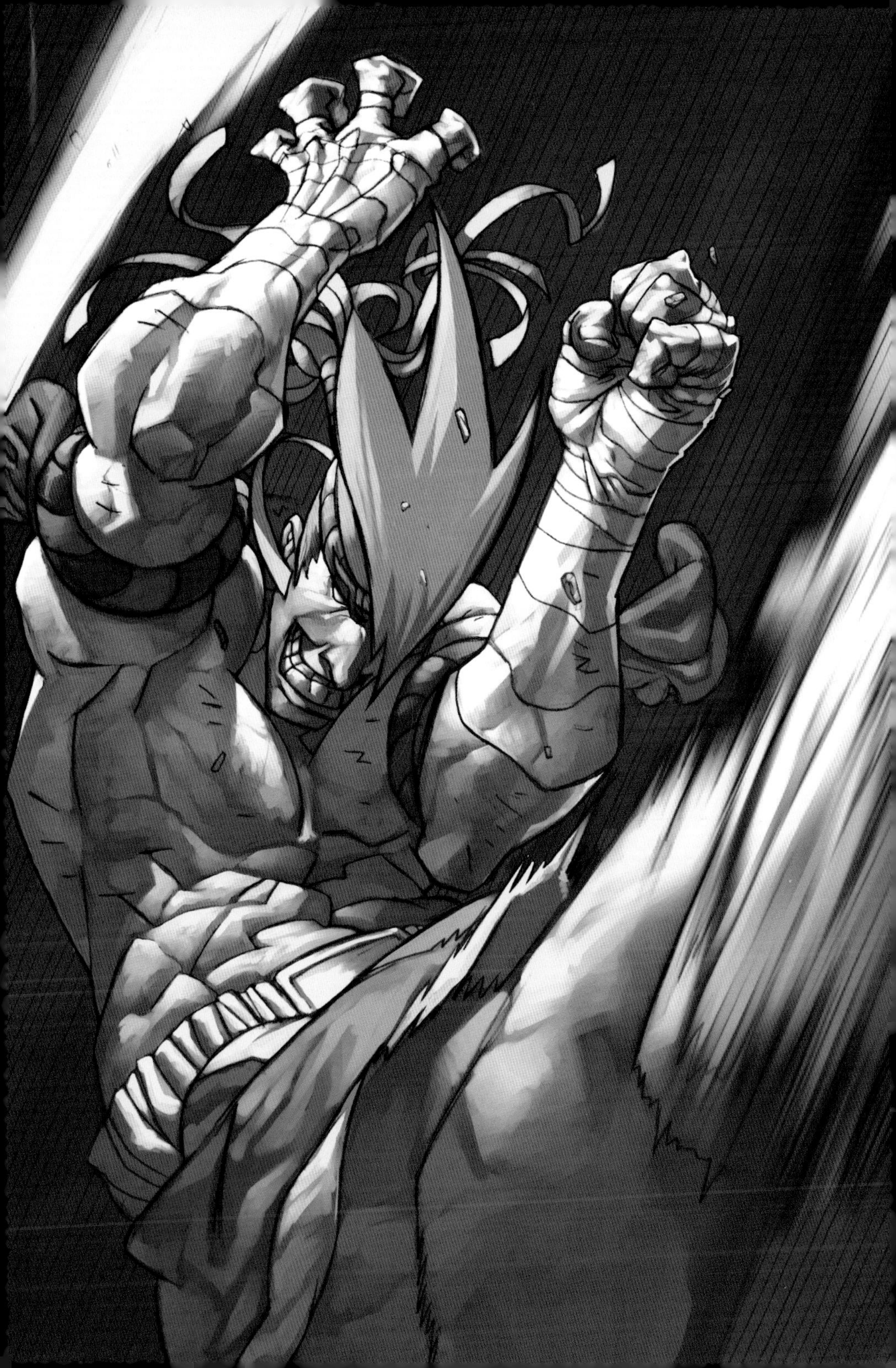

AKUMA
Master of the Fist

BIRTHDAY: Unknown
COUNTRY OF ORIGIN: Japan
FIGHTING STYLE: Martial Arts rooted in Ansatsuken
HEIGHT: 178 cm   **WEIGHT:** 85 kg
MEASUREMENTS: B118/W84/H86
BLOOD TYPE: Unknown
LIKES: Unknown
DISLIKES: Unknown
SPECIAL ABILITIES: Unknown

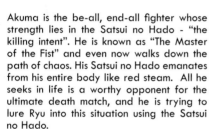

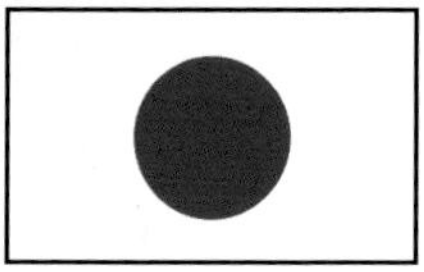

Akuma is the be-all, end-all fighter whose strength lies in the Satsui no Hado - "the killing intent". He is known as "The Master of the Fist" and even now walks down the path of chaos. His Satsui no Hado emanates from his entire body like red steam. All he seeks in life is a worthy opponent for the ultimate death match, and he is trying to lure Ryu into this situation using the Satsui no Hado.

Akuma trained under Goutetsu, alongside his brother Gouken, in the martial art of Ansatsuken (the Assassin's Fist). Overwhelmed by his desire to be the ultimate force, Akuma gave in to the Satsui no Hado and murdered his master. Later, Akuma also killed his brother Gouken, master to Ryu and Ken, using the Satsui no Hado. After committing these extreme acts of betrayal, Akuma vanished without a trace, only to reappear to challenge M. Bison during the Street Fighter Tournament.

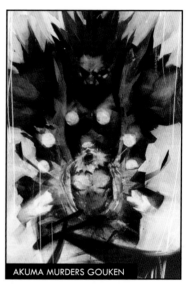

AKUMA MURDERS GOUKEN

Akuma has discovered rare sources of enjoyment in Ryu, who carries within him a potential to unlock the Satsui no Hado, as well as Gen, an assassin who fights using the Ansatsuken.

FIGHTING STYLE

Since he studied the same basic style as Ryu and Ken, a lot of Akuma's techniques are very similar to theirs. However, the evil of the Satsui no Hado augments these moves to make them far more damaging. In addition, Akuma has perfected several unique maneuvers, including his trademark, the dreaded and destructive Shun Goku Satsu, also known as the Raging Demon.

SIGNATURE MOVES: Ashura Senku, Shun Goku Satsu, Zanku Hadoken

豪鬼 AKUMA

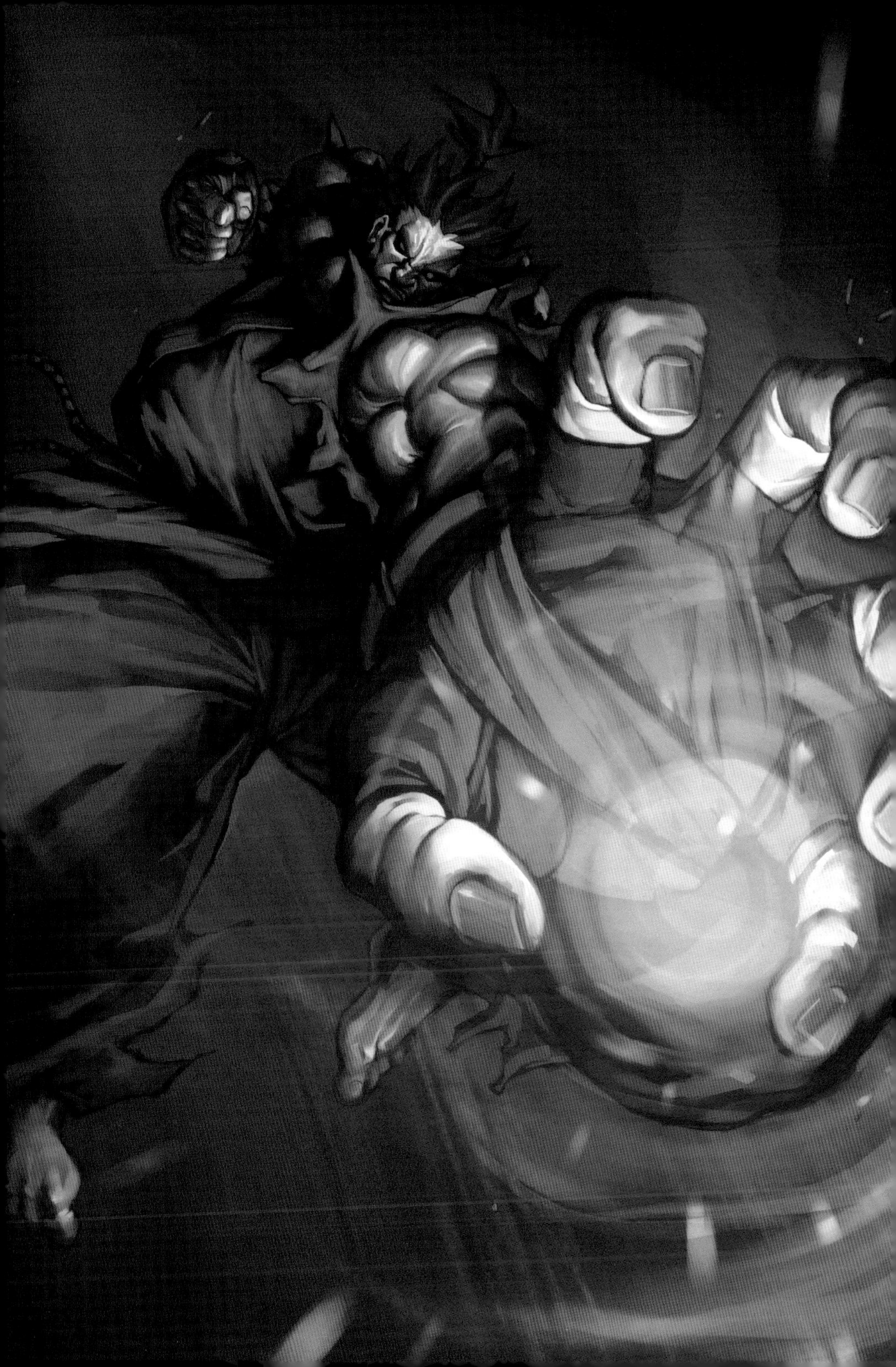

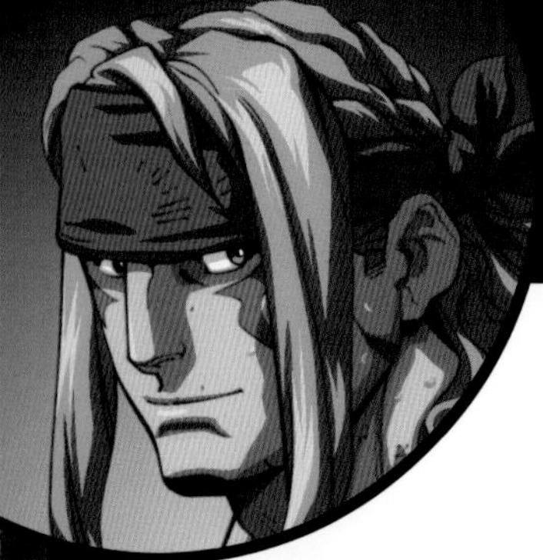

ALEX

The Young Blood

BIRTHDAY: ---------
COUNTRY OF ORIGIN: U.S.A.
FIGHTING STYLE: Wrestling and Kickboxing
HEIGHT: --------- **WEIGHT:** ---------
MEASUREMENTS: ---------
BLOOD TYPE: ---------
LIKES: Military fashion, city life
DISLIKES: Those who prey on the weak
SPECIAL ABILITIES: NYC pizza connoisseur

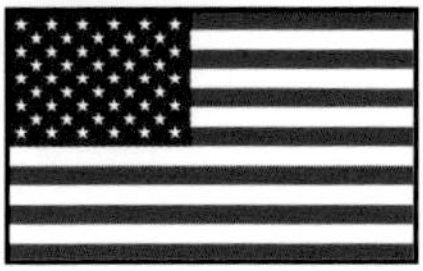

A young fighter living in Manhattan, Alex is a tough guy who keeps his abundant blond hair loosely gathered with a red bandana. Insensitive and a little abrasive, Alex's bold personality tends to get him into trouble.

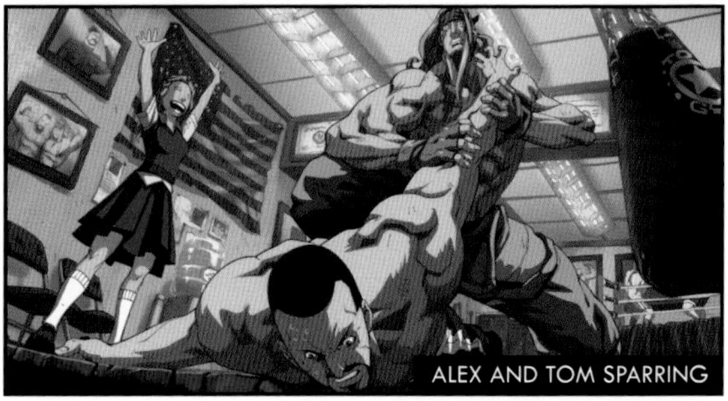

ALEX AND TOM SPARRING

Alex encountered the world of street fighting when his mentor and roommate, Tom, was defeated and hospitalized by an unknown fighter. A friend to Alex's father, Tom had been Alex's trainer, running the local gym where Alex first trained. Alex became obsessed with avenging his mentor, despite Tom's assurances that it had been a fair fight. The unknown fighter turned out to be Gill, the sponsor of the third World Warrior tournament. Alex fought hard, desperate to gain the chance to face down Gill and get revenge.

Alex returned home after the tournament to find Tom recovered from his injuries. With thoughts of vengeance no longer clouding his mind, Alex continues to hone his fighting skills and seek out worthy opponents. At times, this desire to prove himself can overwhelm his common sense, leading him into dangerous situations which push him to the very limits of his abilities.

Tom also has a 14 year-old daughter named Patricia, whom Alex treats like a younger sister. His protective feelings towards this young woman could someday prove to be the biggest weakness in this warrior's defenses.

FIGHTING STYLE

Alex has swift strikes and incredible strength that he wields like a weapon. Jumping into battle, Alex uses powerful throws and crushing blows to grin down his foes. His fighting style combines wrestling, chopping hand strikes and his infamous Power Bomb attack.

SIGNATURE MOVES: Flash Chop, Power Bomb, Spiral DDT

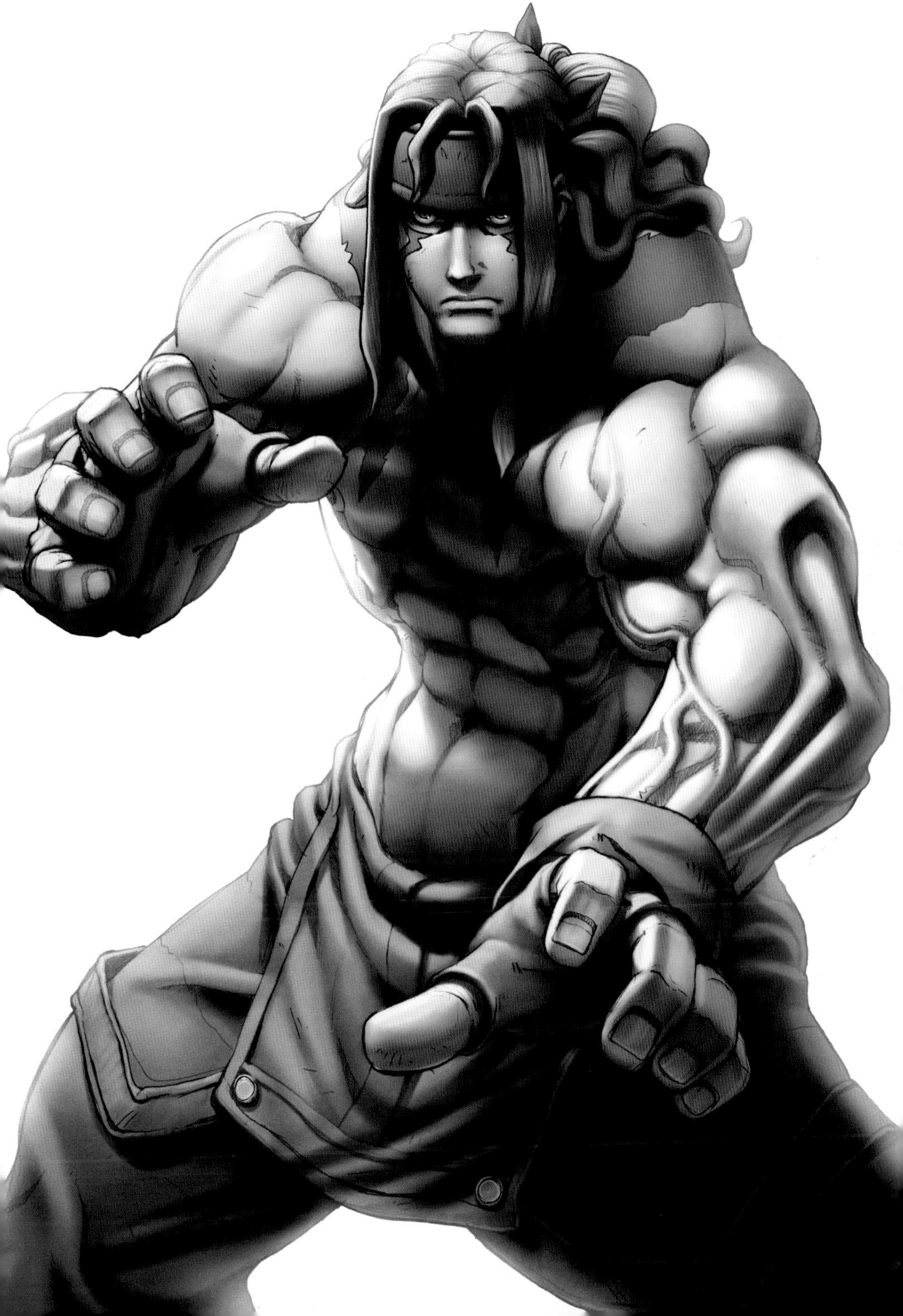

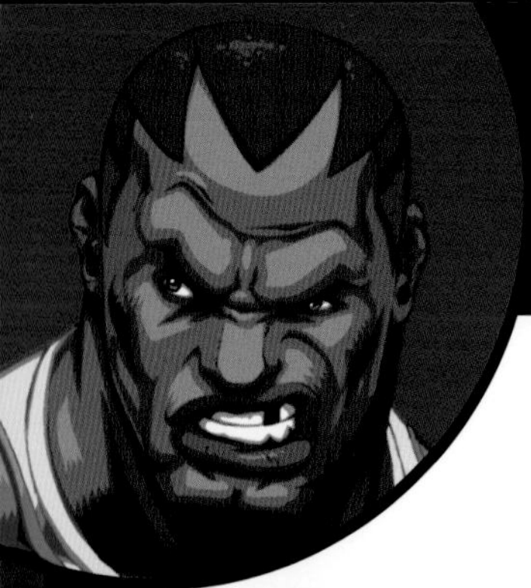

BALROG

The Blood-Crazed Bull

BIRTHDAY: September 4
COUNTRY OF ORIGIN: U.S.A.
FIGHTING STYLE: Boxing
HEIGHT: 198 cm **WEIGHT:** 102 kg
MEASUREMENTS: B120/W89/H100
BLOOD TYPE: A
LIKES: Women, bourbon
DISLIKES: Fish, effort, math
SPECIAL ABILITIES: Gambling

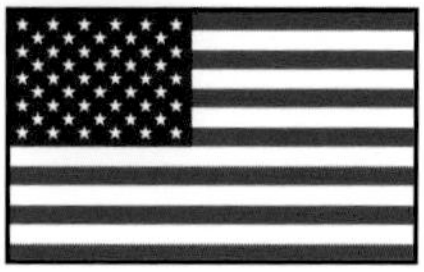

The first of the four Shadaloo bosses, Balrog has some serious fight in him, but his mental capacity is rather limited. Born as the youngest child in a poor family, Balrog spent his childhood fighting in the slums. Unable to hire a professional coach, Balrog's fighting style is best described as "brawling." As a boxer, Balrog does not use any kicks, but the power of his punch is unmatched.

BALROG IN LAS VEGAS

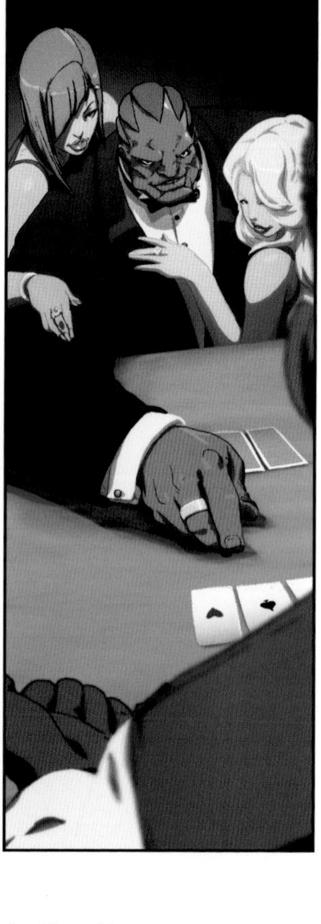

The allure of wealth and glory attracted him to the world of professional boxing, but Balrog was soon denied matches when it became clear that he was unable to restrain himself. Most of Balrog's opponents were hospitalized in critical condition. For a while Balrog participated in money fights in Las Vegas, but even there, he had trouble finding opponents due to his dangerous fighting style.

Having lost his place in the world of boxing, Balrog was making ends meet by working as a bouncer for casinos and bars when he was approached by M. Bison. Blinded by the money M. Bison offered, Balrog joined Shadaloo. By obediently following all of his orders, Balrog was able to fight his way to M. Bison's side as his right hand man.

FIGHTING STYLE

Aside from his below-the belt style and the occasional head butt, Balrog's technique is built around pure boxing. Although he looks bulky and slow, he can burst forward with incredible speed when required. Using all of his weight and momentum, his Dash Straight Punch has amazing reach and power. When he puts his mind to it, Balrog can truly be described as a knock-out king.

SIGNATURE MOVES: Dash Uppercut, Buffalo Headbutt

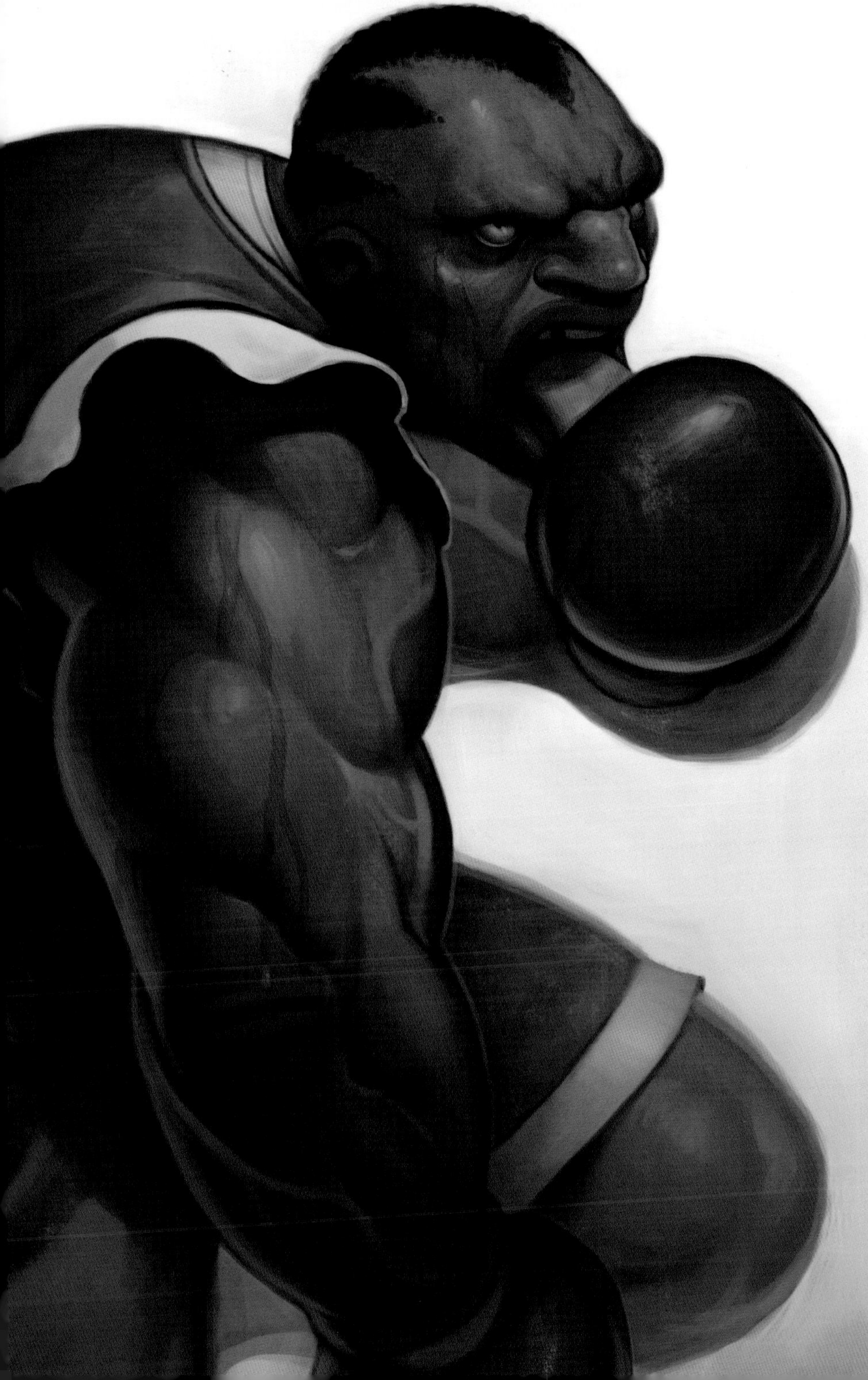

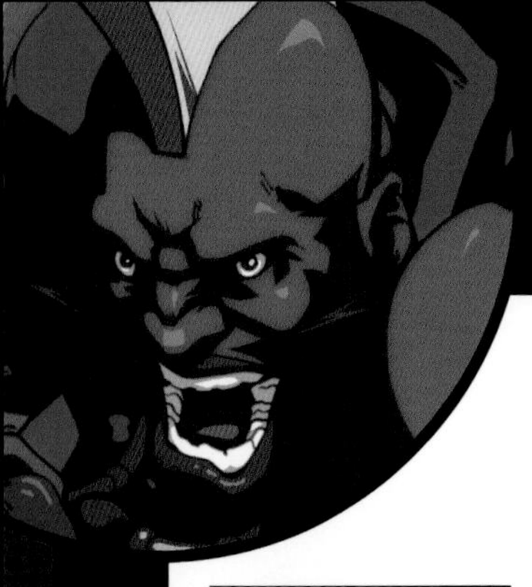

BIRDIE

Number One Thug

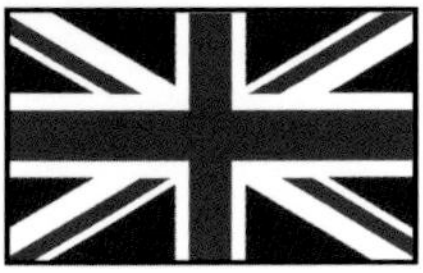

BIRTHDAY: ---------
COUNTRY OF ORIGIN: England
FIGHTING STYLE: Barroom Brawling/Pro Wrestling
HEIGHT: 216 cm **WEIGHT:** 111 kg
MEASUREMENTS: B156/W102/H106
BLOOD TYPE: O
LIKES: Beer, beef jerky, making money
DISLIKES: Children, police
SPECIAL ABILITIES: Gluttony, criminality

Using a variety of fighting styles, the mohawk-topped Birdie made quite a name for himself as a professional wrestler. He was exiled from the sport due to his violent tendencies and dirty tactics.

While eking out a living as a bouncer at a bar, rumors of Shadaloo reached his ears and Birdie started street fighting in the hopes that someone from Shadaloo would take notice of his abilities. He would eventually get his wish and be recruited into Shadaloo, though as a lowly thug his actual duties do not differ that much from his days as a bouncer.

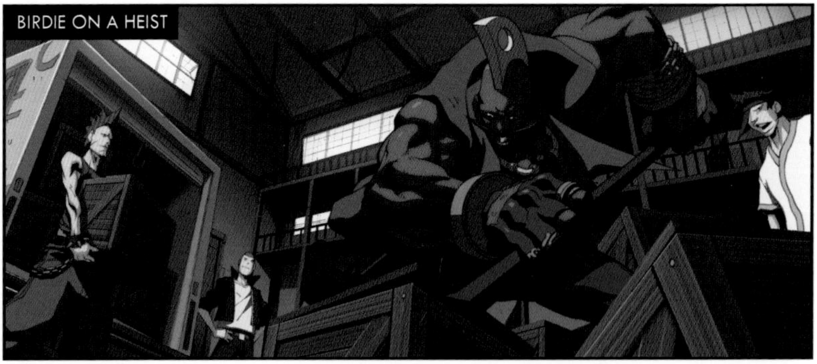

BIRDIE ON A HEIST

He may not seem like the sharpest tool in the shed, but Birdie is well aware that M. Bison is simply using him. He is waiting for just the right opportunity to kill M. Bison while he sleeps and take the throne of Shadaloo for himself. Birdie sees Russian wrestler Zangief as his rival, not because of his wrestling background, but because Birdie perceives Zangief's own mohawk as a personal challenge.

FIGHTING STYLE

A true fighter of the streets, Birdie's fighting style is an unrefined sloppy combination of barroom brawling and crushing wrestling maneuvers. He relies on hitting his opponent hard and fast before they have a chance to evaluate the weaknesses in his technique. With more strength than most of the fighters he faces, his overpowering fists and rock solid head butts are usually enough to ensure his victory.

SIGNATURE MOVES: Bull Horn, Bandit Chain, Murderer Chain

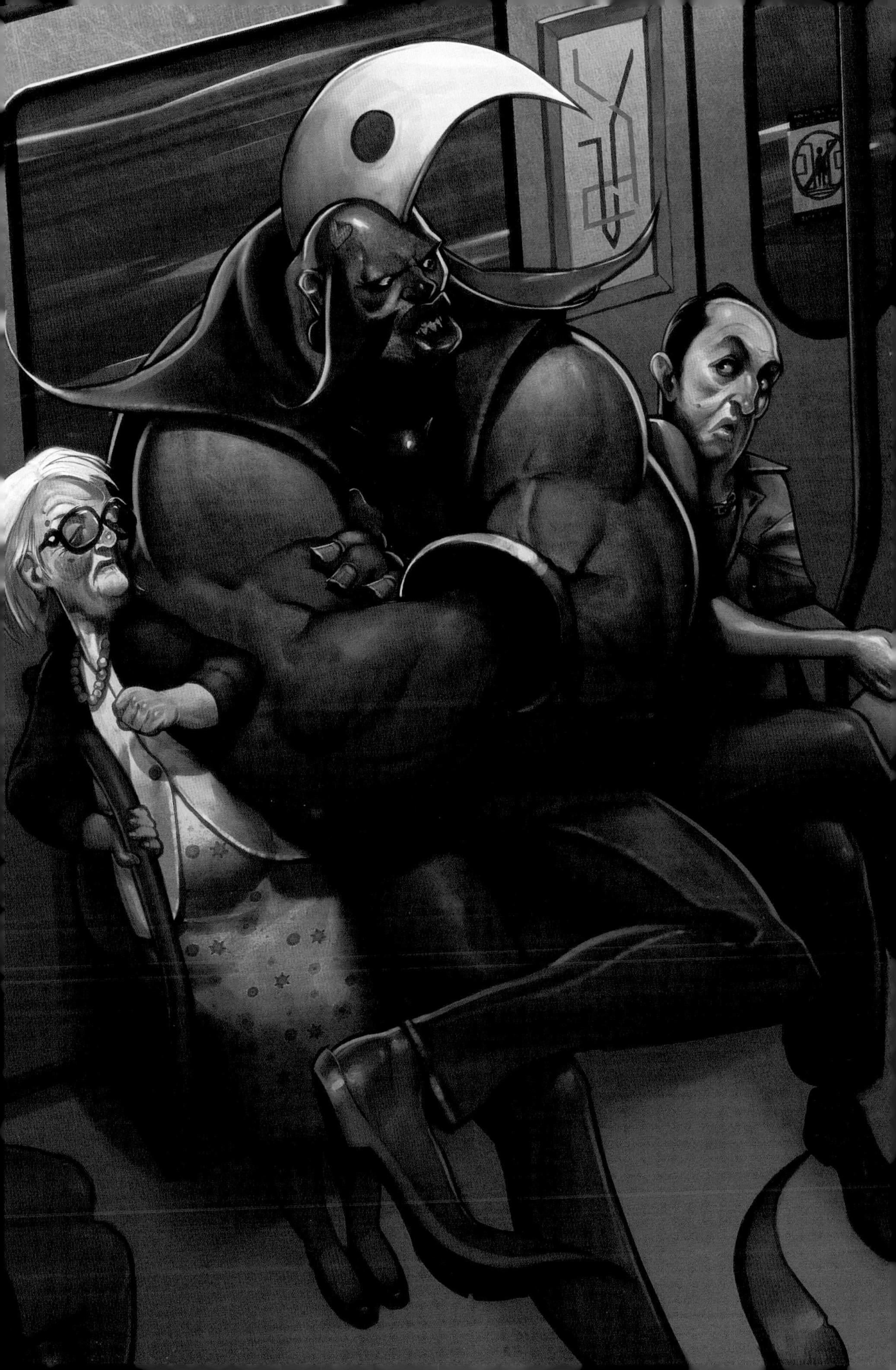

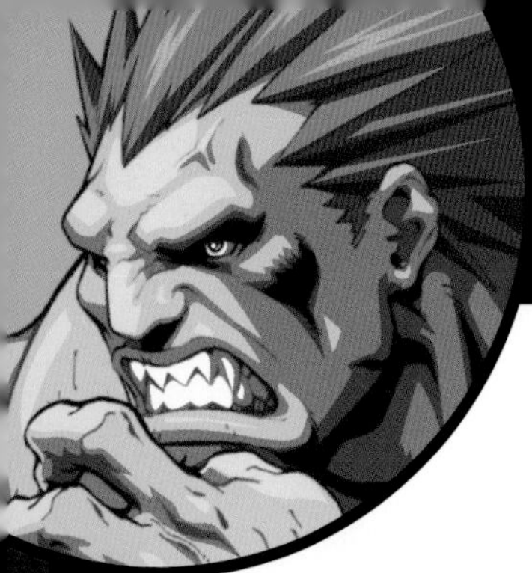

BLANKA

Warrior of the Jungle

BIRTHDAY: February 12
COUNTRY OF ORIGIN: Brazil
FIGHTING STYLE: Electricity, Feral Maneuvers
HEIGHT: 192 cm **WEIGHT:** 98 kg
MEASUREMENTS: B198/W120/H172
BLOOD TYPE: B
LIKES: His mother, arapaima, tropical fruits
DISLIKES: Army ants
SPECIAL ABILITIES: Hunting, discharging electricity

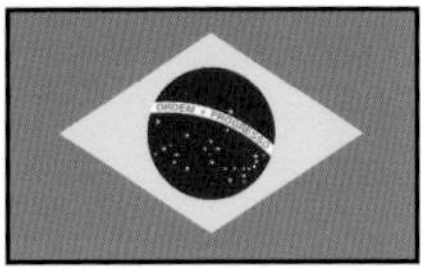

The monstrous-looking Blanka is a true wild child. His sharp claws, spiked fangs, and shocking electrical attacks make him a feral force to be reckoned with.

A 10 year old Blanka was flying to visit his uncle in Brazil when a Shadaloo operation caused the plane to crash. Of all the plane's passengers, Blanka was the only survivor. He was forced to stay alive and eventually grow up on his own deep within a mountainous Brazilian jungle. His green skin tone, long claws, and superhuman speed were all attributes he acquired to help him endure in his new surroundings. His unique electrical abilities are said to have been acquired through a tussle with an electric eel. Blanka eventually became the king of the jungle, but he found peaceful days to be boring and wanted to find someone strong to fight. Combined with Blanka's curiosity about the world outside his jungle, this desire for challenging combat led him to explore a nearby busy city, and later the world.

Blanka wears an anklet at all times, a symbol of his bond with his lost family. This anklet allowed for a dramatic reunion between him and his mother, Samantha, after a chance encounter between the two. Samantha turned out to be a warm and loving individual who accepted her child despite his mutated and inhuman form.

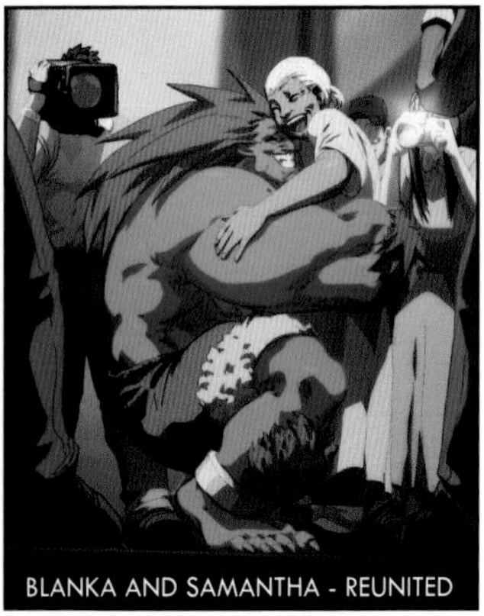

BLANKA AND SAMANTHA - REUNITED

The reason his name is Blanka (Spanish for "white") despite his green coloring is because he was initially a pale Caucasian male, and his "whiteness" was his most prominent trait in the eyes of the indigenous jungle people. Blanka's real name is Jimmy. He once saved the life of fighter Dan Hibiki, and ever since then Dan has called Blanka by his real name. The two are now good friends, and Dan has tried to train Blanka in the art of taunting.

FIGHTING STYLE

Trained to survive in the harsh Amazon jungle, Blanka is capable of long, powerful punches and incredibly quick, fluid motions of his body. He can roll into a ball while in midair and spin toward his opponents for a gravity-defying attack. Stranger still, time spent swimming among deadly electric eels has turned his body into a powerful electricity-charged conductor which can burst forth with light and power. His wild nature gives him an unmistakable fighting style and ferocity.

SIGNATURE MOVES: Electric Thunder, Rolling Attack

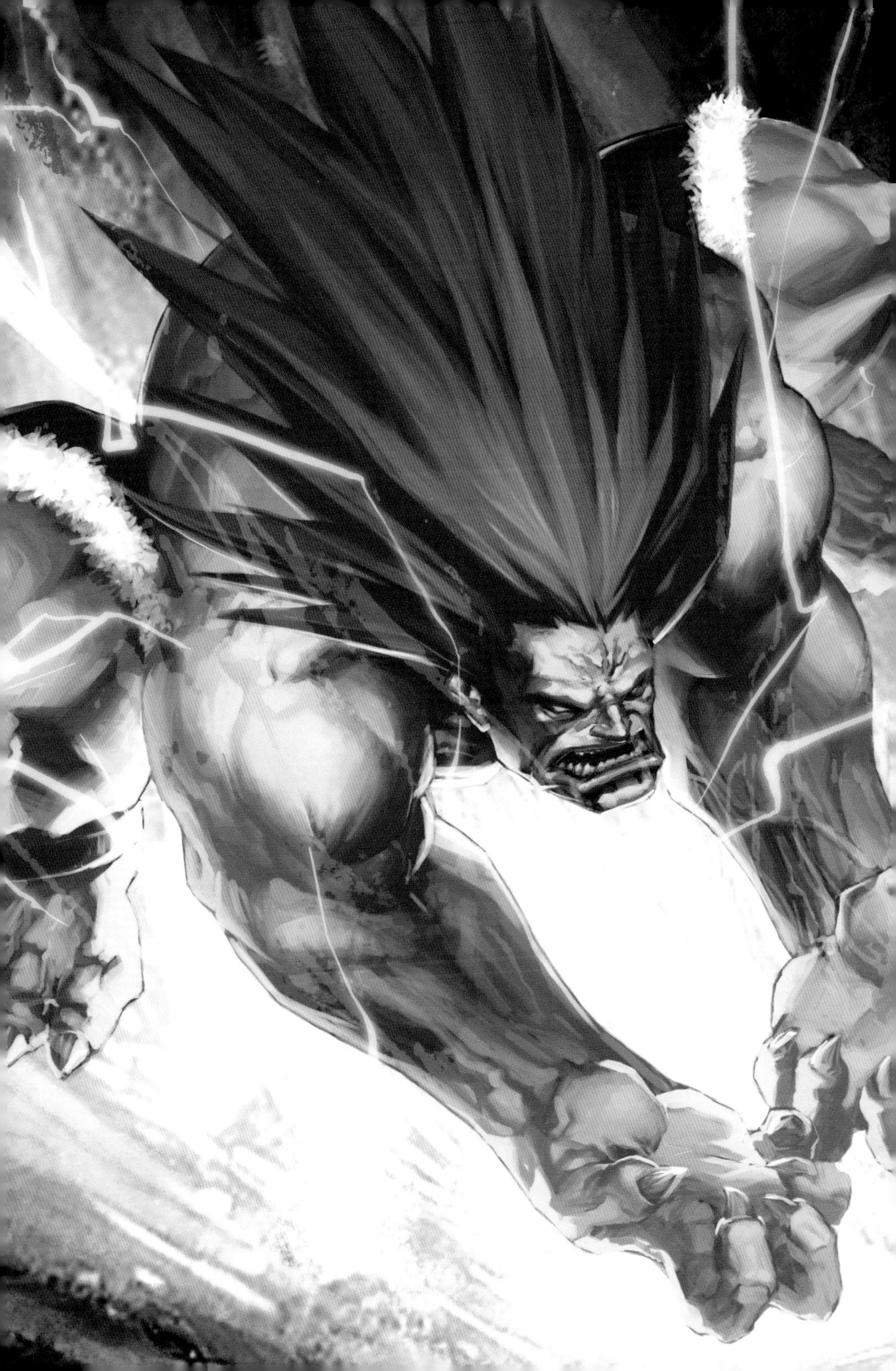

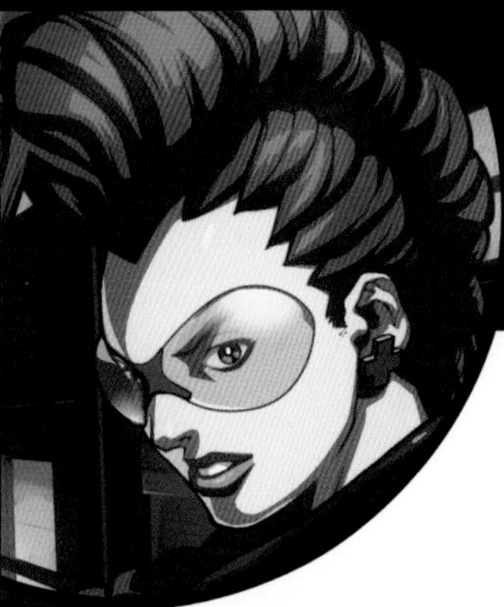

C. VIPER

Miss Perfect

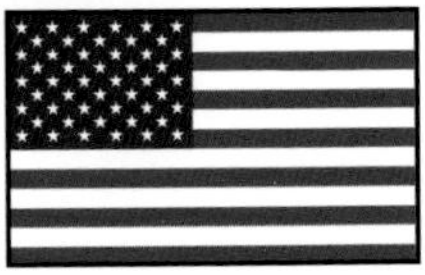

BIRTHDAY: July 18
COUNTRY OF ORIGIN: U.S.A.
FIGHTING STYLE: Use secret spy gadgets
HEIGHT: 175 cm **WEIGHT:** 56 kg
MEASUREMENTS: B98/W60/H90
BLOOD TYPE: AB
LIKES: Her daughter, money
DISLIKES: Working overtime
SPECIAL ABILITIES: Magic tricks

A smart and tough C.I.A. agent, Crimson Viper is all business. She never does anything for emotional reasons, or out of a sense of obligation. Viper works behind the scenes in many places, but her true identity is shrouded in mystery. She can normally hold her own in a fight and is an adept martial artist. However, given the strength and abilities of the fighters she may face in combat, Viper's superiors determined that she should go into combat with a technological advantage in the form of the Battlesuit – an integrated fighting suit sporting concealed gadgetry tuned for hand to hand combat.

At first glance, this suit appears to be an ordinary black suit. Upon closer examination, the suit is revealed to not only play host to a bevy of secret gadgetry, but also be made of a blend of secret materials specially built to resist fire, heat, shock, and friction. Her left glove contains an electrical generator capable of generating 1,000,000 volts of power, while her right glove contains a device that uses high frequency vibrations to cause a localized earthquake. The heels of her boots conceal both a flame thrower and a set of jump jets.

Viper's current mission is to investigate the BLECE project and eliminate the surviving products of the Shadaloo's "Living Incubator" program, including Seth. To this end she infiltrated S.I.N. and has been acting as Seth's personal lackey for some time.

Few know that Viper's real name is Maya, and that she is also a loving mother. Whenever she returns home she is greeted by her young daughter, Lauren.

FIGHTING STYLE

Viper relies more often on her spy gadgets than on pure fighting skill. She can stun opponents with electric bursts from her left glove, while her right glove's Seismic Hammer attack sends a shockwave beneath the ground, hitting opponents from a distance. She can also burn opponents using the flamethrowers in her boots, and can jump much higher than the average fighter with the boots' concealed jets.

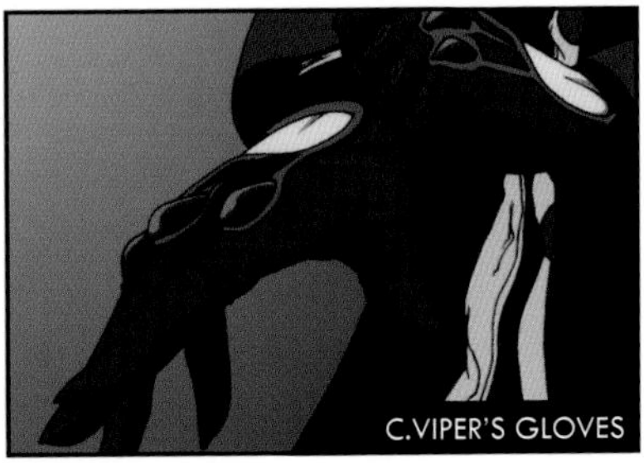

C.VIPER'S GLOVES

SIGNATURE MOVES: Burning Kick, Seismic Hammer, Thunder Knuckle

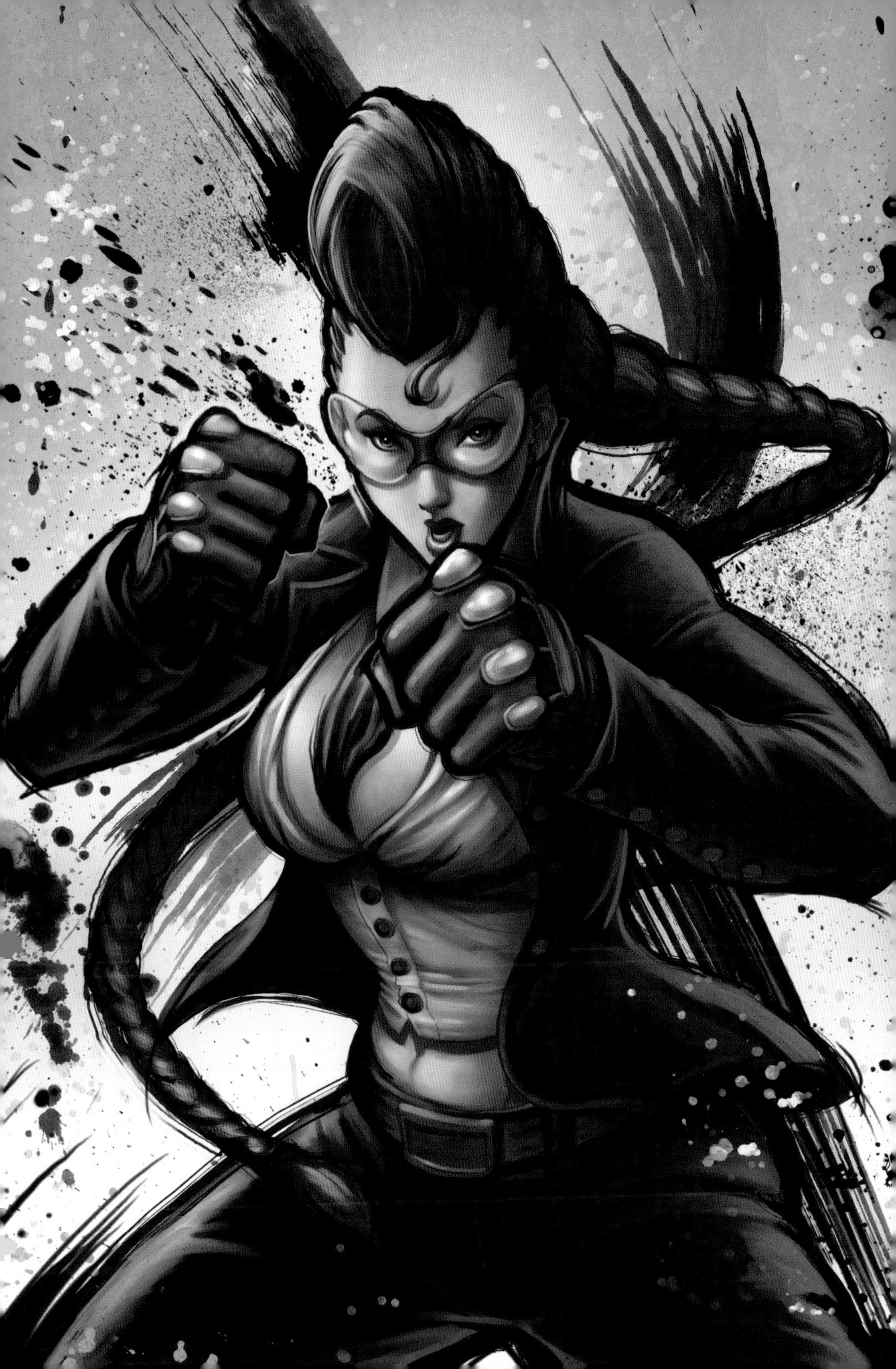

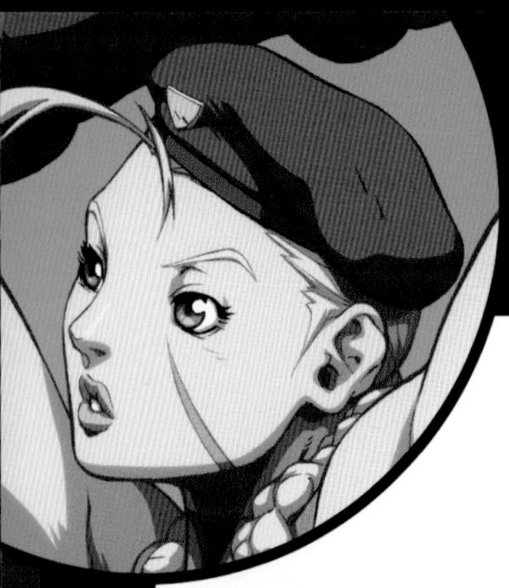

CAMMY

The Stinging Bee

BIRTHDAY: January 6
COUNTRY OF ORIGIN: England
FIGHTING STYLE: Shadaloo Assassination Techniques (Shadaloo), Special Forces Training (Delta Red)
HEIGHT: 164 cm **WEIGHT:** 46 kg
MEASUREMENTS: B86/W57/H88
BLOOD TYPE: B **LIKES:** Cats
DISLIKES: Everything when she's in a bad mood
SPECIAL ABILITIES: Knife throwing

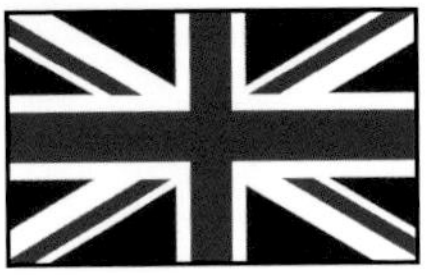

A fighter based in England, Cammy White is a member of the special operations division of the British Secret Intelligence Service (S.I.S.) called Delta Red. Cammy was once a member of M. Bison's personal guard, operating under the codename "Killer Bee".

Bison originally created Killer Bee himself, cloning her from his own genetic material. Brainwashed and modified by Shadaloo, Killer Bee was given orders from M. Bison to collect battle data. As she fought through more battles, Killer Bee began to develop some form of self-awareness. Eventually Bison grew concerned about Killer Bee's independence, and secretly ordered Vega and his other modified doll soldiers to eliminate her.

Though she wasn't sure how, Killer Bee found her way into the arms of Delta Red. They took her into protective custody after they found her passed out with no memory, and she was placed under the care of Delta Red instructor Colonel Wolfman. It was Colonel Wolfman who first gave her the name "Cammy". Cammy received a powerful shock when she found out that she was originally sent into Delta Red as a spy for Shadaloo, but her teammates offered her their support and encouragement, allowing her to regain her stability.

Cammy now has standing orders to kill Shadaloo boss M. Bison. The British military also has their eye on Cammy, considering her, with her unique modifications, to be a valuable and interesting specimen.

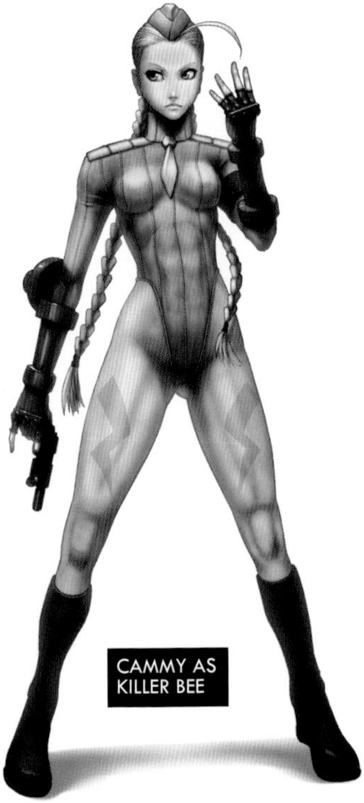

CAMMY AS KILLER BEE

FIGHTING STYLE

Cammy's fighting style consists of quick steps always looking for an opening to use her most powerful attack. Her graceful movements and smooth acrobatics give her incredible maneuverability for taking down her enemies. The enhancements she gained from Shadaloo's experiments have given her rapid reflexes and increased strength. Her deceptively small body possesses incredible fighting abilities.

SIGNATURE MOVES: Cannon Spike, Spiral Arrow

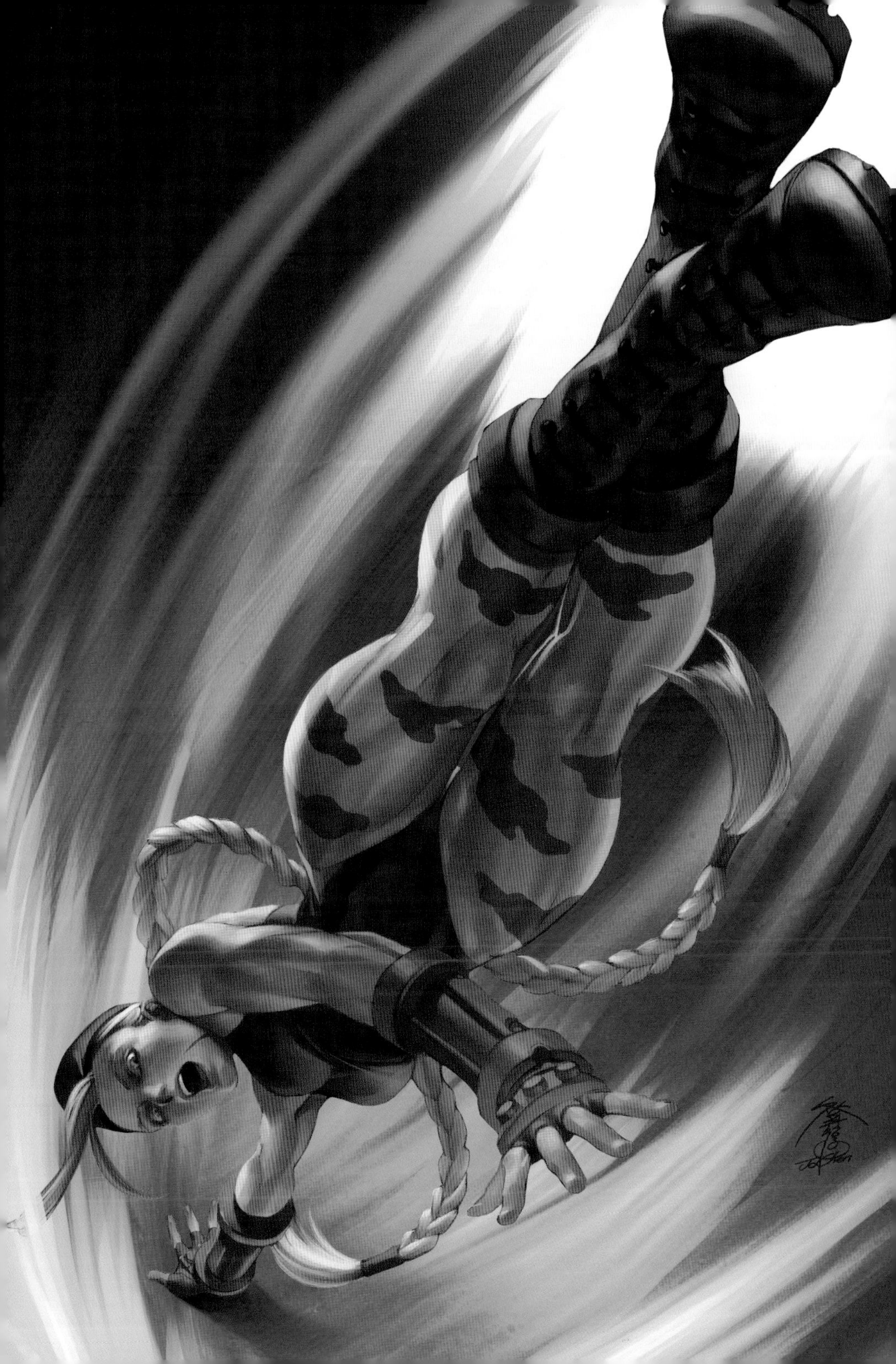

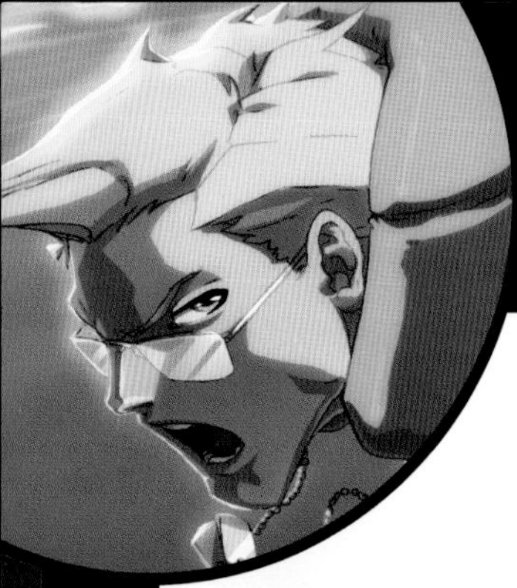

CHARLIE

The Calm Soldier

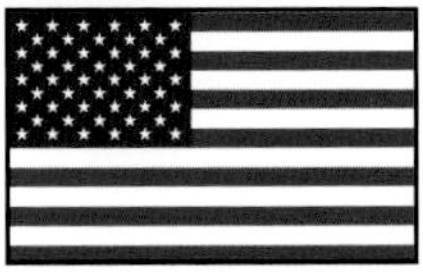

BIRTHDAY: ---------
COUNTRY OF ORIGIN: United States
FIGHTING STYLE: Special Forces Training
HEIGHT: 186 cm **WEIGHT:** 84 kg
MEASUREMENTS: V123/W81/H87
BLOOD TYPE: AB
LIKES: Justice, scotch
DISLIKES: Injustice
SPECIAL ABILITIES: Harrier maintenance, psychology

Charlie Nash is a lieutenant in the U.S. Air Force and a talented fighter, with a cool and straight-edged personality. His glasses give his handsome features an intellectual touch, and he wears his blond hair hardened over his head like a horn. These glasses are purely for aesthetic purposes, since Charlie actually has 20/20 vision. Charlie also always wears his dog tags to identify himself as a soldier in the U.S. Air Force. He is the mentor and best friend of Guile.

While investigating possible corruption within the Air Force, Charlie was discovered by one of the high ranking officers under M. Bison's influence and relegated to a rural post. Refusing to give up, Charlie used his new position to form a small band of like-minded soldiers.

Charlie was able to infiltrate Shadaloo despite the hurdles placed in his way, but was ultimately discovered. He and Guile teamed up to take on Bison, but only Guile escaped from the resulting explosion. Charlie's last words to Guile were "M. Bison" and "Psycho Drive". Because Charlie's body was never found, Guile holds out hope that his friend is still alive.

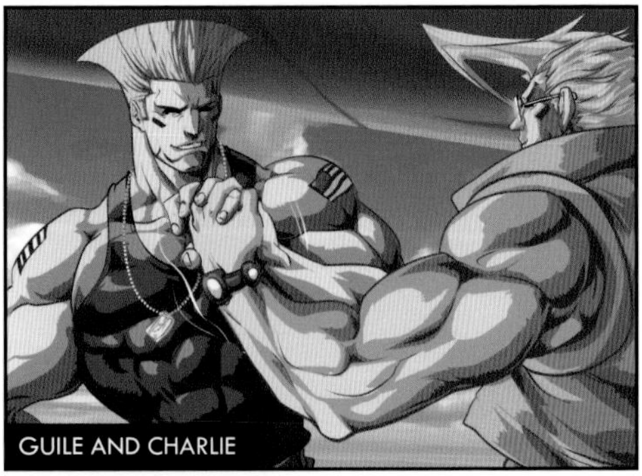

GUILE AND CHARLIE

FIGHTING STYLE

His military-themed martial arts include close range strikes and various wrestling maneuvers. While his moves are nearly identical to Guile's, there are some subtle differences. His attacks favor repeated use of his Somersault Shell attack. He loses out in pure damage dealing capability, favoring quicker counterattacking power instead.

SIGNATURE MOVES: Sonic Boom, Somersault Shell

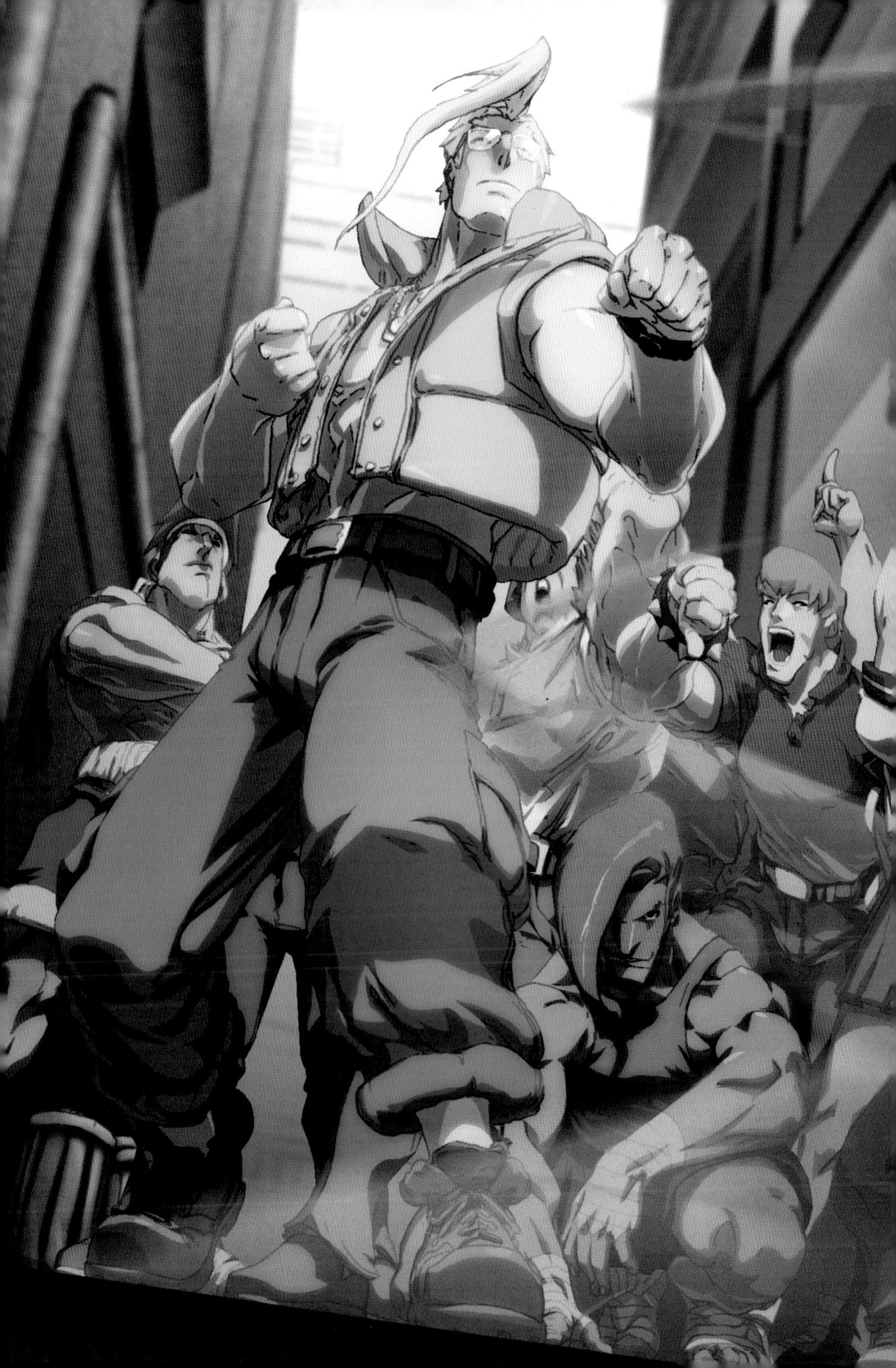

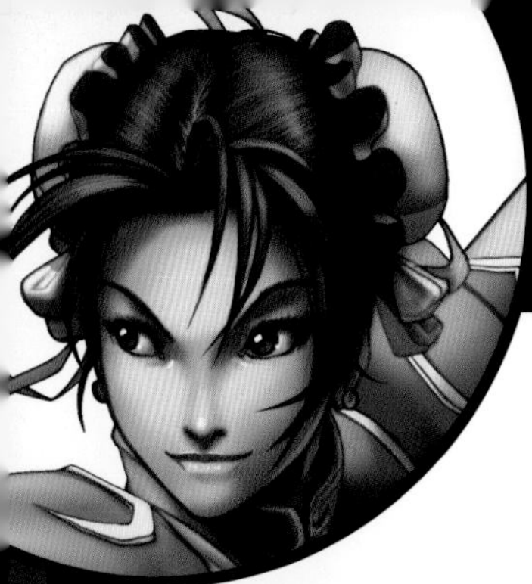

CHUN-LI

The Strongest Woman in the World

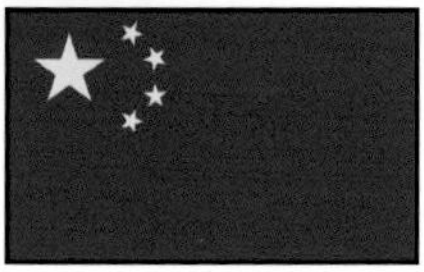

BIRTHDAY: March 1
COUNTRY OF ORIGIN: China
FIGHTING STYLE: Chinese Martial Arts
HEIGHT: 169 cm **WEIGHT:** She'll never tell
MEASUREMENTS: B88/W58/H90
BLOOD TYPE: A
LIKES: Crepe, fruits, and candy
DISLIKES: Vega, crimes, people who can't get to the point
SPECIAL ABILITIES: Shooting

Chun-Li is a police investigator whose attacks mainly revolve around her elegant leg maneuvers. After seeing her first classical Chinese play at age 5, Chun-Li started learning Chinese martial arts and developed her own unique kick technique.

Chun-Li became a detective at the age of 18 in hopes of finding her missing father. She later followed in her father's footsteps and became a narcotics investigator at the ICPO (also known as Interpol). Working as the ICPO's anti-Shadaloo investigator, Chun-Li was known as "the black sheep of the ICPO." She was investigating Shadaloo for the illegal sales of narcotics and weapons when Shadaloo got its claws into the upper levels of the ICPO.

Unable to rely on her own agency, Chun-Li teamed up with Charlie Nash, who was in a similar situation. The two worked together to foil M. Bison's plans. Later, while searching for her father's whereabouts, Chun-Li found a connection between his disappearance and Shadaloo. This only strengthened her resolve to take down Bison and his organization.

After the fall of Shadaloo, Chun-Li resigned from her post as an ICPO investigator and began a Kung Fu class for children. When one of her students was kidnapped by the Illuminati, Chun-Li found herself standing on the field of battle once more.

Chun-Li initially started street fighting as a way to gather useful information, but quickly began enjoying it. She trains in martial arts not only to maintain a level of endurance necessary in her line of work, but also because it is an effective way to control her weight. With her traditional Chinese dress, hair buns and muscular legs, Chun-Li is the perfect balance of beauty and combat power.

FIGHTING STYLE

Over the years Chun-Li has learned many Chinese Martial arts and other elaborate fighting styles. By understanding her own inner self, adapting her father's Chinese martial arts and learning many other Kenpo styles, Chun-Li has built up a powerful array of kicking strikes. She takes pride in her incredible acrobatic balance and uses it to perform various "Hit-and-run" type attacks. Over the years, Chun-Li has also developed several ki-energy attack forms to add to her already impressive abilities.

SIGNATURE MOVES: Kikoken, Lightning Kick, Spinning Bird Kick

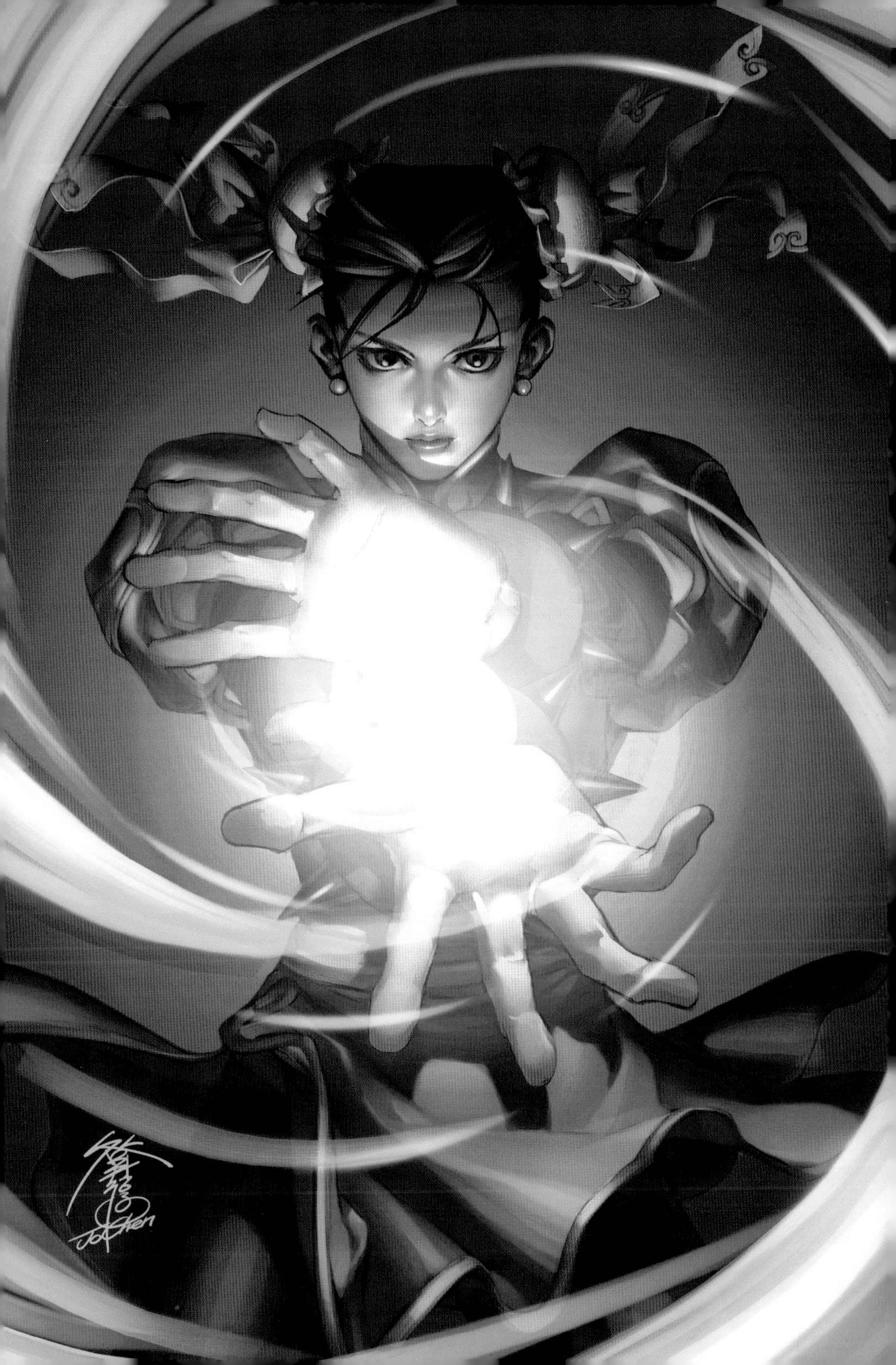

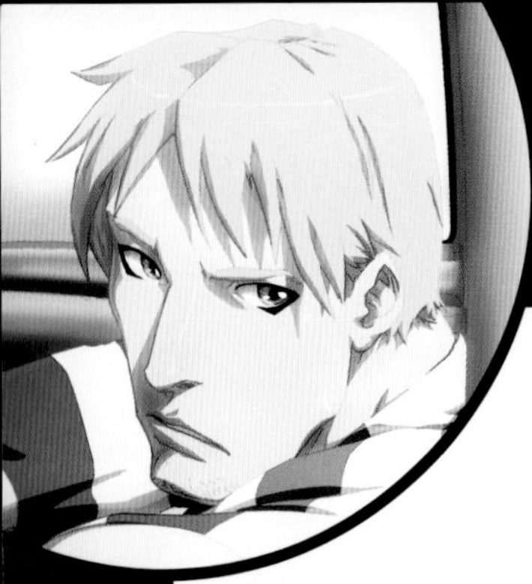

CODY

The Fallen Hero

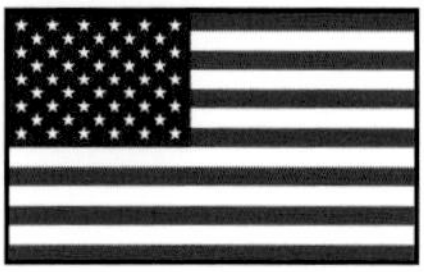

BIRTHDAY: April 18
COUNTRY OF ORIGIN: U.S.A.
FIGHTING STYLE: Underworld Brawling
HEIGHT: 185 cm **WEIGHT:** 80 kg
MEASUREMENTS: B139/W86/H97
BLOOD TYPE: O
LIKES: Starting fights, Metro City street meat
DISLIKES: Lectures
SPECIAL ABILITIES: Knife tricks

Cody Travers was once a celebrated hero in Metro City, alongside his friends Guy and Mayor Mike Haggar. Cody was able to rescue his kidnapped girlfriend, Jessica Haggar, from the clutches of the Mad Gear gang, and helped foil Mad Gear's plans on several occasions. But these days Cody is a near-permanent jailbird, spending most of his time in and out of prison.

Though he saved Metro City from Mad Gear's schemes, Cody quickly grew bored with the peaceful life, and turned to a life of random brawling until he was arrested for assault. He is no longer the pleasant young man he once was, with his perpetual five o'clock shadow and eyes that are devoid of life. Cody now has a pretty pitiful air about him, and even his prison uniform suits him quite well. He manages to live a pretty carefree life behind bars, and will often bust through his 50cm thick concrete cell wall whenever he feels like going out, only to return on his own some time later.

Cody is still quite skilled with his throwing knives, but he has also learned a few dirty fighting tactics like throwing stones and crushing eyes. He has apparently grown apart from Jessica.

FIGHTING STYLE

Cody fights with the viciousness of an underworld brawler. The handcuffs chained to his wrists have become a weapon he uses to hold down his victims. He'll use whatever dirty tricks or weapons he can get his hands on, including throwing rocks, blinding foes or slashing them with a knife.

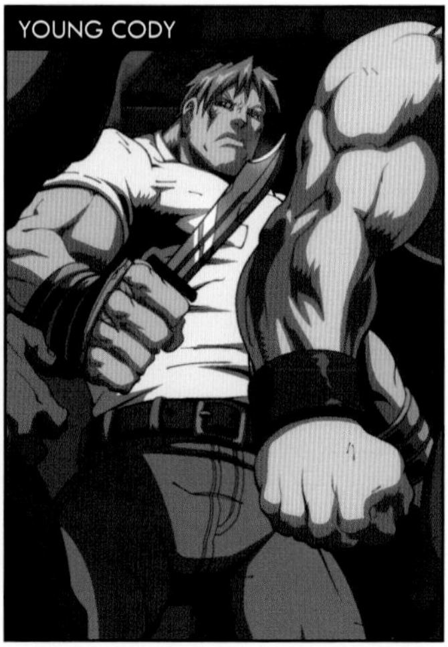

YOUNG CODY

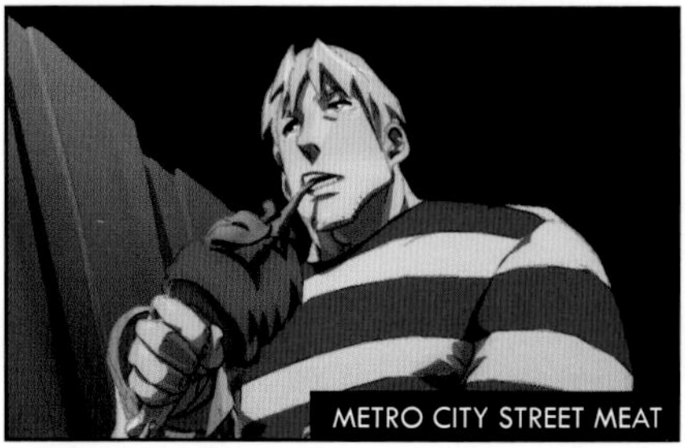

METRO CITY STREET MEAT

SIGNATURE MOVES: Bad Stone, Criminal Uppercut, Ruffian Kick

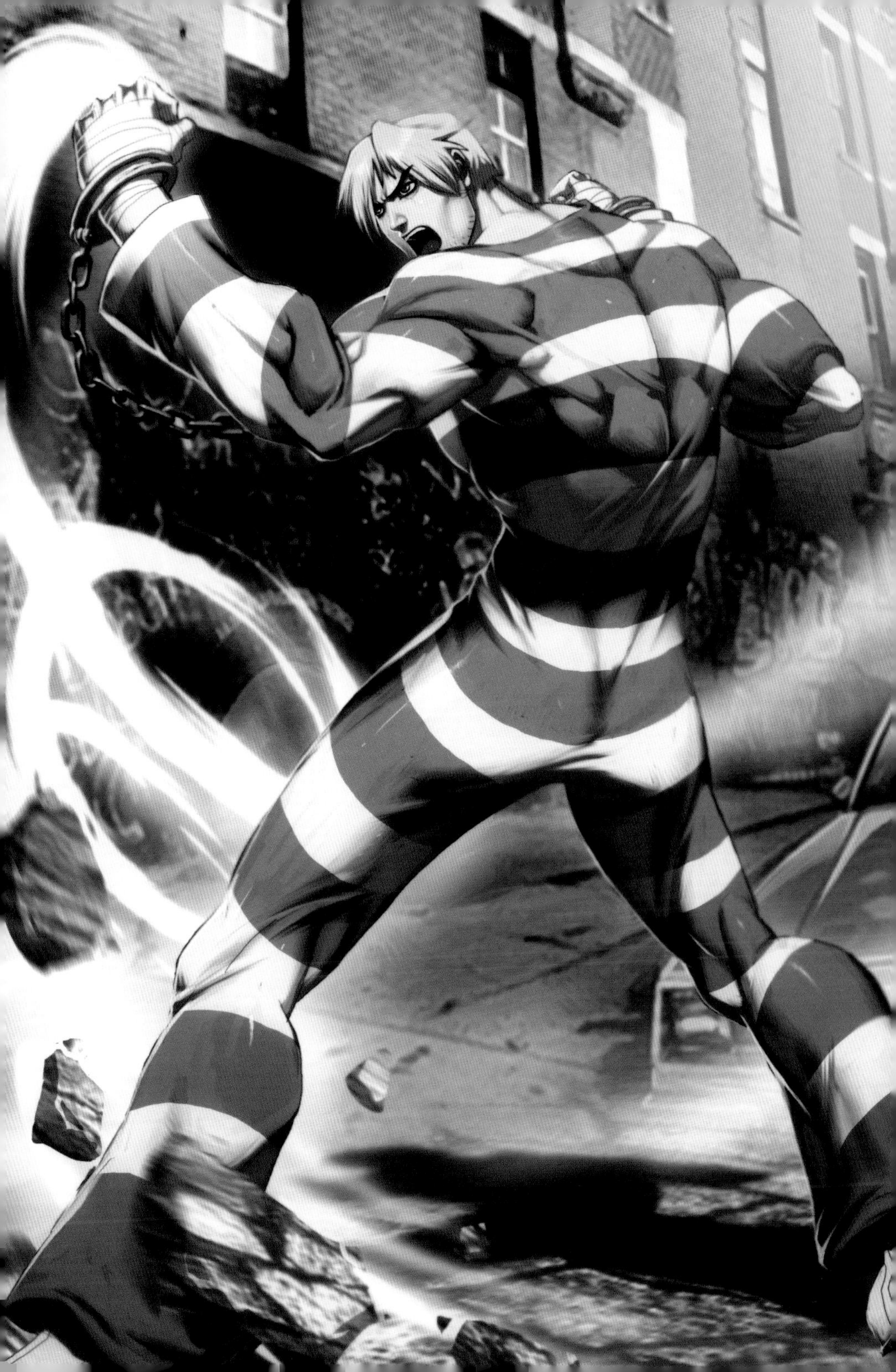

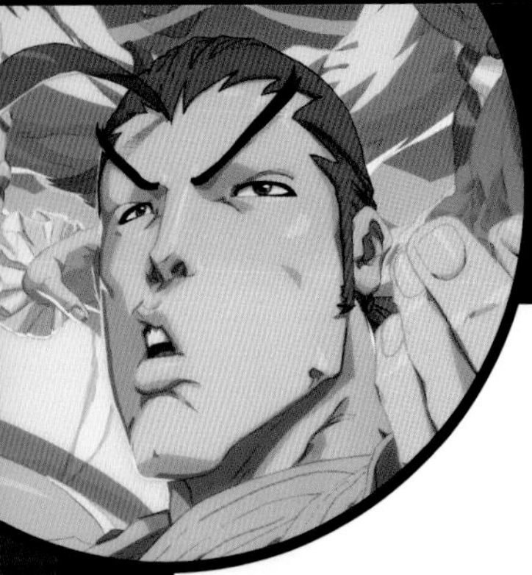

DAN

Legacy of Saikyo Style

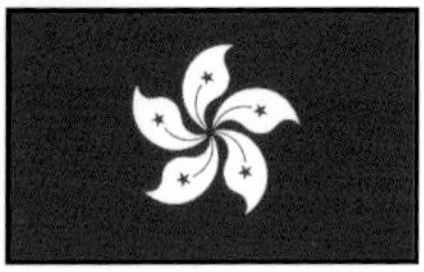

BIRTHDAY: November 25
COUNTRY OF ORIGIN: Hong Kong
FIGHTING STYLE: Saikyo "Ultimate" Style
HEIGHT: 177cm **WEIGHT:** 74kg
MEASUREMENTS: B113/W83/H88
BLOOD TYPE: O
LIKES: Taunting people
DISLIKES: Seaweed, evil-doers, cool guys
SPECIAL ABILITIES: Breaking tiles, karaoke

Dan Hibiki is a second-rate martial artist who specializes in colorful taunts and uniquely half-baked moves. Dan is Japanese by heritage, but was born and raised in Hong Kong. He is overwhelmed with a desire for vengeance against Sagat, the man who was responsible for the killing his father, Go Hibiki.

Dan studied briefly under Gouken, Ryu and Ken's master, but was expelled due to his obviously dark intent. Since Dan was studying under Gouken before Ryu and Ken arrived, Dan is convinced that their techniques are all weak imitations of his own. He holds a particular disdain for Ken, possibly due to Ken's popularity with women.

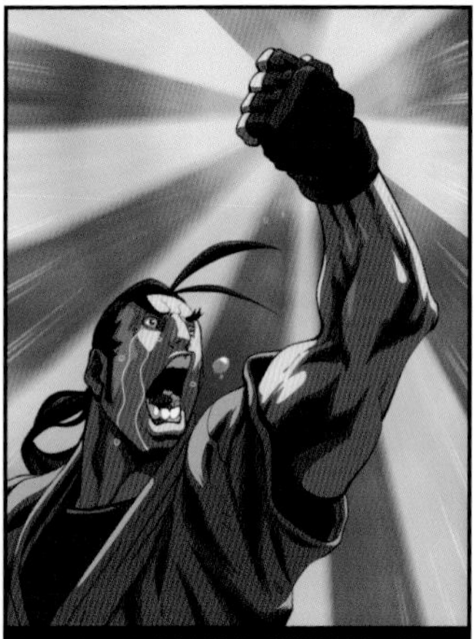

DAN LAMENTS HIS FATHER'S DEATH

Upon hearing rumors of Ryu defeating Sagat in battle, Dan left on a journey, determined to be the one to end Sagat's life. Dan eventually did find Sagat, and defeated him in a fight. In truth, Sagat realized that revenge can lead you down a path you may regret and deliberately lost the match, allowing Dan to satisfy his anger. Dan believes he won fairly, and his exhilaration at defeating Sagat was so extreme that it left even M. Bison speechless. Considering himself as "ultimate" for defeating Sagat, Dan established Saikyo-Ryu (the "Ultimate Style") and opened his own dojo.

Dan's life was once saved by Blanka during an encounter within the Brazilian jungle, which is why Dan treats Blanka as a friend and calls him by his real name, Jimmy. Dan is also quite familiar with Sakura, and treats her like his first student.

FIGHTING STYLE

With his incomplete training, Dan's special attacks are quite strange and not as damaging as they should be, even though they're based on the same powerful moves used by Ken and Ryu. His strongest attacks involve repeated small strikes against his enemy, using them as a way to boost self-confidence. No one is quite sure why Dan is so fond of repetitive attacks, not even Dan himself.

SIGNATURE MOVES: Gadoken, Koryuken, Dankukyaku

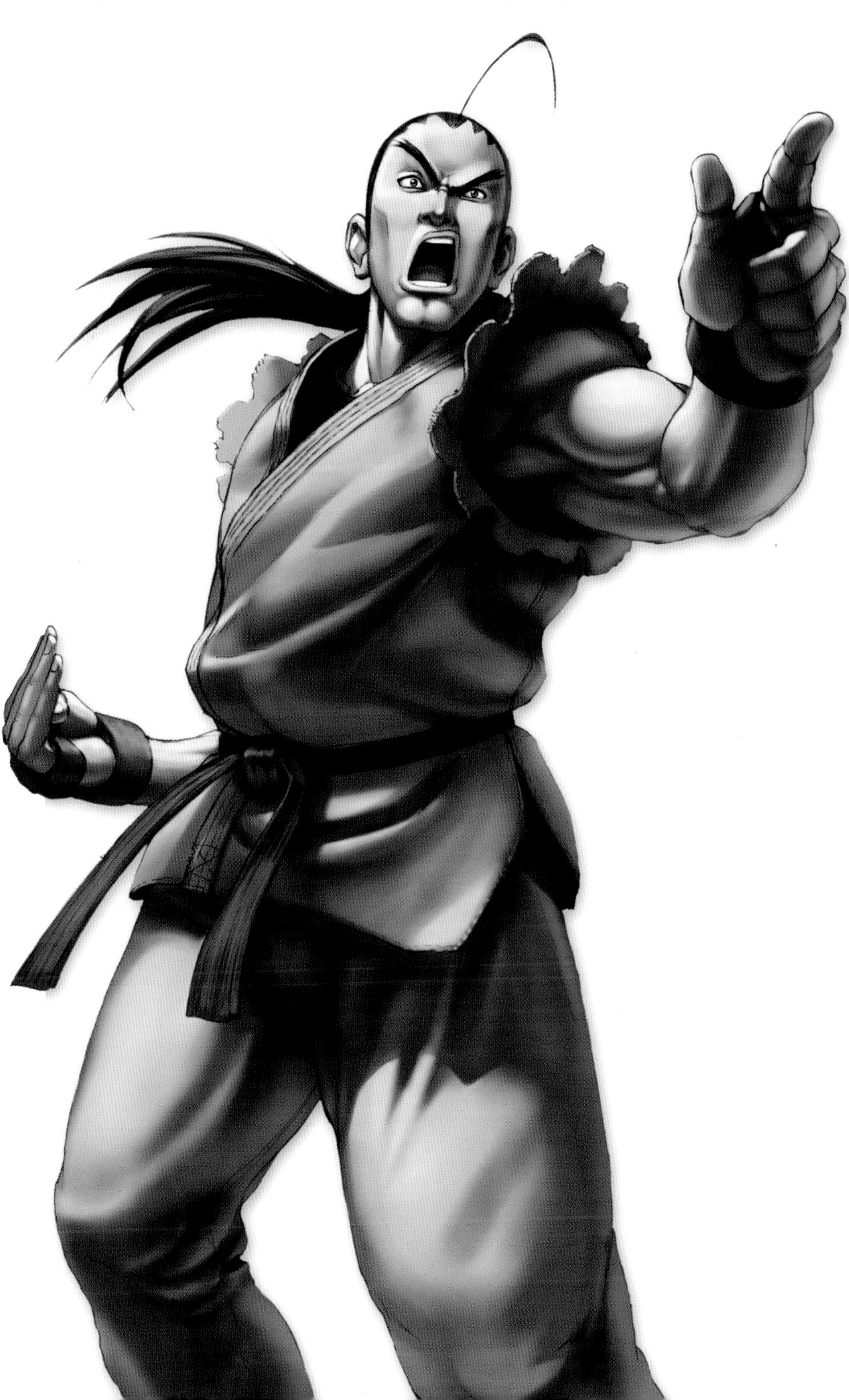

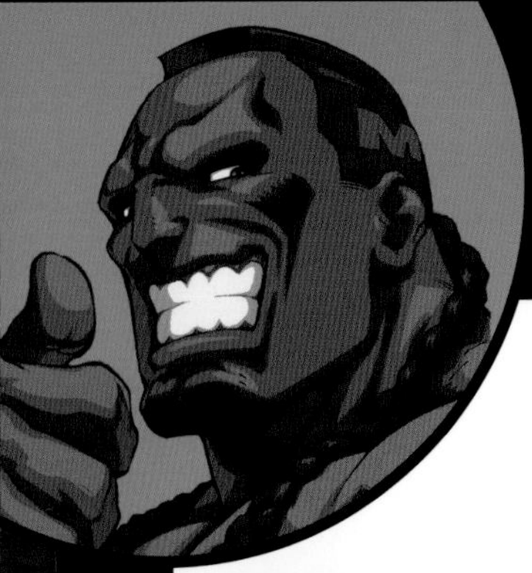

DEEJAY

The Southern Comet

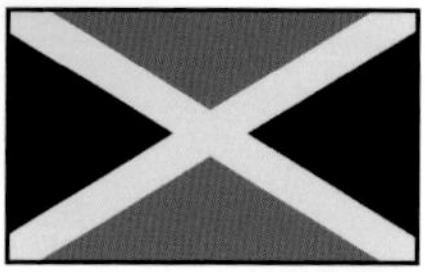

BIRTHDAY: October 31
COUNTRY OF ORIGIN: Jamaica
FIGHTING STYLE: Kickboxing
HEIGHT: 184 cm **WEIGHT:** 92 kg
MEASUREMENTS: B130/W89/H94
BLOOD TYPE: AB
LIKES: Shouting, singing, dancing
DISLIKES: Silence
SPECIAL ABILITIES: Bamboo dancing

Dee Jay is a unique fighter in that he is both a kickboxer representing Jamaica, and a popular musician whose albums have all gone gold. He is probably the only street fighter who can sing, dance and play the maracas. He has an extremely cheerful disposition, which goes well with his muscular physique.

Dee Jay was making his way as a kickboxer, and decided to travel the world in order to be acknowledged as a great fighter. Talent scouts noticed Dee Jay's charismatic attitude during one of his fights and with some time were able to turn him into a top musician. Dee Jay began feeling his musical inspiration waning, until one day, when he saw the potential for a new musical spark in the "rhythm of attacks" in street fighting. Now, he is beyond thrilled to be able to combine his love of music and his love of martial arts into one single journey.

The word "Maximum" on Dee Jay's pant leg is the title of one of his hit songs.

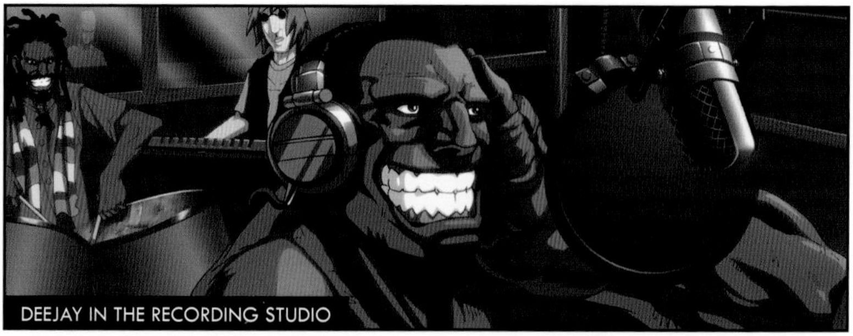

DEEJAY IN THE RECORDING STUDIO

FIGHTING STYLE

His sharp punches and long flowing kicks move with the beat of his music, utilizing an internal rhythm to create his signature move, the Machine Gun Uppercut, which he uses to stun opponents. His Double Rolling Sobat advances with each step and has an incredible reach, making it ideal for hitting opponents from far away.

SIGNATURE MOVES: Double Dread Kick, Hyper Fist, Max Out

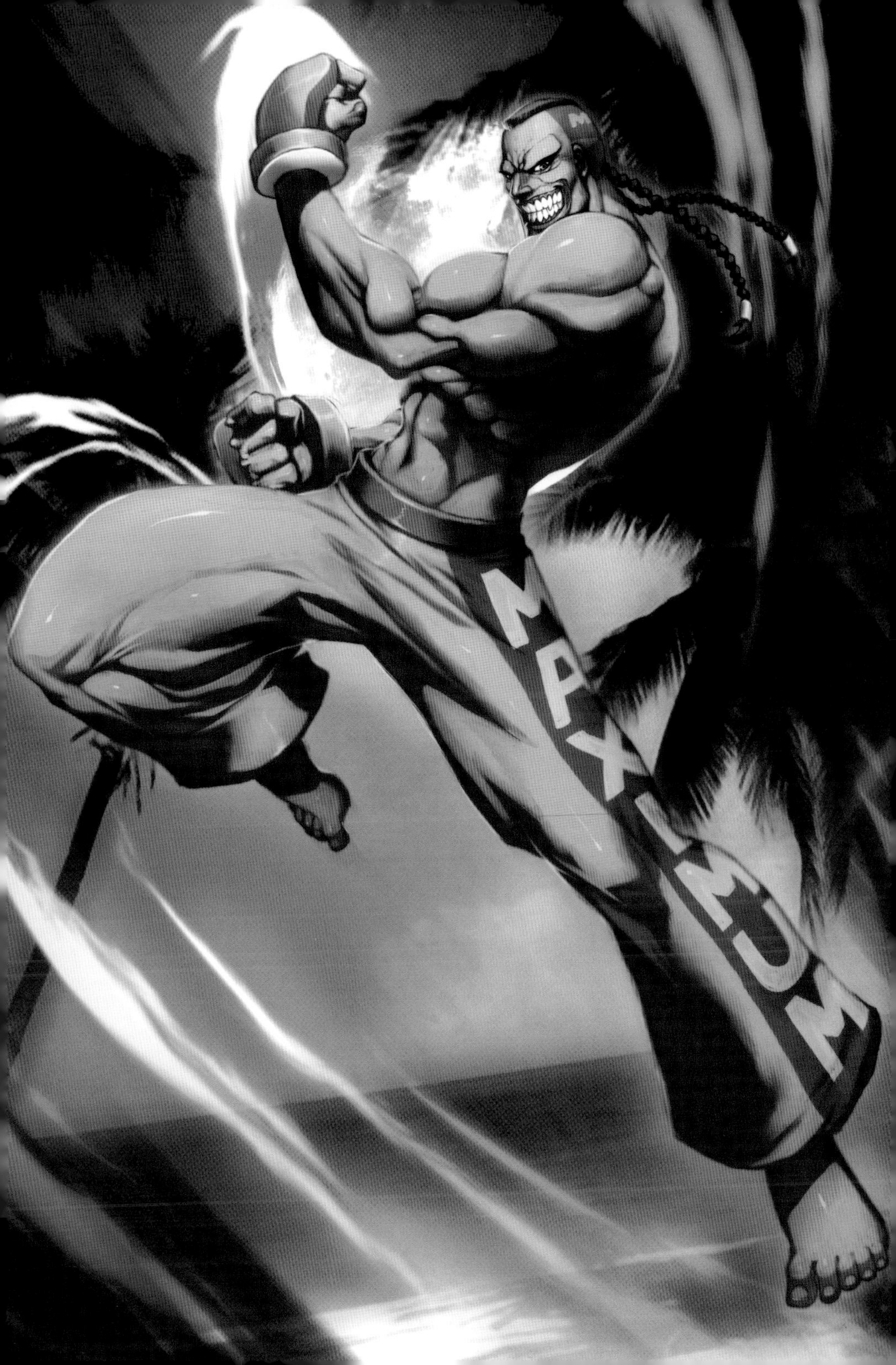

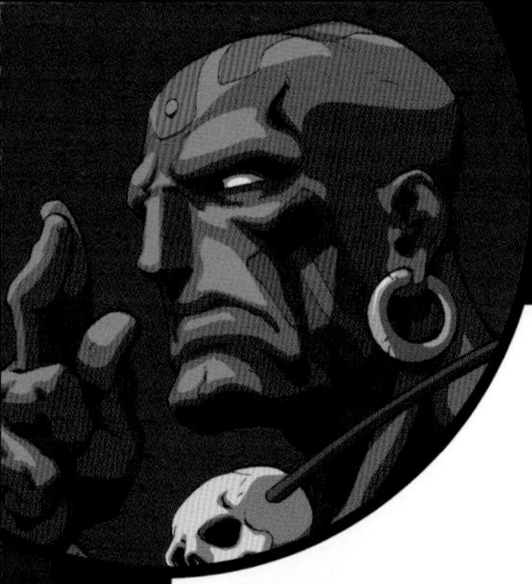

DHALSIM

The Spirit of Yoga

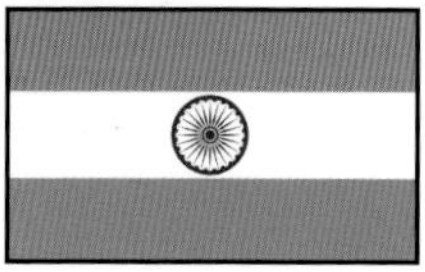

BIRTHDAY: November 22
COUNTRY OF ORIGIN: India
FIGHTING STYLE: Yoga
HEIGHT: 176cm(variable) **WEIGHT:** 48kg(variable)
MEASUREMENTS: B107/W46/H65
BLOOD TYPE: O
LIKES: Curry, meditation
DISLIKES: Sweets, meat
SPECIAL ABILITIES: Preaching and selflessness

Dhalsim is a monk from India who has mastered the ancient art of yoga. In order to cover the medical expenses for the people of his village, who had fallen ill to an epidemic, Dhalsim became involved in street fighting despite his disdain for violence.

Even as he continues to fight, Dhalsim believes that harming others is wrong. This belief is the root of constant grief and confusion over what he does. His ability to stretch his limbs at will comes from his years of yoga training. To avoid harming his opponents more than is absolutely necessary, Dhalsim fights using the power of artificial flames granted to him by the fire god Agni. As he advanced in his understanding of yoga, Dhalsim later acquired the additional ability to read other people's emotions, and the power of teleportation.

Dhalsim had accomplished his initial goal of raising enough money to save his fellow villagers, but he could not simply stand idly by knowing that a wave of negative energy was sweeping across the world. With great conviction, Dhalsim once again stepped onto the field of battle, intent on rooting out the source of this unseen threat.

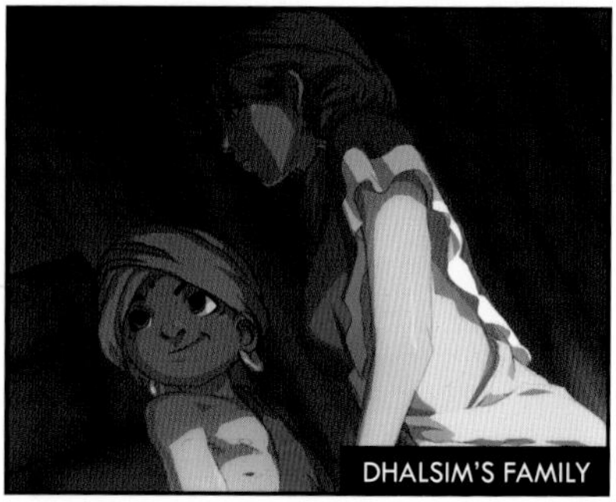
DHALSIM'S FAMILY

Dhalsim's yoga training has allowed him to survive on a minimal amount of food intake. He has a beautiful wife named Sally and a son, Dhatta. Sally studies yoga like her husband, while Dhatta is still too young for such intense devotion. Dhalsim can also often be seen riding an elephant named Kodal.

FIGHTING STYLE

Dhalsim's contorting limbs and mystical yoga-based powers are the product of many years of intense training and meditation. With this unique ability, he can stretch his arms and legs in order to strike at opponents from a great distance. Although his hand and foot attacks don't deal very much damage, he is capable of powerful fire-breathing attacks which he gained by drawing strength from the Indian God of Fire, Agni. Dhalsim never forgets the importance of prayer even when he goes forth to do battle against his enemies.

SIGNATURE MOVES: Yoga Fire, Yoga Flame, Yoga Teleport

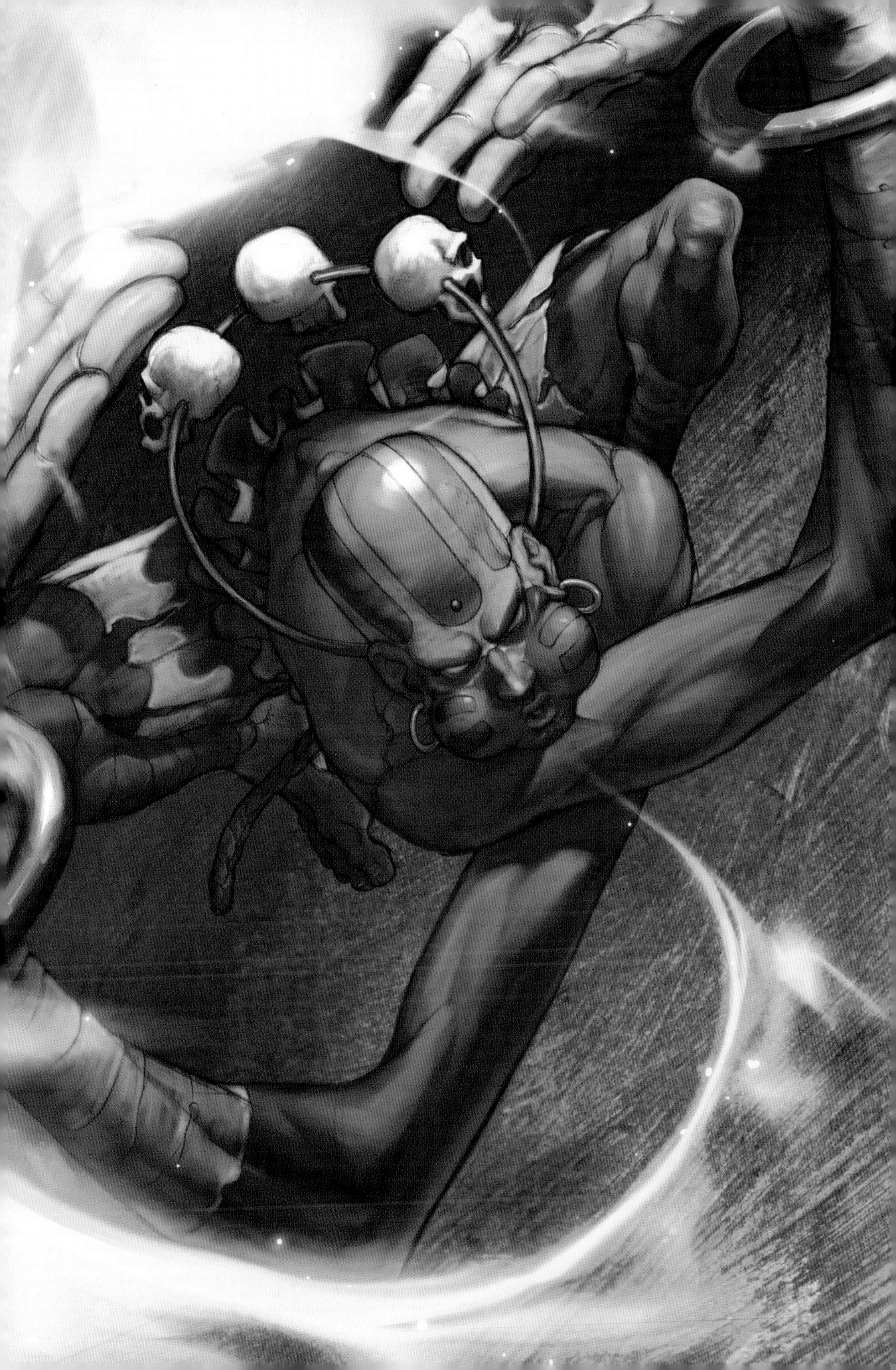

DUDLEY
The Gentleman Boxer

BIRTHDAY: January 27
COUNTRY OF ORIGIN: England
FIGHTING STYLE: Boxing
HEIGHT: 185 cm   **WEIGHT:** 101 kg
MEASUREMENTS: B160/W90/H100
BLOOD TYPE: B
LIKES: Tea, roses
DISLIKES: Uncivilized Behavior
SPECIAL ABILITIES: Pottery appraisal, gardening

Dudley is a gentleman boxer who grew up in England and loves his tea. His father was a successful athlete and prominent businessman, which allowed Dudley to grow up in comfort and luxury. If Dudley has any weaknesses beneath his skilled exterior, it would be compassion for his fellow fighters. He may get sentimental about his past matches and flawless fighting techniques, but he has a great deal of pride that drives him as well.

When Dudley was in university his father made a poor business decision, plunging Dudley into the unfamiliar world of poverty. Dudley managed to claw his way back up in the world as a professional heavyweight boxer, rebuilding his family fortune, but was not able to recover his father's beloved Jaguar sports car. This car has such a special meaning to Dudley that he began a search around the world for it. He eventually did find and regain the car, after finding it in the possession of Gill and the Illuminati.

Due to his training as a professional boxer Dudley only uses punches, even when street fighting. The speed and impact of his punches said to be unmatched. A perfectionist, Dudley is known to be a bit of a dandy, and some would accuse him of becoming soft over the years. Dudley always wears his boxing gloves, even while driving his sports cars or drinking tea.

After claiming his throne as the boxing champion, Dudley was knighted and invited to perform a fight in the royal court of England. Dudley looks nearly identical to his father. He loves roses, and has constructed a huge rose bush labyrinth on his estate. Dudley also has his own butler, a man named Orth K. Gotch, who has a distinctively curled moustache.

FIGHTING STYLE
With swift advances and powerful punches that dominate in close quarters, Dudley is a fierce fighter. A boxing master, he keeps foes pinned down with rapid punches and dashing moves designed to press the offensive.

SIGNATURE MOVES: Machine Gun Blow, Rolling Thunder

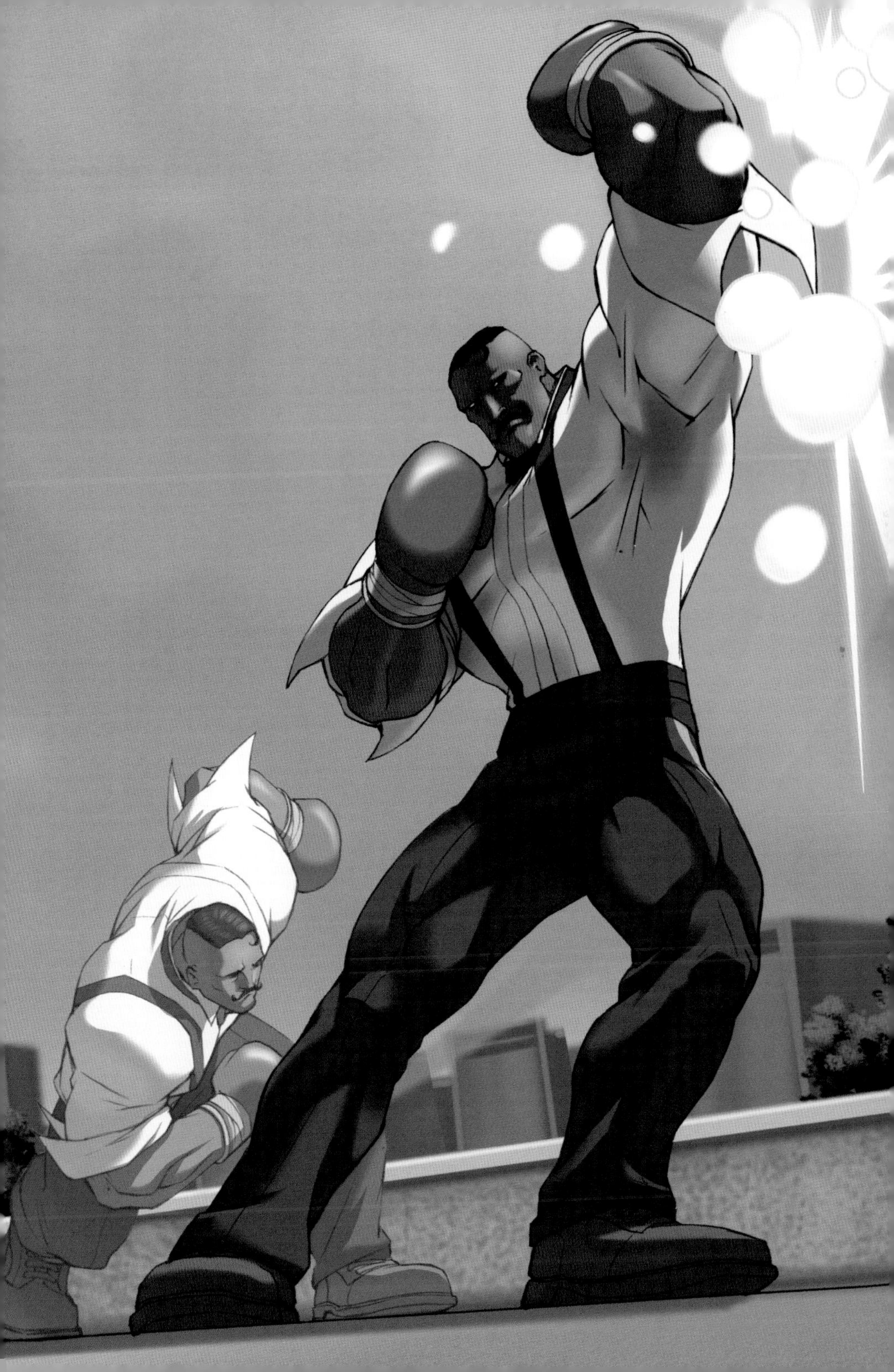

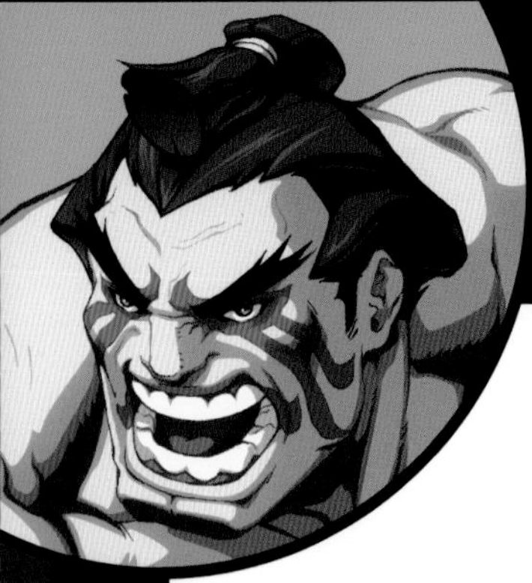

E. HONDA

The Passionate Sumo Wrestler

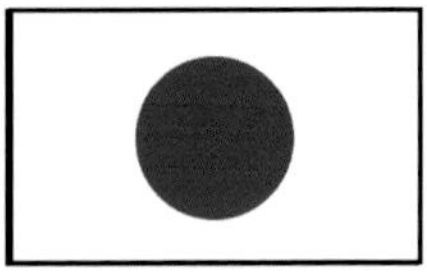

BIRTHDAY: November 3
COUNTRY OF ORIGIN: Japan
FIGHTING STYLE: Japanese Sumo Wrestling
HEIGHT: 185 cm (including his hair) **WEIGHT:** 137 kg
MEASUREMENTS: B212/W180/H210
BLOOD TYPE: A
LIKES: Tira misu, chanko nabe, and baths
DISLIKES: Indecision
SPECIAL ABILITIES: Nabe connoisseur

Edmond Honda is a Japanese wrestler who is said to be unrivaled in the world of sumo. His chaotic fighting style has won him the attention of the masses. He has declared that he will make the whole world acknowledge the greatness of sumo wrestling, and has thrown himself into the world of street fighting to achieve this goal.

Despite the fact that he started street fighting as a way to spread awareness of sumo wrestling, Honda's fighting style is far from that of traditional sumo. He was said to begin his hardcore training regime very early in the morning, which led to more than a few unhappy neighbors around his heya (a sumo wrestling stable). When rumors spread of Edmond's plans to travel the world, the entire neighborhood breathed a collective sigh of relief. This relief did not last long, however, as Edmond never failed to call his students every morning to yell at them over the phone. Following Edmond's instructions, his students set up speakers around the neighborhood so that he could yell at them while they trained. It seemed that sleeping in was not going to be an option for Edmond's neighbors any time soon.

Honda's favorite spot is Kapukon Yu, a public bath in Higashikomagata which has been in business for over 60 years. The old gentleman who mans the counter has known Honda since before his glory days as a sumo wrestler. Honda often faces opponents here in order to drum up some business for Kapukon Yu, which has been going through some hard times. Recently, Honda has come up with the idea that if Sumo were an Olympic sport, its popularity would grow leaps and bounds. To that end, he is seeking to position himself as a member of the International Olympic Committee.

While street fighting, Honda usually wears a red loincloth instead of the blue one he wears when competing in an official sumo match. He also has been known to fight wearing a yukata with the hem tucked up, as if he had just stepped out of the bath. Officially, his rank is that of Ohzeki, but it is said that he is skilled enough to be a Yokozuna. Where he got the Western first name "Edmond" is still a mystery.

The students at Honda's heya include Hatonoyama, Maru No Umi, and Yasuhanada. Honda and Zangief also get along quite well, sharing common ground as warriors who utilize their raw physical strength when fighting.

FIGHTING STYLE

Honda's fighting style includes defensive moves based around his strong palm strikes, and mighty throws. The tremendous blows that come from his enormous hands can break though opponents' defenses with ease. Using his patented Hundred Hand Slap and Super Head Butt maneuvers, Honda can strike far more quickly than his enemies would usually expect.

SIGNATURE MOVES: Hundred Hand Slap, Sumo Smash, Super Headbutt

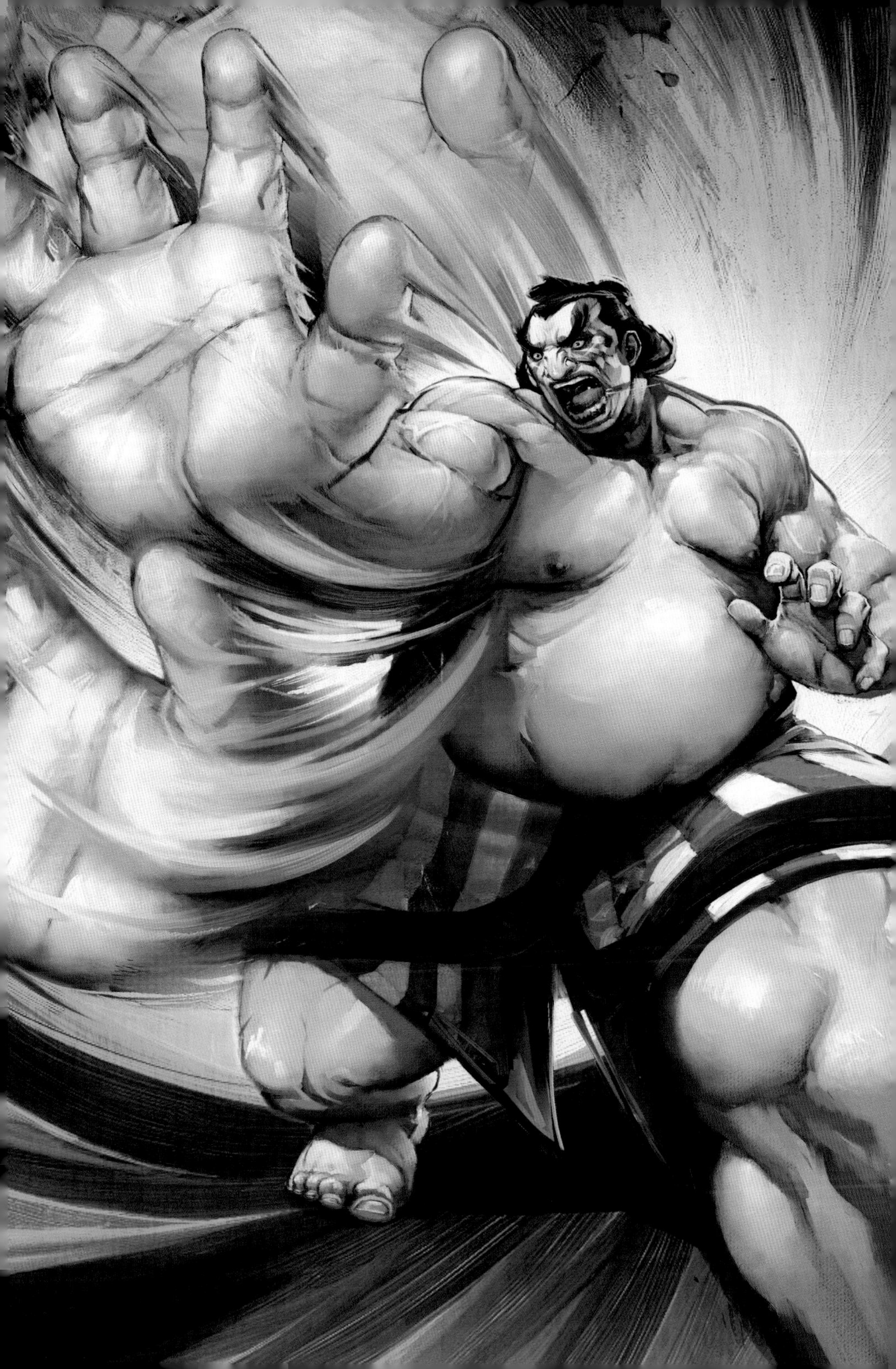

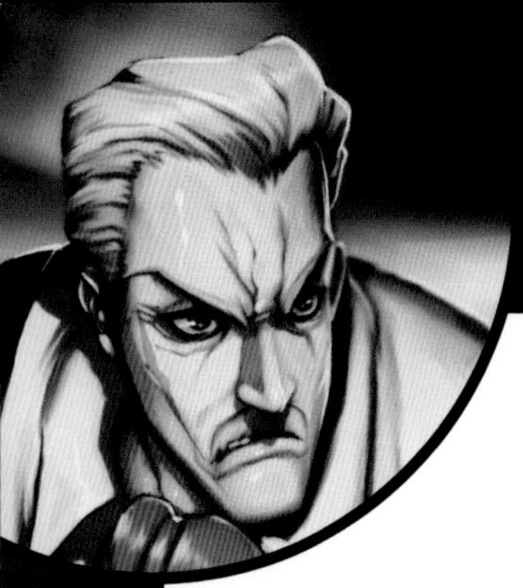

EAGLE

The Fancy Bodyguard

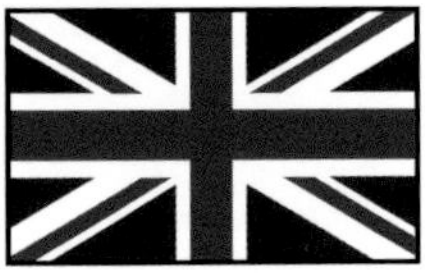

BIRTHDAY: ---------
COUNTRY OF ORIGIN: England
FIGHTING STYLE: Bojutsu
HEIGHT: 183 cm **WEIGHT:** 75 kg
MEASUREMENTS: B105/W80/H86
BLOOD TYPE: AB
LIKES: Dancing, roast beef
DISLIKES: Ungentlemanly behavior, unrefined fellows
SPECIAL ABILITIES: Golf

This steel club wielding fighter hails from England, working as both a bouncer and bodyguard-for-hire. He craves to experience all of the fighting arts. His desire for the perfect duel has set his eyes on the world.

With his moustache, bow tie and impeccable fashion sense, Eagle may seem like a gentleman at first glance, but will quickly reveal himself to be a cold hearted fighter who is willing to beat his opponent to within an inch of their life and sometimes beyond. He was once hired by an unknown party to defeat Sagat during the first Street Fighter tournament, but was unsuccessful.

Being a bouncer is more than just a side job for Eagle, as he loves dancing and the night club scene.

FIGHTING STYLE

Eagle's whole fighting style is based around his two steel clubs. He mixes up quick individual jabs with a flurry of lighting fast repetitive club strikes. Eagle views his fights as a performance, and is just as concerned about the entertainment factor of his fighting style as he is its effectiveness. He takes great care to put some showmanship in all his moves.

SIGNATURE MOVES: Liverpool White, Manchester Black,
Oxford Red, St. Andrew Green

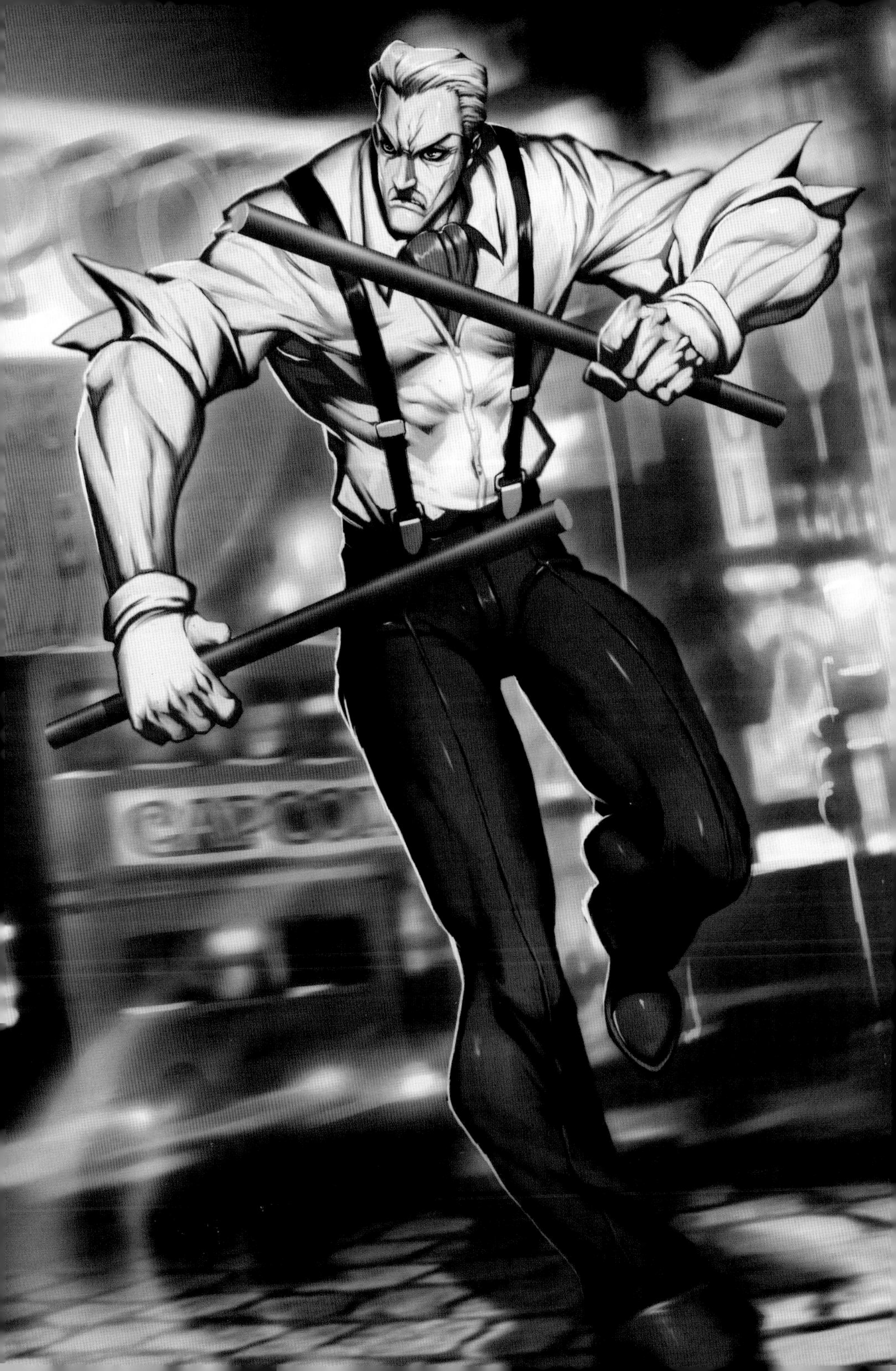

EL FUERTE
The Spicy Hurricane

BIRTHDAY: October 29
COUNTRY OF ORIGIN: Mexico
FIGHTING STYLE: Lucha Libre (Mexican Wrestling)
HEIGHT: 168 cm   **WEIGHT:** 70 kg
MEASUREMENTS: B120/W82/H90
BLOOD TYPE: B
LIKES: Prickly pears   **DISLIKES:** Additives
SPECIAL ABILITIES: Can hold a neck bridge position for 2 hours

As a luchador and a cook, El Fuerte has a foot in each world. It is said that El Fuerte's passion and spirit rival even that of the Red Cyclone's. El Fuerte travels the globe in search of the ultimate recipe, but his cooking skills often leave something to be desired.

El Fuerte decided to become a chef when he was only five years old. While visiting a friend, the friend's father had served the two boys a meal of tortilla soup. It was the most delicious meal he had ever tasted, and from that point on El Fuerte strove to recapture the spirit of that meal in his own dishes. The friend's family later moved away to another village, but El Fuerte would as an adult be reunited with his childhood companion — better known as Native American martial artist T. Hawk.

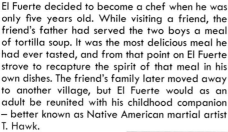

EL FUERTE IN THE KITCHEN

FIGHTING STYLE
As a luchador, El Fuerte combines rapid holds and hits with high-flying air moves. He uses a variety of unexpected attacks to surprise opponents and hit them where it hurts. His Habanero Dash can transition into several very different attacks, always keeping his opponents guessing.

SIGNATURE MOVES:
Guacamole Leg Throw, Habanero Dash, Quesadilla Bomb

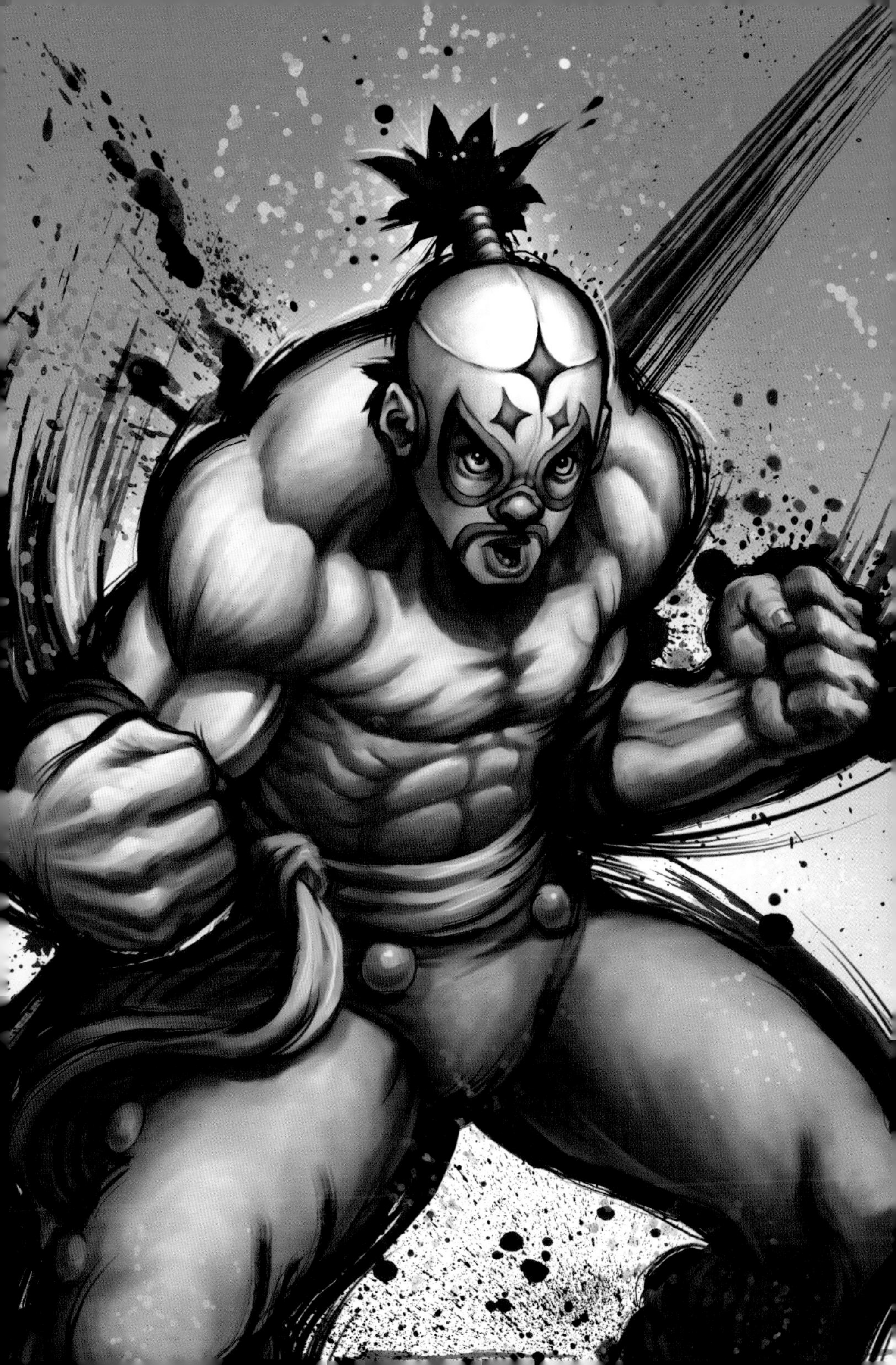

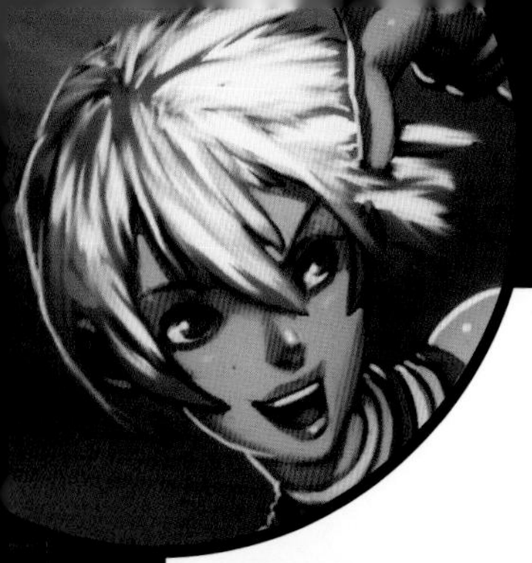

ELENA

Princess of the Savannah

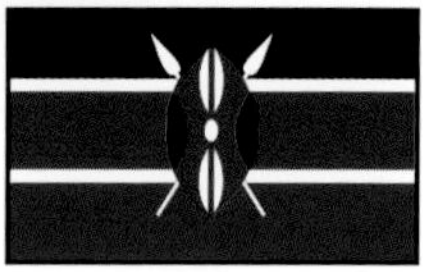

BIRTHDAY: ---------
COUNTRY OF ORIGIN: Kenya
FIGHTING STYLE: Capoeira
HEIGHT: --------- **WEIGHT:** ---------
MEASUREMENTS: ---------
BLOOD TYPE: ---------
LIKES: Travelling, animals
DISLIKES: Damage to the environment
SPECIAL ABILITIES: Communication with nature, holistic healing

Daughter to the elder of a small tribe living in the African savannah, Elena is a happy, energetic girl who never forgets to be moved by, and feel gratitude for, everything around her. Her special talents include her ability to become friends with her opponent after a match. As a member of a warrior tribe, Elena was told by her father to learn the culture of battle. Elena took up Capoeira, moving to the rhythm of the earth and kicking out with her long legs.

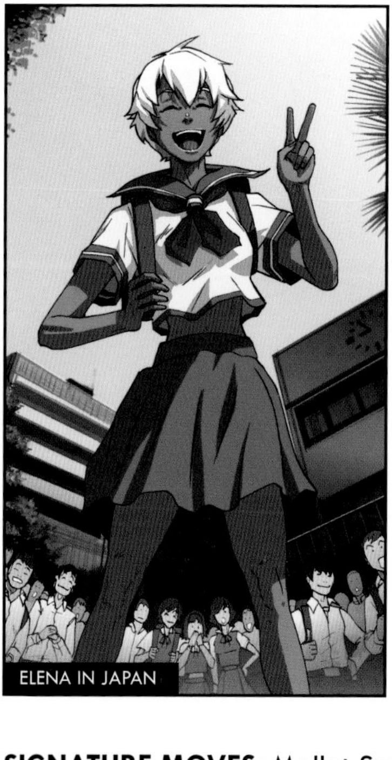

ELENA IN JAPAN

Admiring her father for earning a doctorate at a university in France, Elena dreamed of one day following in her father's footsteps and studying abroad. In the end, she chose to attend school in Japan, where she made a new best friend – Narumi. Elena calls this petite and shy girl by the endearing nickname "Naruchan."

Once she finished her school term in Japan, Elena looked forward to studying next in France. Hoping to make more "friends" before school starts, Elena found her way into the world of street fighting.

Elena is a senior in high school - one year younger than Ibuki.

FIGHTING STYLE

Elena's fighting style is Capoeira, a leg based martial art developed by shackled slaves. Using her long legs and natural springing movements to make up for her lack of strength, she fights as well as foes much stronger than she is. Her flowing and rhythmic dance-like maneuvers play with her opponents as she lets loose confusing, artistic kicks.

SIGNATURE MOVES: Mallet Smash, Scratch Wheel, Spin Scythe

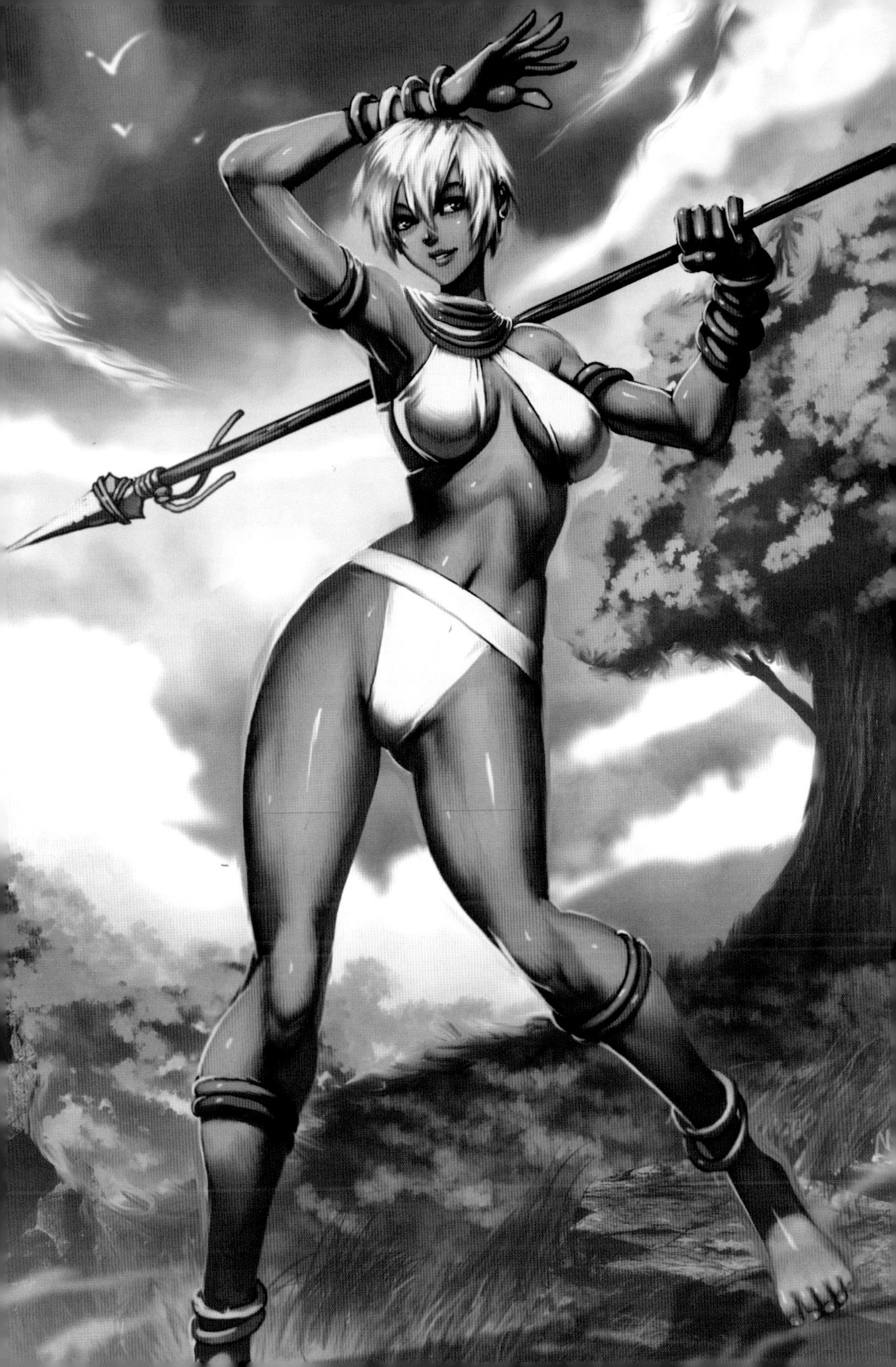

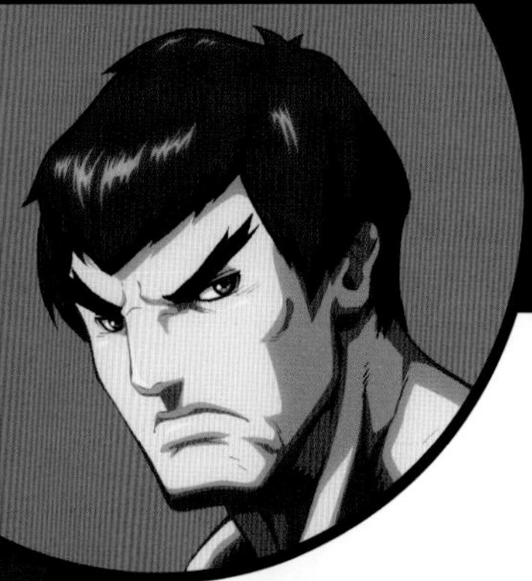

FEI LONG

Fists of Fury

BIRTHDAY: April 23
COUNTRY OF ORIGIN: Hong Kong
FIGHTING STYLE: Kung Fu
HEIGHT: 172 cm **WEIGHT:** 60 kg
MEASUREMENTS: B108/W76/H80
BLOOD TYPE: O
LIKES: Kung Fu, self-assertiveness
DISLIKES: Lethargy, apathy, indifference
SPECIAL ABILITIES: Performs all his own stunts

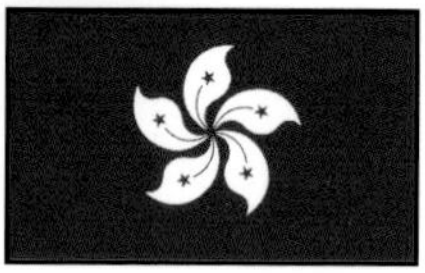

No man in Hong Kong can face Fei Long as an equal when it comes to Kung Fu. Born and raised in Hong Kong, Fei Long makes good use of the Kung Fu skills he has been developing since he was 6 years old and made his debut as an action movie star. He was sometimes said to be carrying the future of the Hong Kong movie industry on his shoulders.

Early on in his career as a movie star, Fei Long heard of the World Fighting Tournament and thought it would be a great opportunity to hone his skills in fighting and acting. By the end, Fei Long came to realize that his true passion was fighting rather than acting, and proceeded to turn down an offer for a main role from a movie director.

After leaving the movie industry for good, Fei Long established the "Hiten Style" of Kung Fu and gathered over 3,000,000 students under his banner.

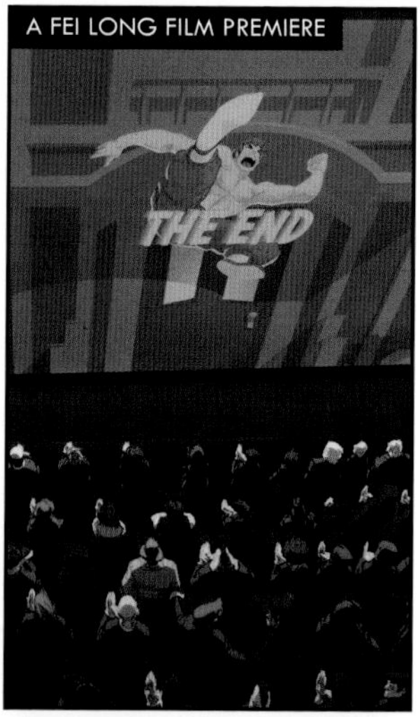
THE END
A FEI LONG FILM PREMIERE

FIGHTING STYLE

With his swift, graceful movements, Fei Long can take advantage of any momentary openings his opponents leave. After striking with many of his powerful blows, Fei Long lets out a piercing shout that increases his power and confidence.

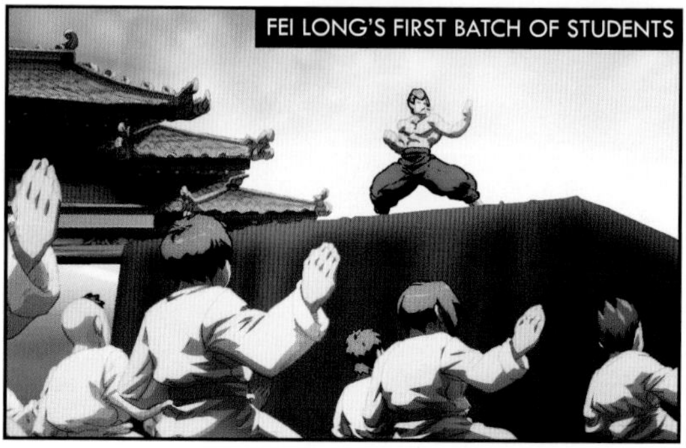
FEI LONG'S FIRST BATCH OF STUDENTS

SIGNATURE MOVES: Rekkaken, Rekkukyaku, Shienkyaku

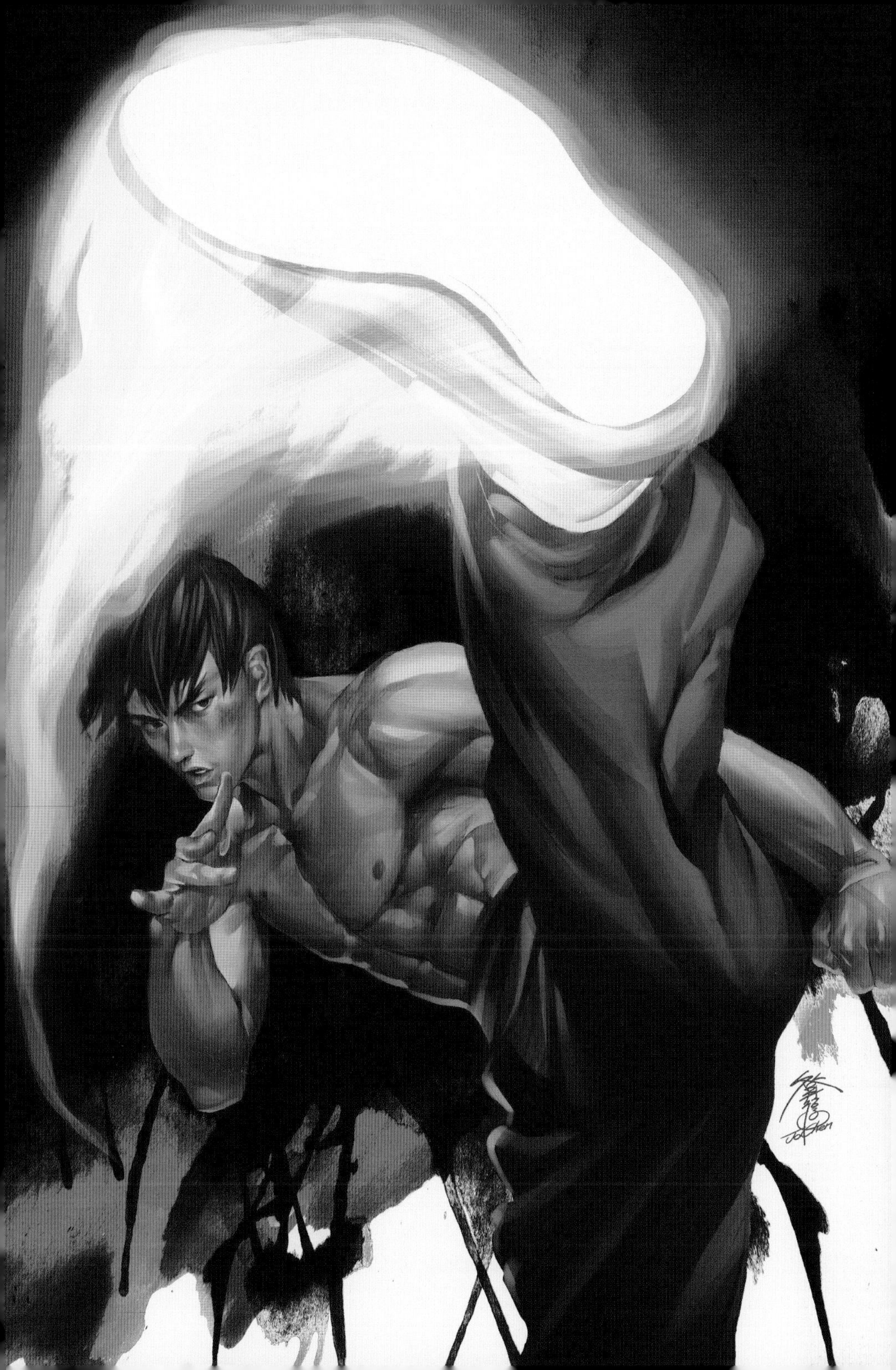

GEN
The Silent Assassin

BIRTHDAY: March 10
COUNTRY OF ORIGIN: China
FIGHTING STYLE: Chinese Martial Arts, Sou & Ki Styles
HEIGHT: 166 cm   **WEIGHT:** 61 kg
MEASUREMENTS: B106/W75/H80
BLOOD TYPE: O
LIKES: Meat buns, writing Chinese poems
DISLIKES: Crowds
SPECIAL ABILITIES: Chinese medicine

Gen is known and feared in the dark underbelly of Hong Kong as "Gen the Invincible, the man of 100 bloody battles." He is an elderly assassin who uses both the Sou and Ki styles with masterful ease to instantaneously end his target's life with his bare hands.

What most people do not know is that Gen is terminally ill, and he is throwing himself into fight after fight because he wishes to greet the end of his life through a blaze of glory. The only joy this 70-something year-old finds in life lies in his "death matches" against challenging opponents, which is why, despite his illness, he will not hesitate to walk out onto a field of battle. He considers Akuma, who practices an extremely deadly art of his own, to be his only true rival. Gen found greater joy in a battle against Akuma than he had in his entire lifetime, and walked away from Akuma's defeated form without executing a killing blow.

Gen was a good friend of Chun-Li's missing father, and as such he feels the need to watch over her when he can. Some of Gen's techniques were taught to Chun-Li's father, and in turn passed down to her.

CHUN-LI TRAINS WITH GEN

FIGHTING STYLE
After mastering countless martial arts over the years, Gen created two distinct fighting styles of his own, the Sou and Ki styles. Once Gen found out that he had contracted a fatal disease he embarked on a quest to find the ultimate opponent, one worthy enough to slay him. Gen's unique death wish makes him a very deadly opponent and also sets him apart from the rest of the street fighters.

SIGNATURE MOVES: Hyakurenkou, Jasen, Zanei

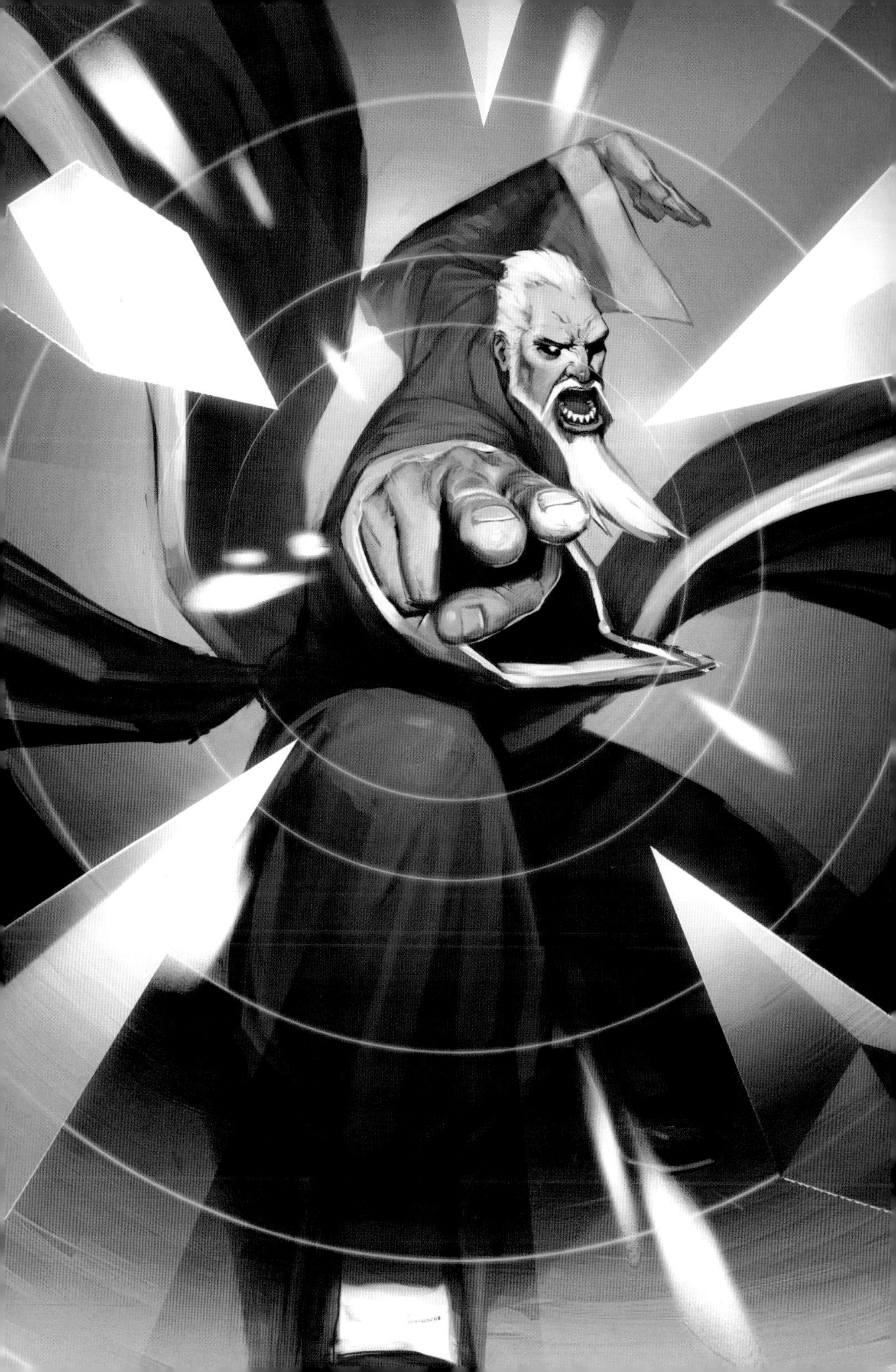

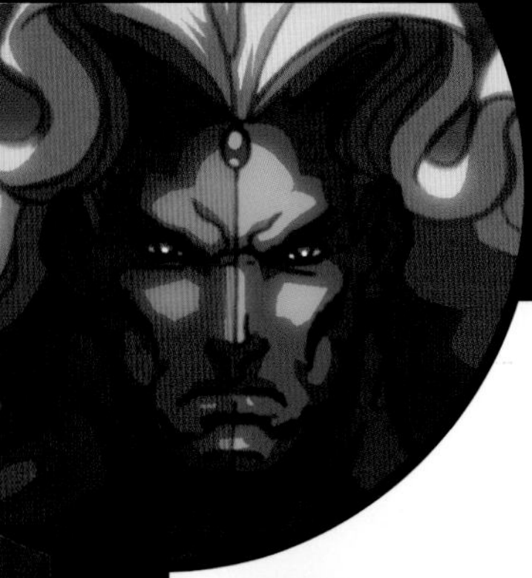

GILL

The Dark Messiah

BIRTHDAY: Unknown
COUNTRY OF ORIGIN: Unknown
FIGHTING STYLE: Illuminati Secret Techniques
HEIGHT: --------- **WEIGHT:** ---------
MEASUREMENTS: ---------
BLOOD TYPE: ---------
LIKES: Order
DISLIKES: Disobedience
SPECIAL ABILITIES: Pyrokinesis/cryokinesis

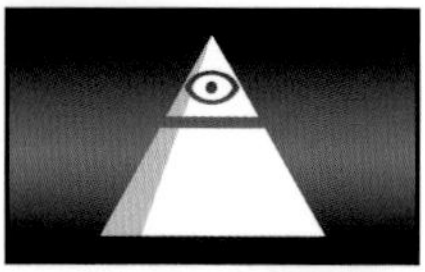

As the president of the 2000+ year old secret society known as the Illuminati, Gill has been behind the scenes, manipulating every aspect of the world. His goal is to build the perfect world by the year 2200. The president of the Illuminati is said to be the elite of the elite, determined by an investigative selection process that happens once every 24 years... but with his long golden locks flowing over his nearly naked, briefs-clad body colored half red and half blue, Gill looks like anything but someone who could be described as "elite".

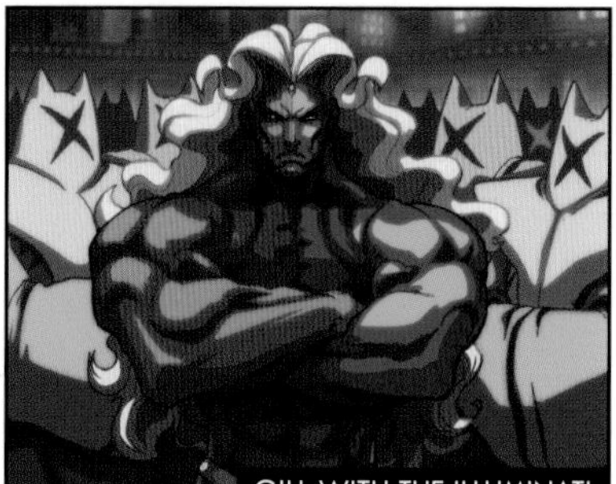

GILL WITH THE ILLUMINATI

Gill's younger brother Urien was also once a candidate for Illuminati presidency, and has become quite jealous of Gill's position. Urien eventually defeated Gill in battle and took the title of president for himself, only to find out that Gill was not only acting as president of the Illuminati, but is also its current emperor. Though he may have given his title of president to his Urien, Gill still holds ultimate control over the Illuminati as their emperor. With the goal of creating a world where life and death, love and hate can all coexist, Gill continues to further his plans.

Gill and the Illuminati hope to usher in a new era known as the "Age of God". The secret society's prophecies foretell that the clash of two primal and opposing forces will collide to devastating effect. They are hoping that the ascension and ultimate control of an emperor figure will bring harmonious balance to these forces. It is said that Gill's body is split between two colors to sublimate the conflict that comes with making the necessary decisions to create his ideal world, and to represents the absolute balance of two opposing forces.

Gill's blue side emits the element of ice and his red side emits the element of fire.

FIGHTING STYLE

Like Urien, Gill is a student of the Illuminati's 66 secret fighting techniques, though he has chosen to focus on different aspects of the form than his brother. He is extremely powerful, wielding the energies of both fire and ice to devastating effects. He also has mastered the Resurrection technique, which allows him to rise again at partial strength if he is defeated in battle.

SIGNATURE MOVES: Pyro-kinesis, Cryo-kinesis, Meteor Smash

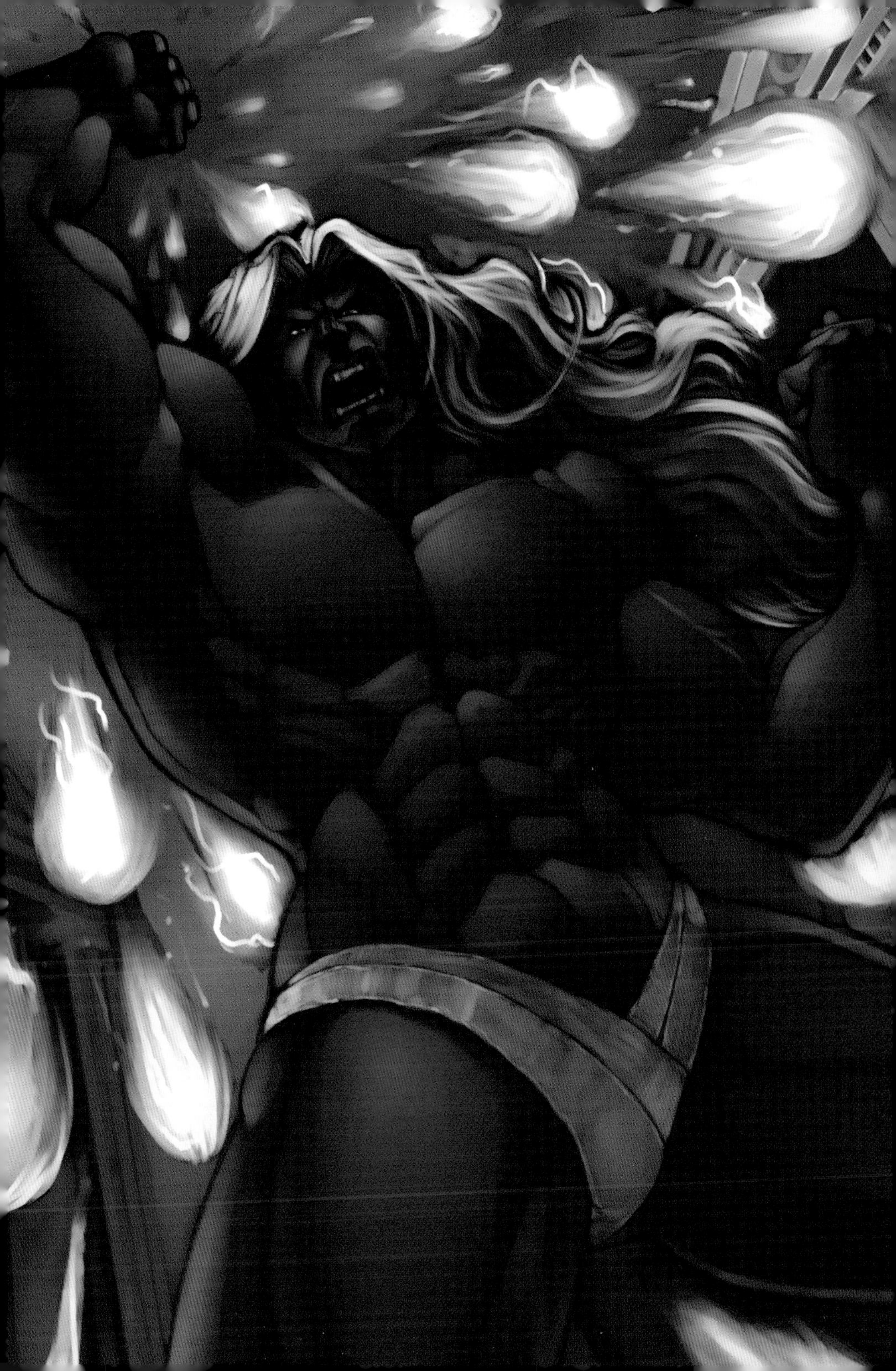

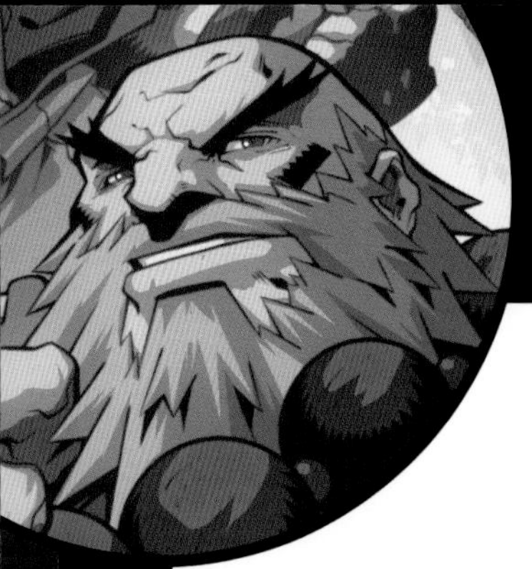

GOUKEN

Built Like a Holy Mountain

BIRTHDAY: Unknown
COUNTRY OF ORIGIN: Japan
FIGHTING STYLE: Martial Arts rooted in Ansatsuken
HEIGHT: 185 cm **WEIGHT:** 90 kg
MEASUREMENTS: B125/W95/H90
BLOOD TYPE: Unknown
LIKES: Dumplings
DISLIKES: Mosquitoes
SPECIAL ABILITIES: Fishing

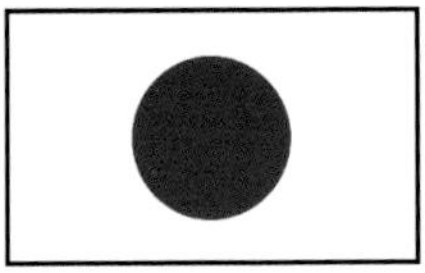

Gouken is master to Ryu and Ken, and the brother of Akuma. Having purified what was originally known as the Ansatsuken (the Assassin's Fist), he established a new style of martial arts around it and passed it on to Ryu and Ken.

Gouken and Akuma learned the Shoryuken, Hadoken, and Tatsumaki Senpukyaku from their master, Goutetsu. These three moves were originally the basis of Ansatsuken. Reveling in the deadly origins of the fighting style, Akuma embraced the dark and destructive "Satsui no Hado" and killed his former Master. Gouken however was able to cleanse all traces of the Satsui no Hado from the martial arts form before passing it on to his students twenty years later.

Akuma would eventually return to challenge his brother as well. In their final match, Akuma unleashed his ultimate technique, the Shun Goku Satsu (Instant Hell Murder), killing Gouken... or so it seemed. At the moment of death, Gouken called on the power of Mu or "nothingness," protecting his life force while his body was destroyed. While it took considerable time and effort, Gouken's spirit was able to rebuild his body, and he returned years later to face Akuma once again. Whether he has been permanently resurrected, or has only returned for a limited time is yet to be revealed.

Gouken has only recently made his presence known to Ryu and Ken. Upon first re-encountering Ryu, Gouken learned of Ryu's struggle with the Satsui no Hado. Gouken used the power of Mu once again to seal the Satsui no Hado within Ryu, and finally end Ryu's constant struggle to maintain control of that dark power. Though he is glad to be reunited with his former pupils, he has made it clear that his role as their master is complete as they are now grown men.

In addition to Ryu and Ken, Gouken also trained Dan for a short time, but expelled him once it was clear he was motivated only by revenge.

FIGHTING STYLE

Gouken is the oldest and most skilled living practitioner of Ansatsuken, and as such is able to use this ancient martial art in many unexpected ways. For instance, he has harnessed the power of the Shoryuken punch into a new horizontal assault, and conversely turned the Tatsumaki kick into a vertical attack. Gouken is also a master of the Hadoken fireball, which he can fire in multiple directions. He can pull off Hadokens using only one hand, a skill achieved by only one other known fighter - Akuma.

SIGNATURE MOVES: Gohadoken, Forbidden Shoryuken, Tatsumaki Gorasen

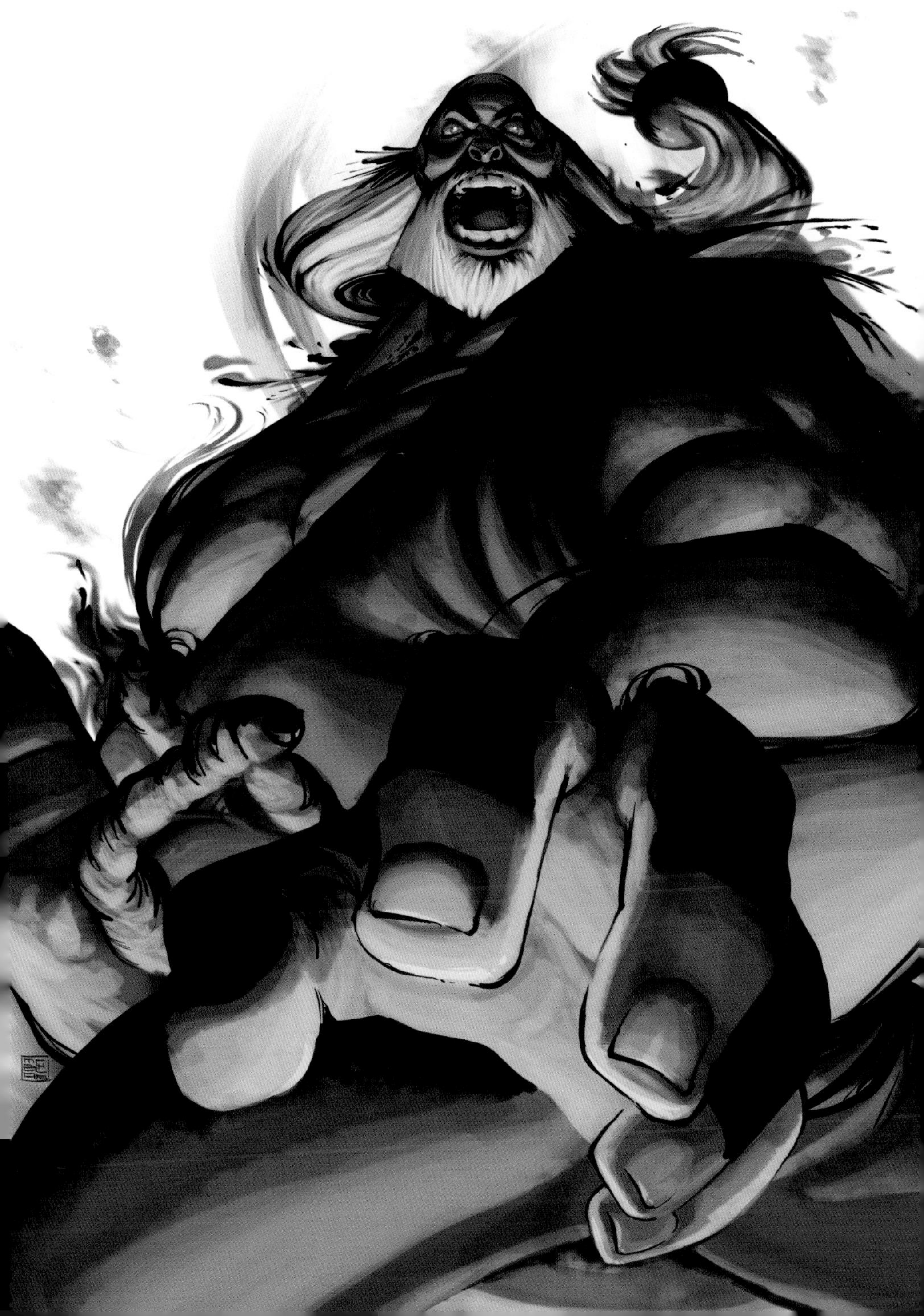

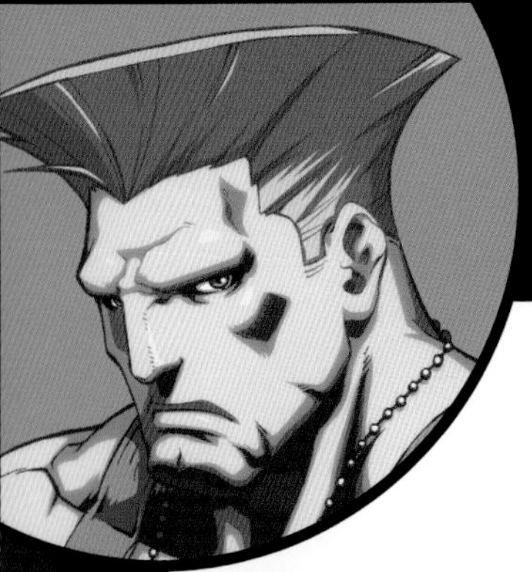

GUILE

The Sonic Blade

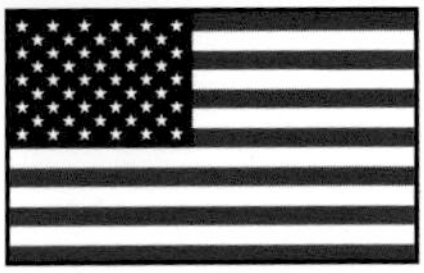

BIRTHDAY: December 23
COUNTRY OF ORIGIN: U.S.A.
FIGHTING STYLE: Martial arts and professional wrestling
HEIGHT: 182 cm **WEIGHT:** 86 kg
MEASUREMENTS: B125/W83/H89
BLOOD TYPE: O
LIKES: American Coffee
DISLIKES: The nattou Ryu fed him while he was in Japan
SPECIAL ABILITIES: Darts

A member of the U.S. Air Force, Guile has sworn to avenge his friend Charlie Nash, who was killed by M. Bison. It is said that Guile's fighting style, a uniquely personal adaptation of martial arts, is capable of cutting through anything and anyone.

Guile and Charlie were both lieutenants in the Air Force, when Charlie left to infiltrate Shadaloo and prove they were connected to corruption within the force. At the time Guile tried to stop Charlie, thinking his actions were too rash and even dangerous, but was unable to keep his friend from leaving. In the end Charlie was discovered by M. Bison, and never returned from the mission.

Upon learning of his friend's death, Guile decided to first go after Bison through legal avenues. After a detailed investigation he was able to produce evidence that M. Bison was responsible for Charlie's murder. Upon taking Bison to court, however, Guile soon found out that Bison had the entire court in the palm of his hand. Realizing that he could not depend on the American legal system to serve justice in this case, Guile made the decision to go after Bison himself, on his own terms.

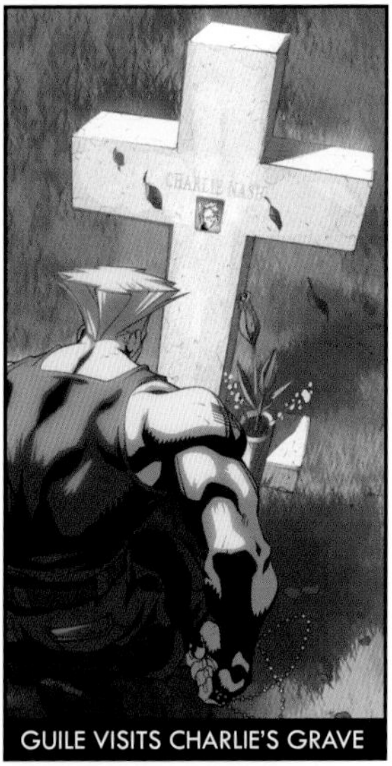
CHARLIE NASH
GUILE VISITS CHARLIE'S GRAVE

Guile not only has his own dog tags with him, but also carries the dog tags of the departed Charlie. He also often visits Charlie's grave to lay flowers and honor his fallen comrade. Deep down, he harbors a hope that his friend may still be alive, as Charlie's body was never found.

Guile's family includes his wife, Julia, a daughter named Amy, and a dog named Sabu. His family often worries that he is too involved in a dangerous career, and wishes he would spend more time at home. Julia also happens to be the sister of Ken Master's wife, Eliza, making Ken and Guile brothers-in-law.

FIGHTING STYLE

Guile's fighting style requires precise judgment and perception of his enemy's movements. By blending martial arts moves with wrestling, he's found a strong array of offensive and defensive maneuvers, including the Sonic Boom and Somersault Kick attack forms.

SIGNATURE MOVES: Flash Kick, Sonic Boom

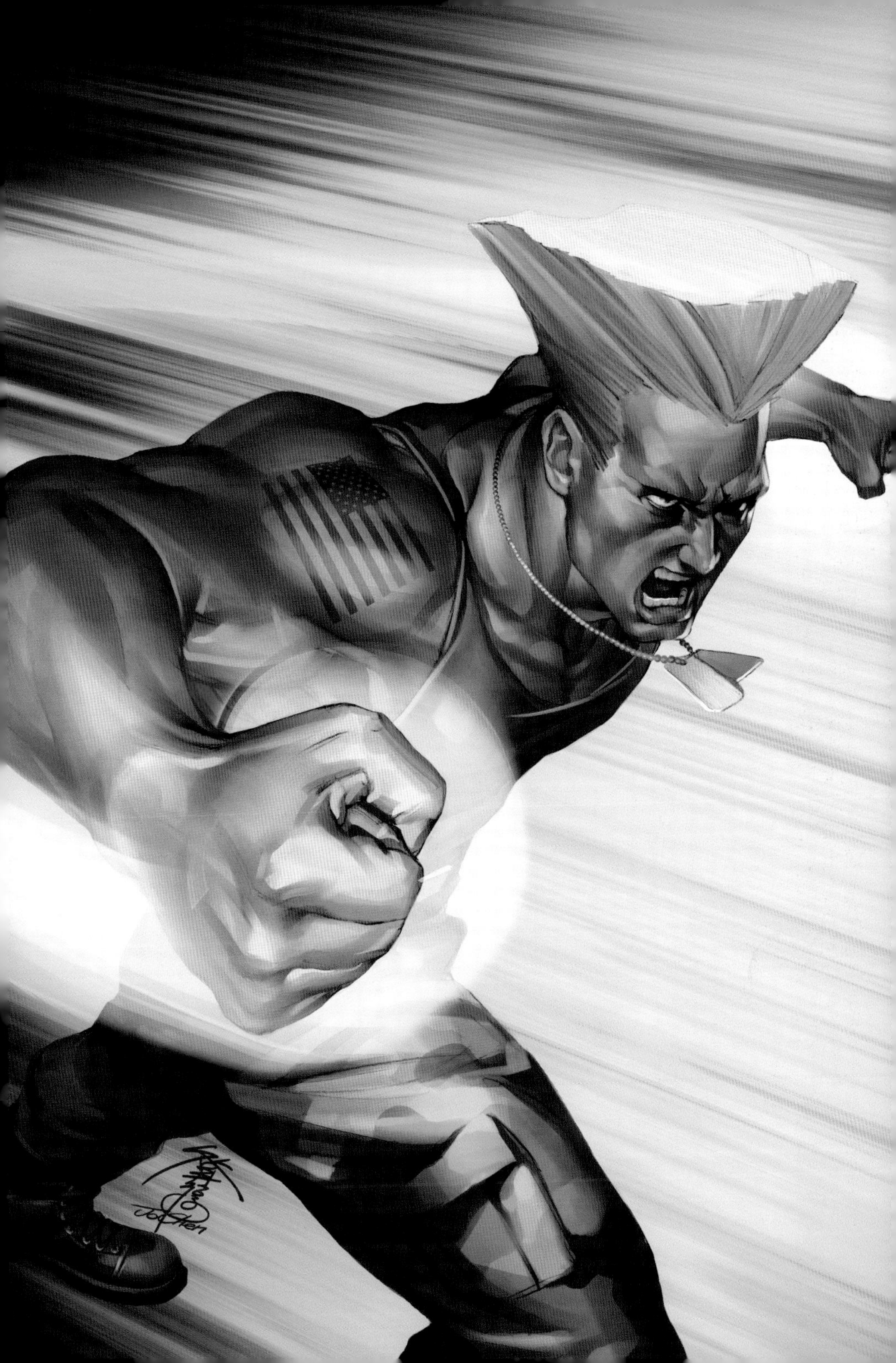

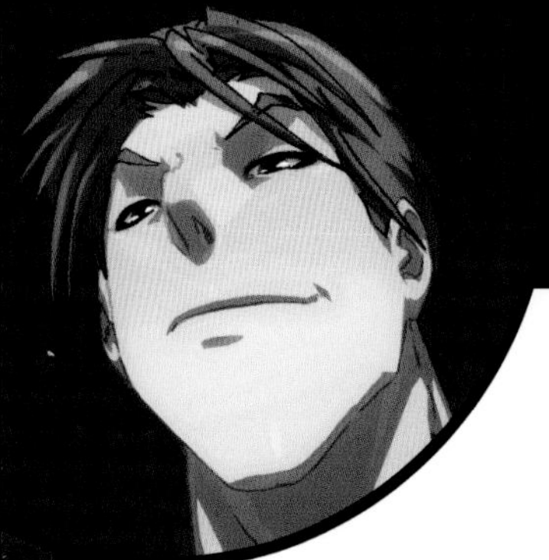

GUY

The 39th Bushin-ryu Master

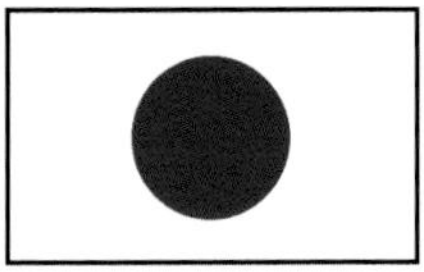

BIRTHDAY: August 12
COUNTRY OF ORIGIN: Japan
FIGHTING STYLE: Bushin-ryu Ninjutsu
HEIGHT: 179 cm **WEIGHT:** 72 kg
MEASUREMENTS: B108/W77/H82
BLOOD TYPE: O
LIKES: Salmon Ochazuke, chilled tofu, sneakers
DISLIKES: Western(horizontal) writing
SPECIAL ABILITIES: Bonsai tending

Guy is the 39th generation master of Bushin-ryu, a 500+ year old practical form of ninjutsu based on multi-opponent tactics.

Guy was still a boy when he was taken in by his master, Zeku. It was from Zeku, 38th generation master of Bushin-ryu, that Guy learned the Bushin style. Guy was just a young hooligan when Zeku found him on the streets of Japan, but Zeku saw a natural talent in Guy and decided to pass the Bushin style down to him. Just before Guy left for America, Zeku told him to "overcome all" before disappearing without a trace.

Guy first headed to Metro City in America in search of some first-hand fighting experience. When he heard that Cody, a young fighter Guy had met while training, was planning on rescuing his kidnapped girlfriend, Guy decided to lend a hand in the fight against Mad Gear. Learning from his experiences in Metro City, Guy realized that he needed to make the Bushin style of ninjutsu more geared towards real battle situations. In order to gain the experience he needed, Guy jumped into the world of street fighting. Through his many battles against strong opponents, Guy succeeded in shaping a new Bushin style.

Zeku once told Guy, "When he who would bring chaos to the world appears, the shadow of Bushin shall be there." Guy was intent on figuring out what this prophetic message was referring to. Once he found out that "he who would bring chaos" was M. Bison, Guy felt it was his duty as the heir of the Bushin style to challenge Bison.

Despite his youth, Guy speaks and acts in a distinctively dated way, possibly due to his training as a ninja. He has trouble with English and other European languages, despite his time spent in America. Though born in America, Guy grew up in Japan.

While he has always worried about his friend Cody's disorderly life, Guy has refrained from meddling. Guy's fiancée, Rena, is the older sister of fellow Bushin style fighter Maki. Guy is also viewed as a rival by former Mad Gear member Sodom, whom he has known since his Metro City days.

FIGHTING STYLE

Guy's unique application of Bushin martial arts utilizes speed and rapid attacks to wear down opponents until he can find an opening for his deadliest maneuvers. Guy labels some of his special attacks with the preface Bushin, even though his master felt it might make the young fighter too egotistical and assume that he'd mastered the deepest secrets of Bushin martial arts.

SIGNATURE MOVES: Bushin Senpukyaku, Hayagake, Kubukari

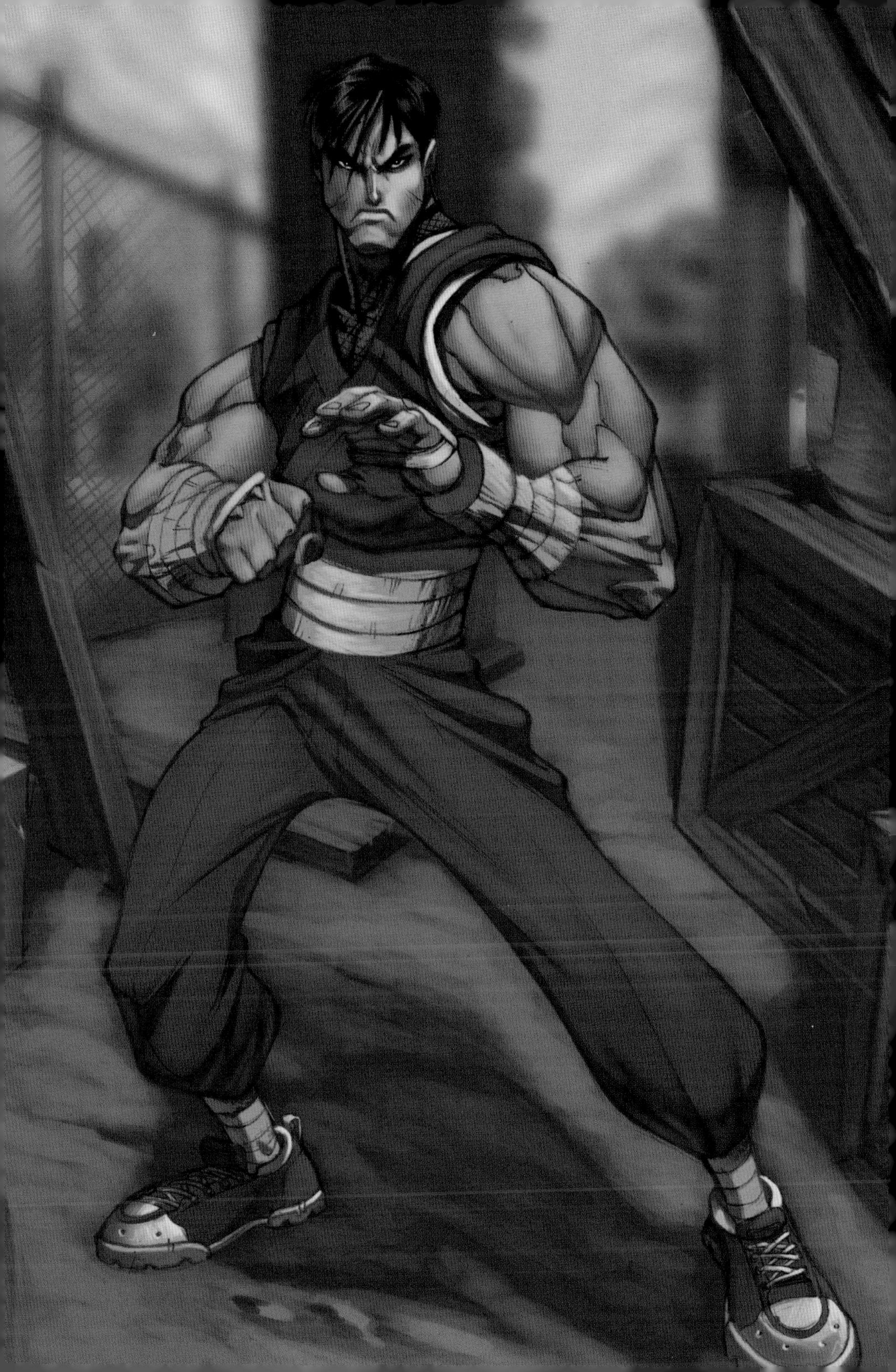

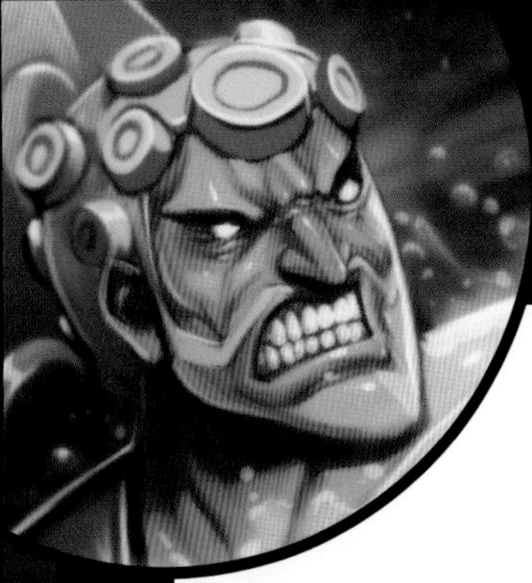

HAKAN

The Invincible Czar

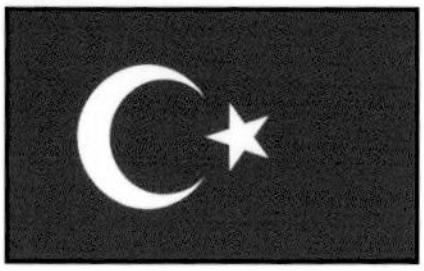

BIRTHDAY: November 13
COUNTRY OF ORIGIN: Turkey
FIGHTING STYLE: Yaglı güreş (Turkish Oil Wrestling)
HEIGHT: 190 cm **WEIGHT:** 110 kg
MEASUREMENTS: B172/W160/H165
BLOOD TYPE: O
LIKES: His wife, daughters, chanko, oil
DISLIKES: Cigarettes, fire
SPECIAL ABILITIES: Enka (Japanese singing style)

Hakan is a huge Turkish oil wrestler with deep red skin and curly turquoise hair, paired with a large moustache. He wears a modified version of traditional Turkish wrestling garb, customized with gold chain, leather bands, and a large belt with a golden lion's head buckle. Hakan often carries a massive barrel which contains a large quantity of oil, which he uses to enhance his unique combat style.

Hakan is the president of the world's leading edible oil manufacturer and a leader in Turkey's national sport of Yaglı güres, oil wrestling. His success in both fields have made him a beloved hero in Turkey.

His drive to fight in the Street Fighter tournament is not fueled by revenge or honor, but in a desire to have fun. He is a very lively sort, and easily makes new friends. Hakan also hopes his victories will make his cherished wife and seven daughters proud. When not seeking out new opponents, Hakan is on a quest to discover the world's perfect oil recipe.

Family is a top priority for him, along with proving the merits of Turkish-style wrestling. He is constantly trying to find worthy husbands for his many daughters to one day marry, despite the fact that they are only 7 to 9 years old.

FIGHTING STYLE

Hakan's best moves revolve around the application of oil to his body. This very unique technique often confuses not only his opponent but the spectators as well. His slippery combat style allows him to grapple and throw opponents with surprising effectiveness. Slide attacks and a unique throw style make him a challenging opponent for fighters more accustomed to facing traditional street fighting styles.

SIGNATURE MOVES: Oil up!, Oil Coaster, Oil Combination Hold

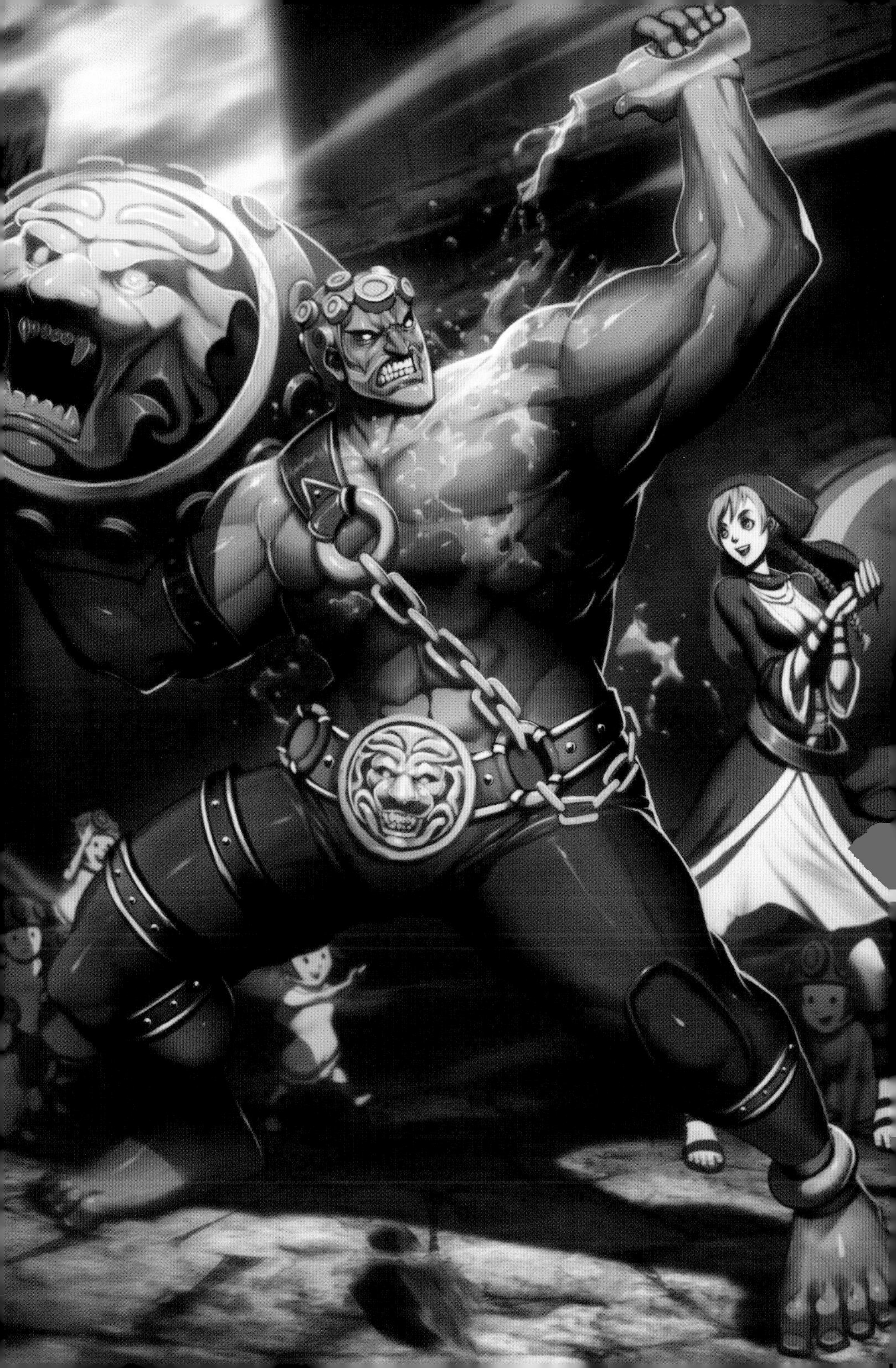

HUGO
The Towering Behemoth

BIRTHDAY: ---------
COUNTRY OF ORIGIN: Germany
FIGHTING STYLE: Pro Wrestling
HEIGHT: --------- **WEIGHT:** ---------
MEASUREMENTS: ---------
BLOOD TYPE: ---------
LIKES: Poison, tag teaming
DISLIKES: Complex decisions
SPECIAL ABILITIES: Weight lifting

Hugo Andore is a giant man raised on a farm in Germany, and a former member of the Mad Gear gang. He crossed over to North America when he was 20 years old, and was able to use his sheer size and strength to start a career in professional wrestling. Hugo was undefeated in both the wrestling world as well as the ultimate fighting world.

HUGO WITH POISON

Hugo was planning on making his debut in tag team wrestling when he lost his partner to a rival's scheme. With only a few months left before the tag team tournament, Hugo and his manager Poison (another former Mad Gear member) decided to make the rounds to various regions in order to find a worthy tag team partner.

Hugo later returned to a solo career, but due to his overwhelming victories, he found that people had started distancing themselves from him, leading to a very short list of willing opponents. Poison came up with the idea for the H.W.A. (the Huge Wrestling Army) to ensure that Hugo always had someone to fight. She would pick fights with any tough fighters they came across, and the unfortunate target would be drafted into the H.W.A. if they were defeated by Hugo. The H.W.A eventually grew to include over 50 fighters.

Though he is a little slow, Hugo has an amiable personality and can be emotionally sensitive at times. He has family in Germany, including two younger sisters, but has not returned to see them since running away from home. He also has several male relatives in Metro City, most of who operate as street thugs.

FIGHTING STYLE

Hugo's fighting style reflects the simple but destructive power of his wrestling background. His speed and jumping abilities are incredible for his size. With his crushing throws he can attack effectively even from above, giving him more than enough opportunity to demolish his foes.

SIGNATURE MOVES: Giant Palm Bomber, Summersault Press

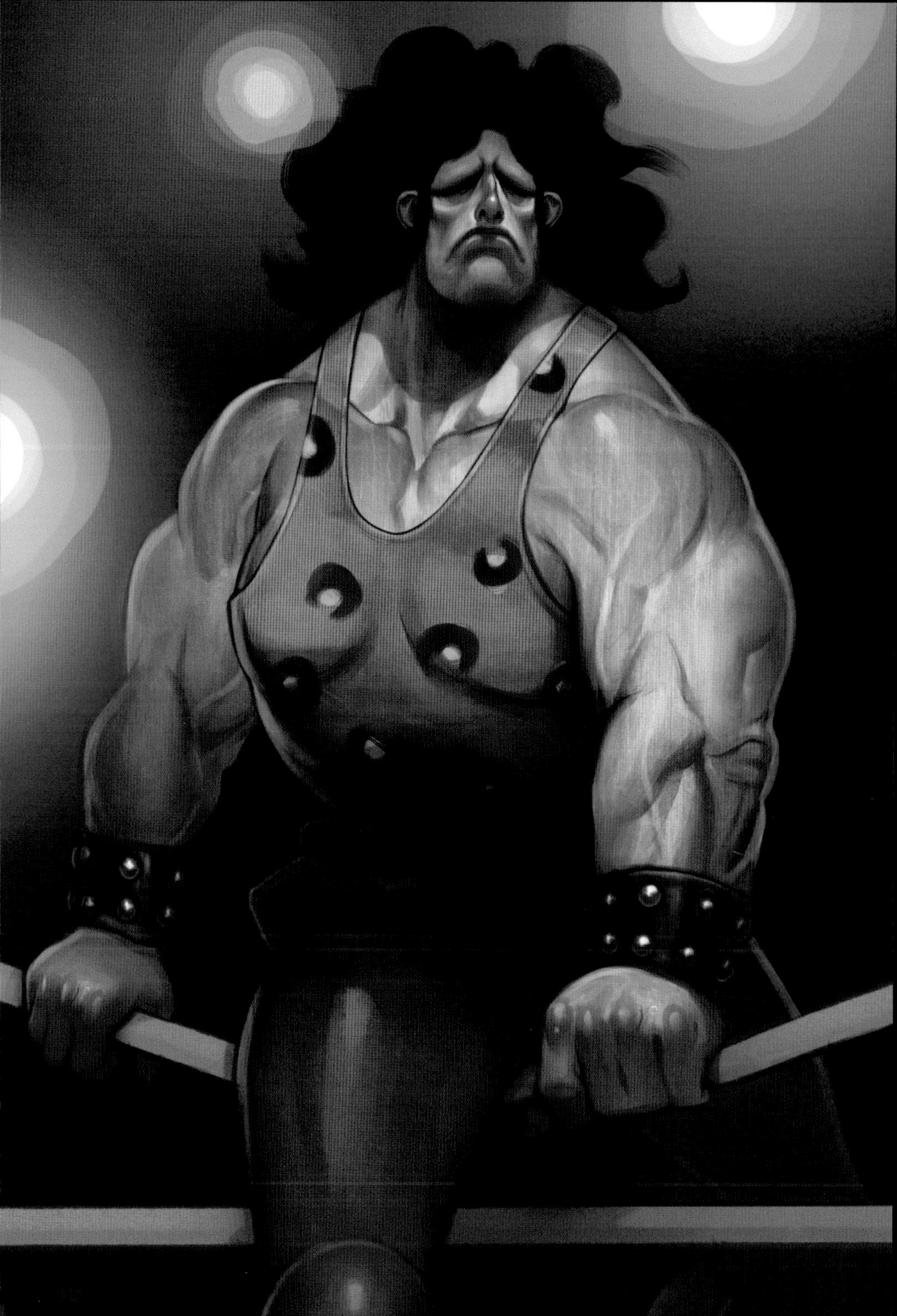

IBUKI
High School Ninja

BIRTHDAY: December 6
COUNTRY OF ORIGIN: Japan
FIGHTING STYLE: Ninjutsu
HEIGHT: 162 cm   **WEIGHT:** 46 kg
MEASUREMENTS: B95/W57/H90
BLOOD TYPE: A
LIKES: Don, roasted sweet potatoes, midwife toads
DISLIKES: Ninja training, detention
SPECIAL ABILITIES: Fast eater

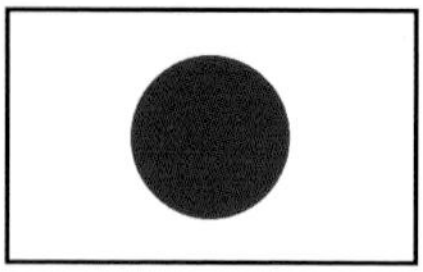

A high school girl living in the Glade of Ninjas, Ibuki has been trained in the ancient Japanese fighting style of ninjutsu since she was very young. Though her physical skills are far superior to the average human's, she is still just a regular high school girl behind the ninja mask. While she is on duty, Ibuki always has her lower face covered with cloth.

On her first major ninja mission, Ibuki was set upon the world with orders to find and retrieve the mysterious G File. Many rumors surrounded the content of the G File, but according to its creator, Gill, "No layman will be able to make any sense of the file just by reading it." In the end, Ibuki was successful in acquiring the G File, but it left an unsettling feeling in her heart.

High school graduation was closing in on Ibuki, but instead of preparing to find employment as her school suggested, she signed up to attend college. She hoped to finally get away from her daily ninja training, find a nice boyfriend, and enjoy campus life. Ibuki successfully

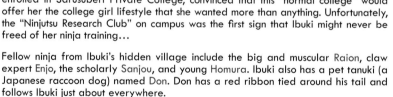

IBUKI AT SCHOOL

enrolled in Sarusuberi Private College, convinced that this "normal college" would offer her the college girl lifestyle that she wanted more than anything. Unfortunately, the "Ninjutsu Research Club" on campus was the first sign that Ibuki might never be freed of her ninja training...

Fellow ninja from Ibuki's hidden village include the big and muscular Raion, claw expert Enjo, the scholarly Sanjou, and young Homura. Ibuki also has a pet tanuki (a Japanese raccoon dog) named Don. Don has a red ribbon tied around his tail and follows Ibuki just about everywhere.

FIGHTING STYLE
Ibuki's fighting style is a combination of ancient martial arts and secret Ninjutsu techniques. Her personal style is based around quick, efficient movements, aiming for weak points on her opponents so she wins before they know what hit them. Her power and reach are less than many other fighters due to her small size, but through training she's been able to overcome this weakness with incredible agility. Ibuki also carries a variety of ninja weapons, but prefers her Kunai daggers.

SIGNATURE MOVES: Kunai, Kasumi Sujyaku, Tsumuji

いぶき IBUKI

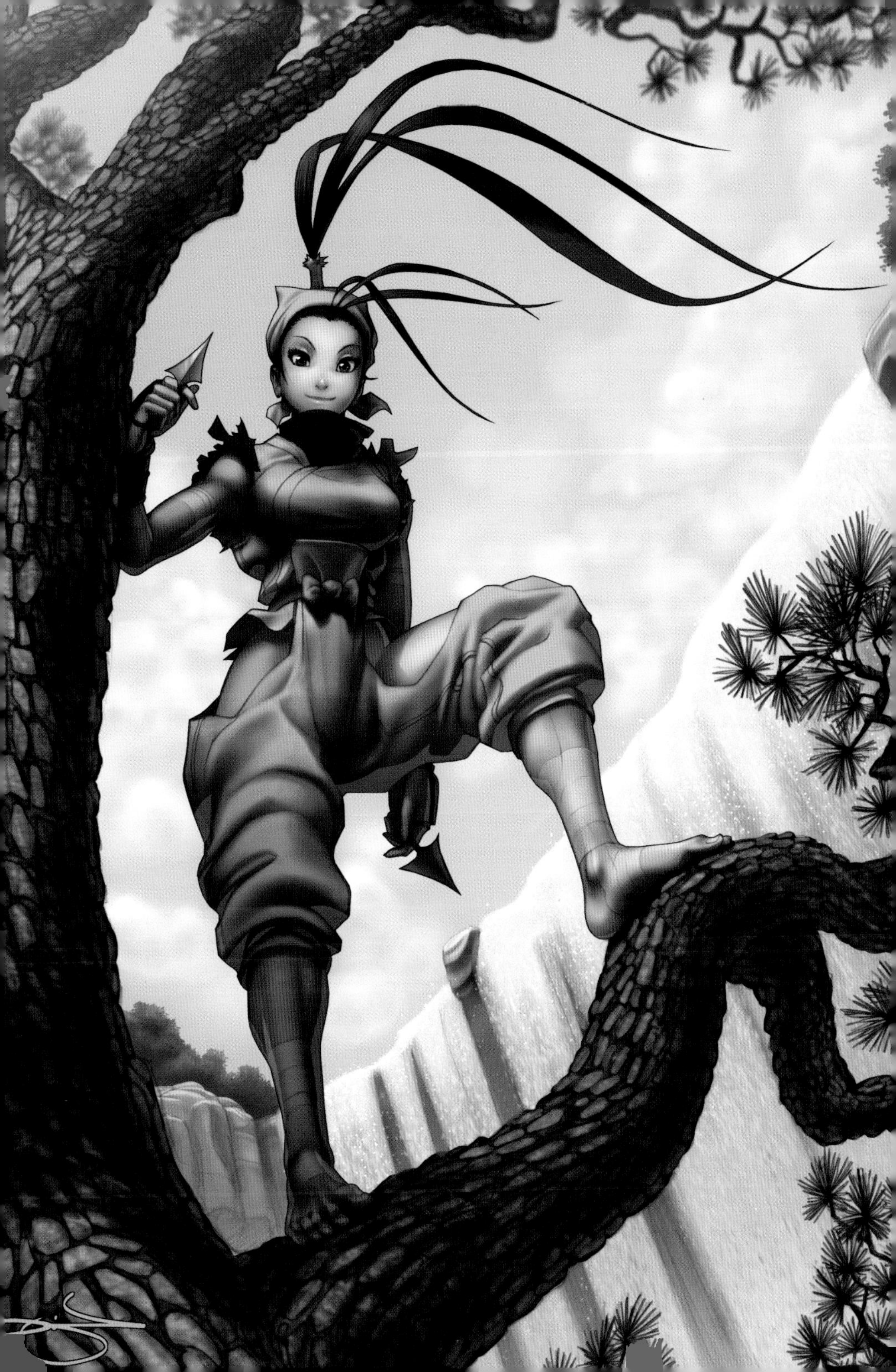

INGRID
The Eternal Goddess

BIRTHDAY: Unknown
COUNTRY OF ORIGIN: Unknown
FIGHTING STYLE: Energy Manipulation
HEIGHT: 179 cm   **WEIGHT:** 49 kg
MEASUREMENTS: B78/W54/H80
BLOOD TYPE: Unknown
LIKES: Unknown
DISLIKES: Unknown
SPECIAL ABILITIES: Unknown

ORIGIN UNKNOWN

Ingrid is a white haired beauty clad in a mysterious aura. Even the fortune teller Rose has been unable to divine anything about her past or future. While her origin and goals are uncertain, she appears to at least be on the side of good. Ingrid claims to be a "messenger from the stars", and the true master of M. Bison's Psycho Power. She has even displayed the ability to travel through time.

Despite her seemingly important mission to regain sole mastery of Psycho Power from Bison, Ingrid is still a vivacious and playful girl. She grows bored easily and is disappointed when a match ends too quickly or was not much fun. She even has a habit of tickling downed opponents.

One thing is certain - Ingrid is an incredibly powerful being in this or any other time.

FIGHTING STYLE
Ingrid fights using an unknown power that infuses all her attacks with a mystical energy. Telekinesis, energy blasts, and strange magical sigils are all parts of her fighting style. Ingrid almost seems to toy with her opponents, and with such powerful abilities at her disposal, she certainly gives the impression of being from a higher plane than the average fighter.

ONE OF INGRID'S MYSTICAL SIGILS

SIGNATURE MOVES: Sun Shot, Sun Rise, Sun Arch, Sun Dive

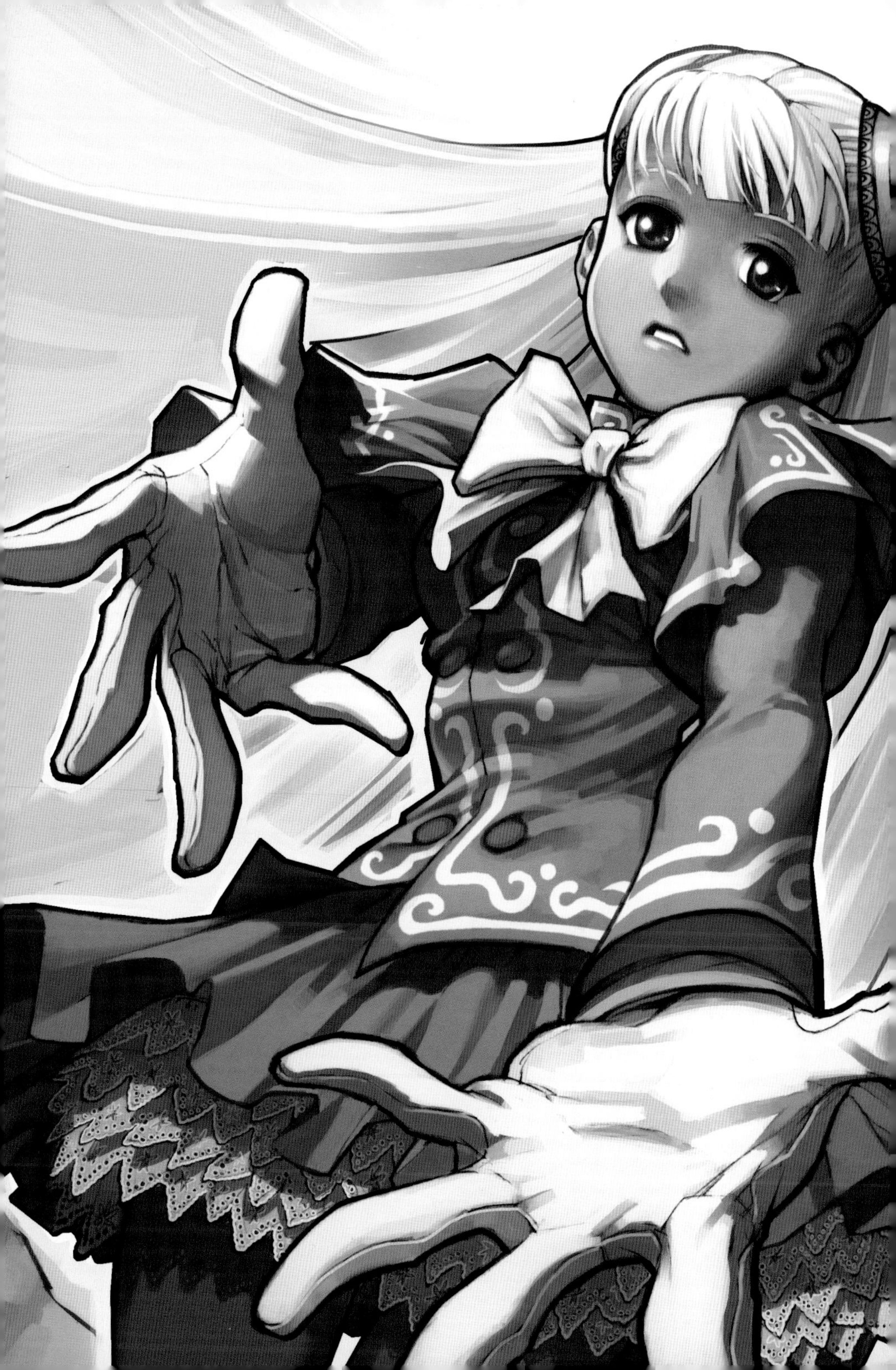

JULI
The Cold-Hearted Assassin

BIRTHDAY: ---------
COUNTRY OF ORIGIN: Germany
FIGHTING STYLE: Shadaloo Elite Forces Training
HEIGHT: 164 cm   **WEIGHT:** 49 kg
MEASUREMENTS: B92/W59/H84
BLOOD TYPE: B
LIKES: Unknown
DISLIKES: Unknown
SPECIAL ABILITIES: Unknown

Similar to her partner Juni, Juli is one of the twelve genetically enhanced women in M. Bison's elite "Doll" soldier unit. Before Shadaloo wiped her mind, she was known as Julia and was the lover of T. Hawk. Though she lived in the Thunderfoot Tribe's village, she is originally German.

After being kidnapped and experimented upon, she received amazing combat abilities. These same enhancements have also shortened her life expectancy considerably. She always shows up alongside Juni, Juli being the full-bosomed girl with chestnut hair and slightly angled eyes.

Although not as powerful or slavishly loyal as Juni, Juli carries out her missions according to Bison's wishes as best she can. After receiving orders to track down and assassinate the traitorous Cammy, Juli left Shadaloo headquarters in search of her prey. Along the way she crossed paths with many other street fighters.

Though she uses many of the same moves as Juni, she has a smaller variety of moves in total, possibly due to the fact that her generous physique limits her versatility. Whether or not Juli will ever escape Shadaloo's brainwashing, only time will tell. Her name, "Juli," is based on the German word for July.

FIGHTING STYLE
Her Shadaloo martial arts training and inner strength make Juli deadly in combat with a distinct specialty in jump kicks. While she possesses a smaller catalog of individual moves than her partner Juni, Juli's combination attacks are still fairly destructive. In addition to this, Juni can team-up with Juni to perform the powerful Psycho Charge Beta duo attack.

SIGNATURE MOVES: Cannon Strike, Earth Direct, Psycho Shield

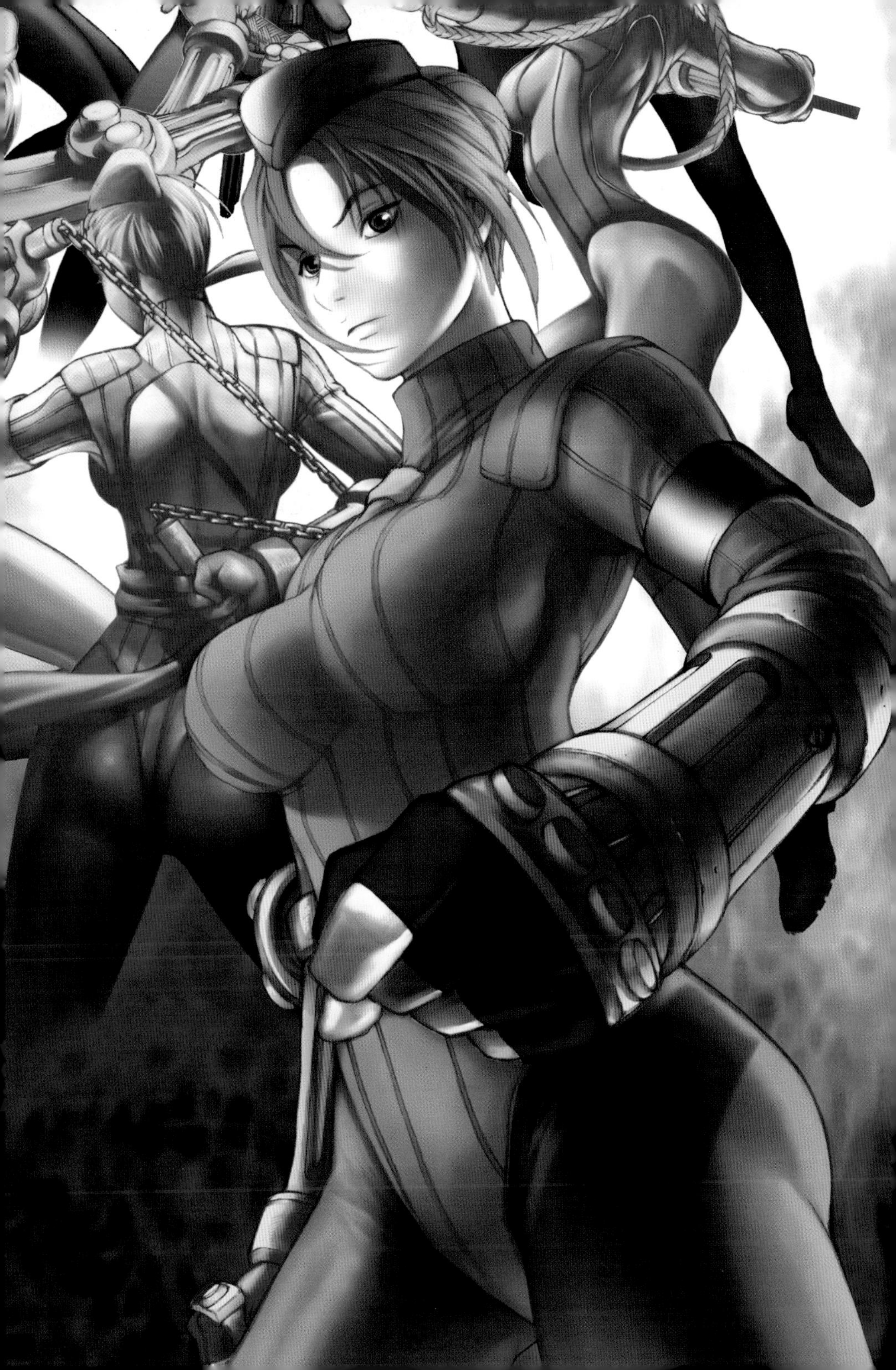

JUNI
The Quiet Killer

BIRTHDAY: ---------
COUNTRY OF ORIGIN: Germany
FIGHTING STYLE: Shadaloo Elite Forces Training
HEIGHT: 162 cm   **WEIGHT:** 46 kg
MEASUREMENTS: B84/W56/H83
BLOOD TYPE: AB
LIKES: Unknown
DISLIKES: Unknown
SPECIAL ABILITIES: Unknown

Altered by Shadaloo's superior genetic technology, including body enhancements and extensive brainwashing, Juni is a near-invincible soldier of Shadaloo. As one of the twelve women in M. Bison's elite "Doll" unit, Juni was built to carry out dangerous tasks without hesitation. She always shows up alongside Juli, Juni being the slim girl with the short light brown hair and large eyes.

Her brainwashing was possibly the most thorough of all the Dolls and in turn she receives many of the most important missions from Bison. One of these missions was to pursue and analyze the fighting data of Ryu.

Juni is a soulless automation in the dark, with only M. Bison there to light her way. Originally from Germany, Juni's name is based on the German word for June.

FIGHTING STYLE

Beyond the martial arts training she received as a member of Shadaloo, Juni has also analyzed combat data gathered from several of the world's top fighters, including Akuma. This data has enhanced her already impressive fighting abilities to create a unique style. Her individual strikes may not carry much strength, but when she strings hits together into devastating combinations she can deal massive damage. In addition to this, Juni can team-up with her teammate Juli to perform the powerful Psycho Charge Beta duo attack.

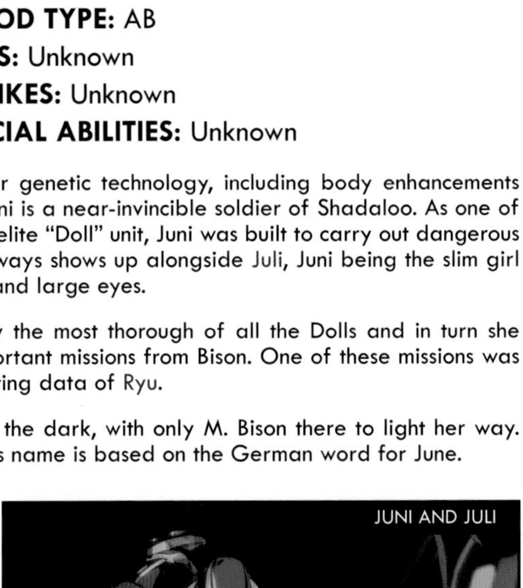

JUNI AND JULI

SIGNATURE MOVES: Cannon Spike, Sniping Arrow, Spin Knuckle

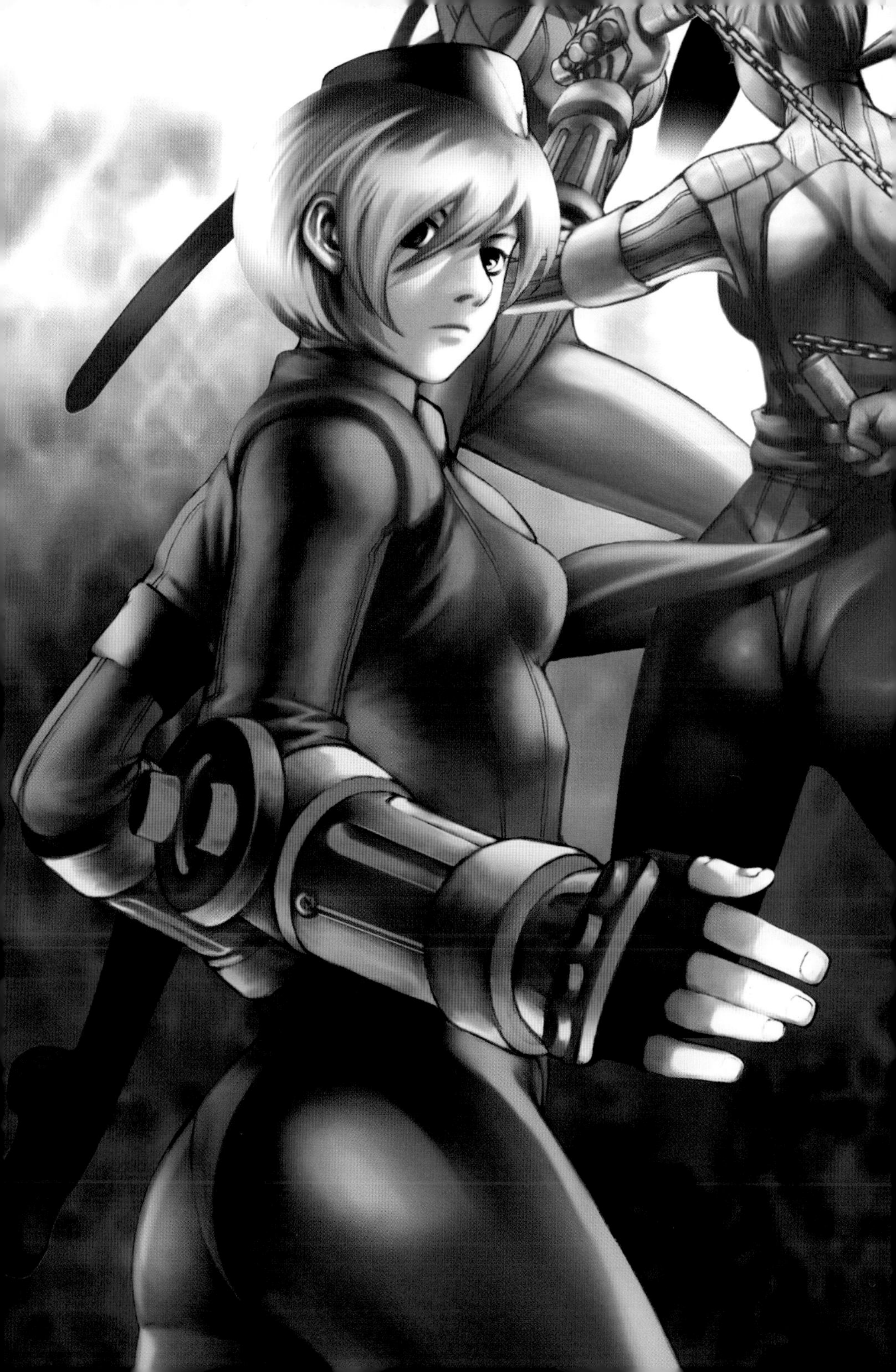

JURI
The Spider

BIRTHDAY: January 1
COUNTRY OF ORIGIN: Korea
FIGHTING STYLE: Taekwondo, Ki attacks
HEIGHT: 165 cm **WEIGHT:** 46 kg
MEASUREMENTS: B83/W56/H85
BLOOD TYPE: AB
LIKES: Spicy foods, spiders
DISLIKES: Boring people, rules
SPECIAL ABILITIES: Photographic memory

Originally from South Korea, Juri Han is a vicious S.I.N. agent who goes by the codename "Spider", and works under Seth. Juri is a provocative fighter who loves violence, and thoroughly enjoys tormenting her prey. Uninterested to say the least in the usual trappings of honor, money, and social prestige, Juri tends to get involved in events that she finds fun or interesting (which almost always means it is dangerous and outside of society's norm).

Juri's parents were murdered by Shadaloo. She joined S.I.N. with the hope of getting close to Shadaloo, and destroying it and M. Bison from the inside. Her motives are purely revenge based, and she doesn't care who she has to cut through, on either side of the law, to reach her goals.

A ki booster called the Feng Shui Engine has been fitted into her left eye socket, and acts as a prosthetic eye. It is a miniature version of the Tanden Engine used by Seth, however the Feng Shui Engine only enhances Juri's existing skills and does not give her Seth's fight data recording abilities.

FIGHTING STYLE
Juri is relentless when on the offensive and worries little about defending herself. She is a sadistic, reckless, and certainly dangerous opponent. A Taekwondo expert, Juri focuses on flashy, fast, and furious kicks and rarely throws a punch. She also has a range of ki-based attacks at her disposal including fireballs and her trademark pinwheel kick.

SIGNATURE MOVES: Fireball Kick, Pinwheel, Feng Shui Engine

ジュリ JURI

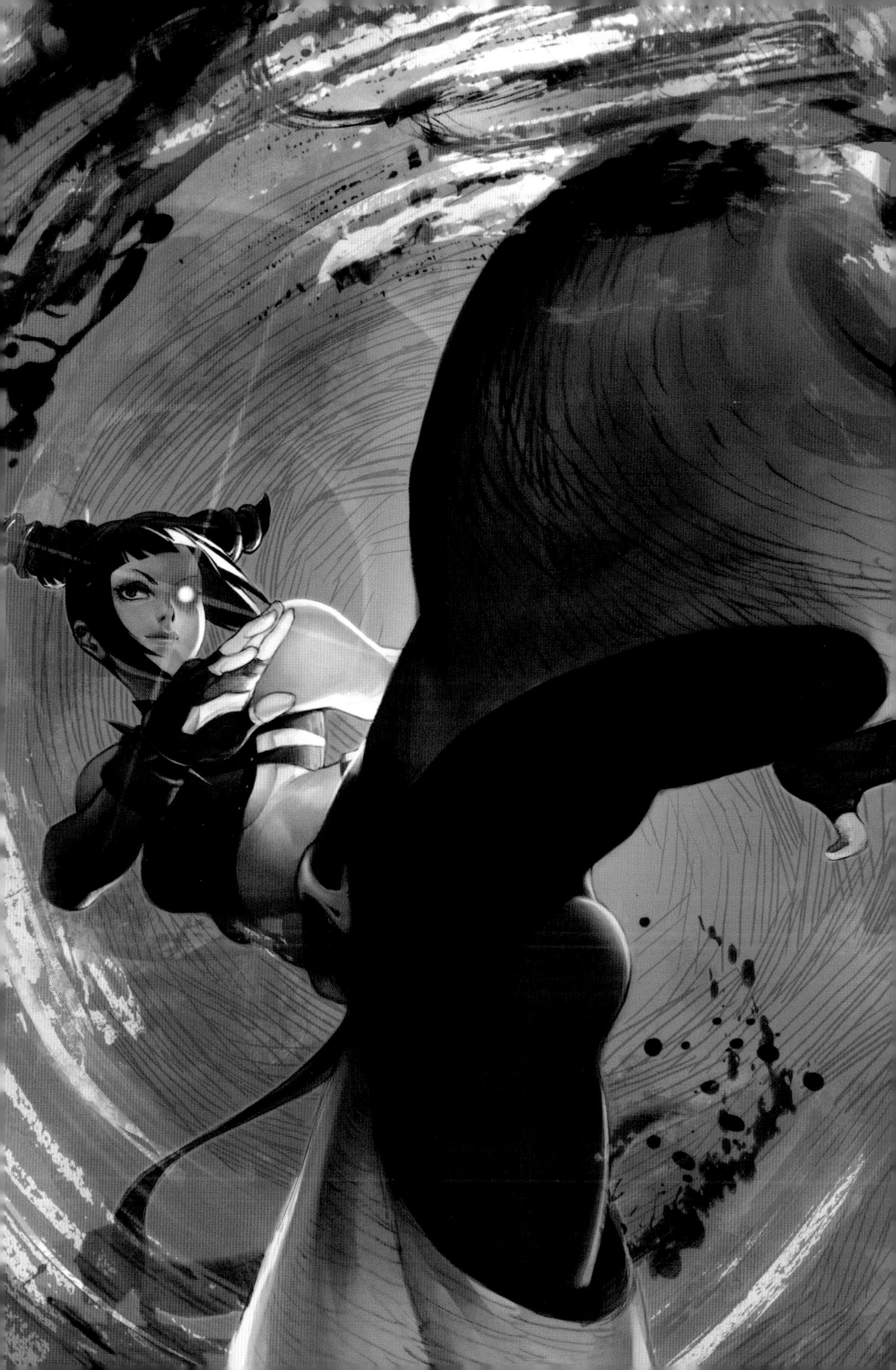

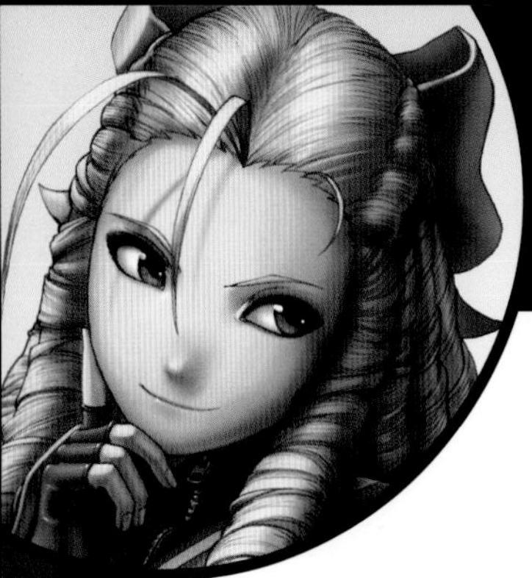

KARIN

The Flawless Rose

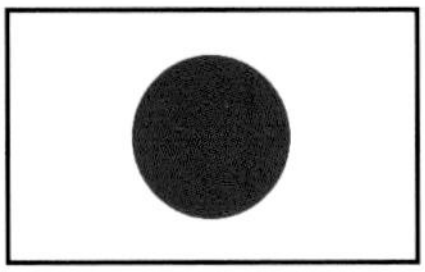

BIRTHDAY: ---------
COUNTRY OF ORIGIN: Japan
FIGHTING STYLE: Kanzuki Style Martial Arts
HEIGHT: 162 cm **WEIGHT:** 48 kg
MEASUREMENTS: B83/W57/H85
BLOOD TYPE: B
LIKES: Absolute victory
DISLIKES: Middle class ideals
SPECIAL ABILITIES: Secret moves of the Kanzuki household

The heiress to the world famous Kanzuki fortune, Karin possesses all three of the golden criteria that an immensely wealthy heiress must have: sharp wit, physical beauty, and a high-maintenance attitude. Her gorgeous golden locks and big hair ribbon are her trademarks. Her family expects nothing less than complete victory from her and she pushes herself to meet their lofty expectations.

Karin's elite household built the global financial conglomerate known as the Kanzuki Zaibatsu (the Kanzuki "financial clique"). The motto of the Kanzuki household, "In all things be victorious!" has never allowed for anyone carrying the Kanzuki name to fail in any endeavor. The Kanzukis are even wealthier than the Masters, so rich that they have their own satellite called "Red Spider Lily".

In accordance with the traditions of her household, Karin is well-versed in all kinds of martial arts. The sum of all of her accomplishments in the field of martial arts is equivalent to 100 dan and 8 kyu (the Japanese ranking system for martial arts, among other things). Karin has taken all of her martial arts knowledge to form the "Kanzuki style", which she has also mastered.

Sakura is a schoolmate whom Karin considers to be her rival. The two girls had a match in the past, and Sakura came out victorious. Hoping for an eventual rematch, Karin set off on a trip across the world to hone her fighting skills. She wears her school uniform when she fights because Sakura does, but Karin's school uniform is a red version that was custom made for her.

FIGHTING STYLE

Karin has a wide array of strikes, throws and potent reversals, and she prides herself on being able to handle any opponent she faces. She keeps her opponents guessing by varying the speed of her attacks, and also makes them second guess their own choice of moves for fear of her powerful counterattacks.

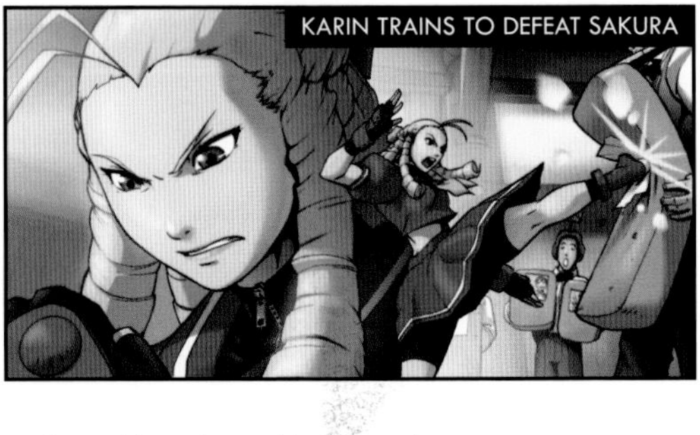
KARIN TRAINS TO DEFEAT SAKURA

SIGNATURE MOVES: Korenken, Kouoken, Mujinkyaku

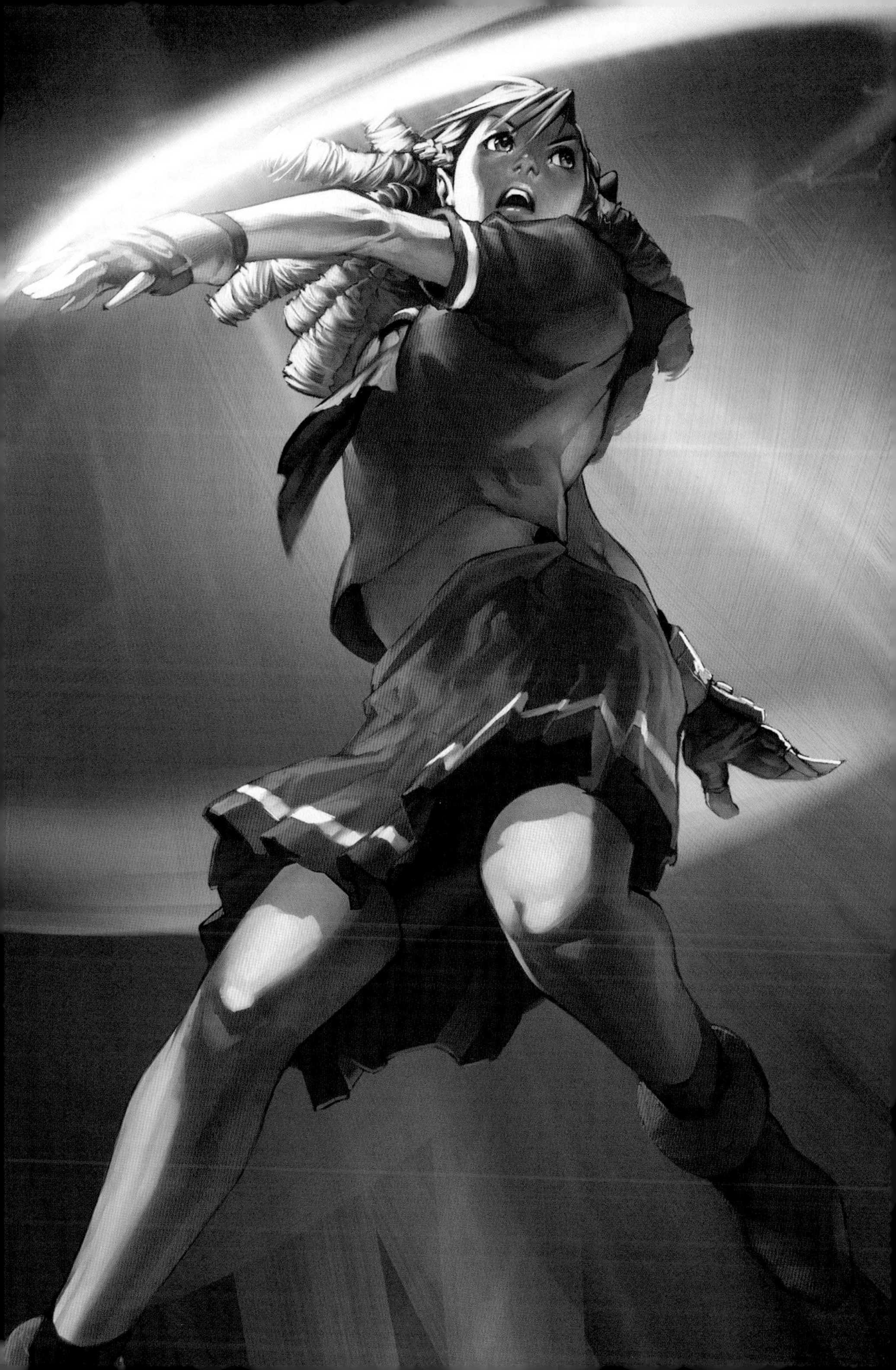

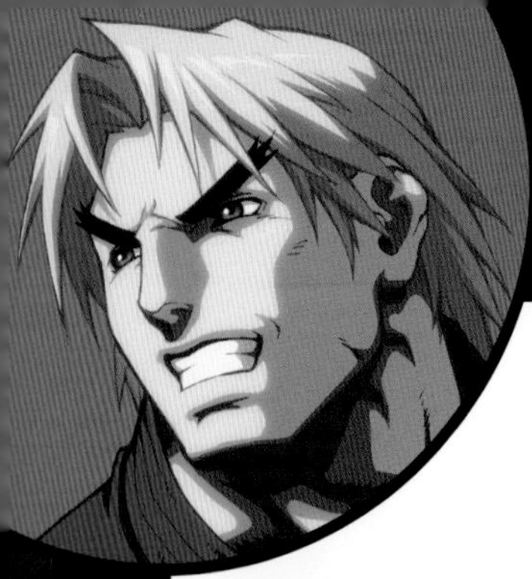

KEN

Fire of the Rising Dragon

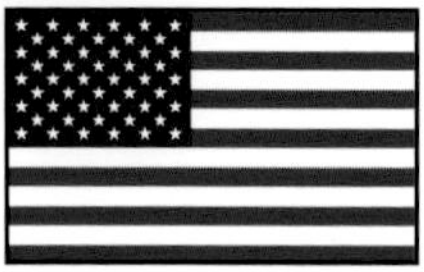

BIRTHDAY: February 14
COUNTRY OF ORIGIN: U.S.A.
FIGHTING STYLE: Martial Arts rooted in Ansatsuken
HEIGHT: 175 cm **WEIGHT:** 72 kg
MEASUREMENTS: B114/W82/H86
BLOOD TYPE: B
LIKES: Skateboarding and pasta
DISLIKES: Pickled plums, soap operas
SPECIAL ABILITIES: Cooking pasta dishes

Ryu's brother in training and his oldest rival, Ken Masters is the heir to the Masters family fortune and the reigning champion of the All American Martial Arts Tournament. This intensely passionate, blonde haired young man wears a bright red dougi, and shares Ryu's goal of becoming the greatest martial artist in the world.

Ken and Ryu have both studied under the same master, Gouken, since they were very young. It was with these young and innocent eyes that they watched the deadly battle between Akuma and Gouken, in which Gouken was ultimately killed. The two friends eventually parted ways in order to find out who would gain global fame as a martial artist first. Ken went to America planning to focus entirely on training. Instead, he met and fell in love with Eliza, the woman whom he would eventually marry.

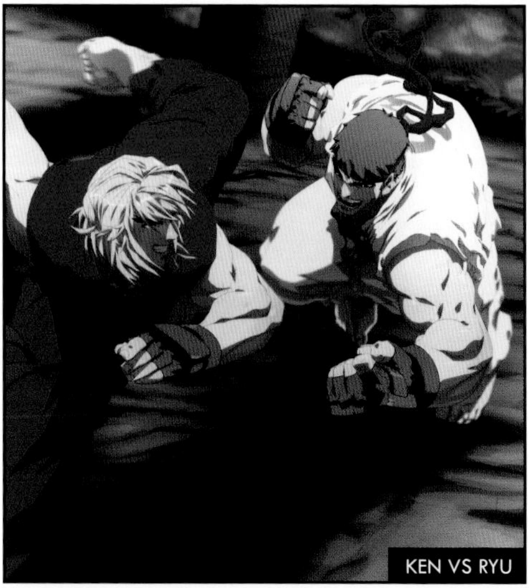

KEN VS RYU

Even after winning his throne as the King of American Fighters, all Ken could think about was his rival, Ryu. In order to clear his mind and rediscover his path, Ken set off on a trip during which he successfully came to understand the meaning of fighting, and once again settled into the training that he hoped would one day lead to a rematch with Ryu. It was at this time when Ken received news that Ryu had fought and defeated Sagat, the emperor of Muay Thai. This event was a serious wake up call for Ken, and he immediately made his way to Japan with the intent to challenge Ryu to a match. When Ken finally found him, it turned out Ryu had lost sight of his purpose, but his oldest friend was able to knock some sense into him again. Ryu and Ken had promised to face off in an ultimate match to find out who is superior, but Ken made the difficult decision to leave the world of fighting for the sake of his beloved wife, and the child they were expecting.

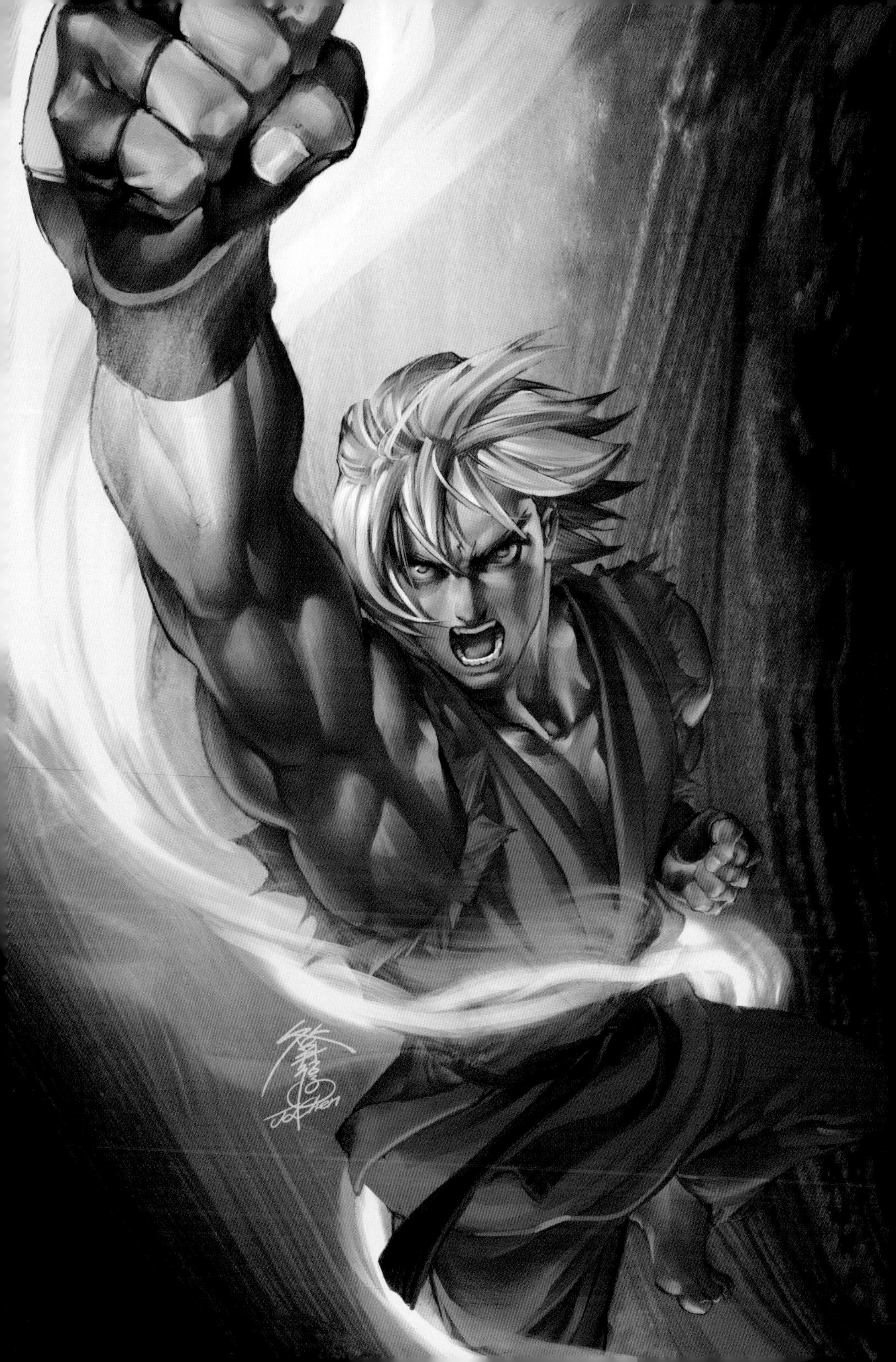

KEN (CONTINUED...)
Fire of the Rising Dragon

ELIZA PREGNANT WITH MEL

KEN CHARGES
A FIREBALL

The pull of street fighting was just too strong, and it was not long before Ken returned to the competitive fighting scene. Ken also gained a student by the name of Sean, who forced his way into Ken's life after seeing him fighting in a tournament. The honest truth is that Ken feels a bit overwhelmed by his die-hard fan turned student, and is hoping to find some way to pawn Sean off on Ryu.

Ken and Eliza have a young son, Mel, whom Ken also trains alongside Sean. Eliza is the younger sister of Guile's wife Julia, making Ken and Guile brothers-in-law. Though born in the United States, Ken is actually only one quarter American and three quarters Japanese. His natural hair color is black, which he dyes blonde.

FIGHTING STYLE
Although his core fighting techniques are similar to Ryu's, their current training methods and overall personalities create subtle differences between them. While Ryu specializes in using his projectile-based attacks, Ken has mastered the Shoryuken to deadly effect, modifying it into the Dragon Punch, Shoryu Reppa, and Shinryuken attacks. His improved Shoryuken techniques, mixed with the many other attacks at his disposal, make him a very capable opponent.

SIGNATURE MOVES:
Hadoken(aka Fireball), Tatsumaki Senpukyaku(aka Hurricane Kick), Shoryuken(aka Dragon Punch), Shinryuken

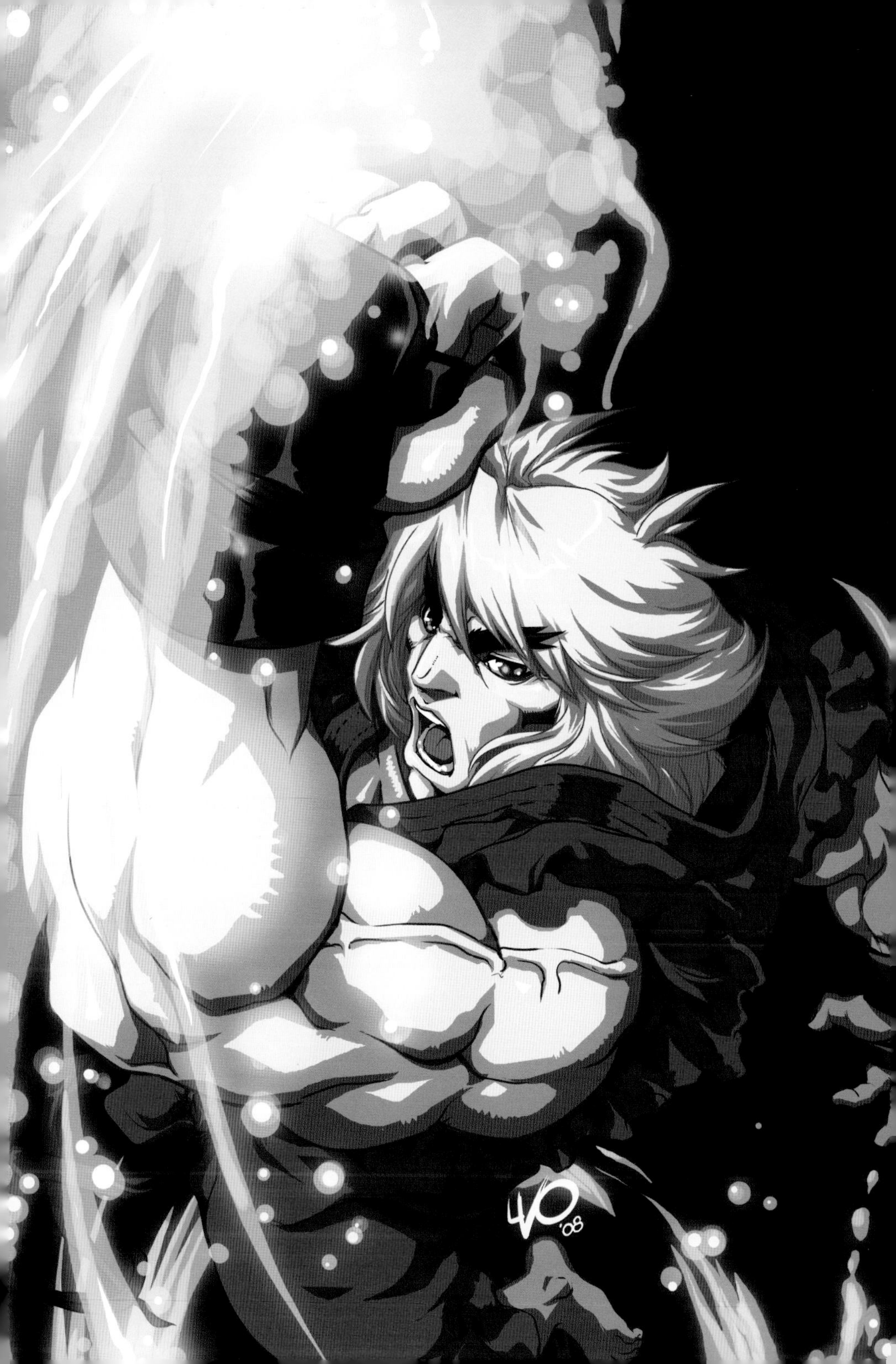

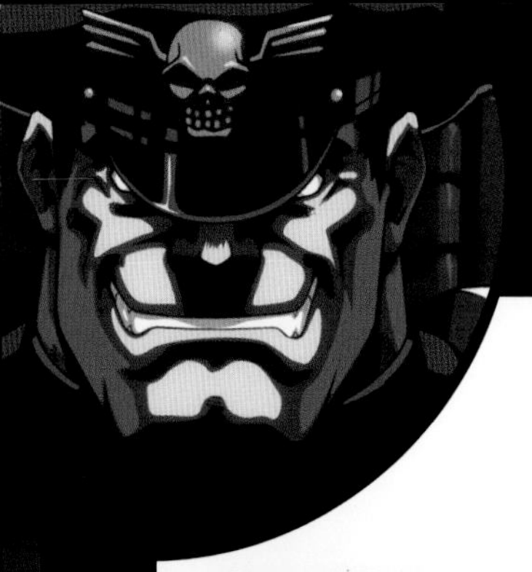

M. BISON

King of Darkness

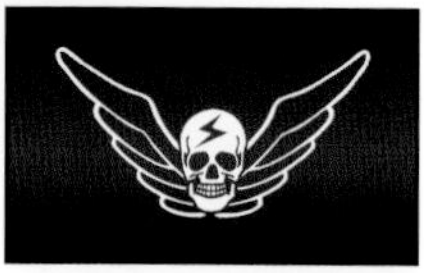

BIRTHDAY: April 17
COUNTRY OF ORIGIN: Unknown
FIGHTING STYLE: Psycho Power
HEIGHT: 182 cm **WEIGHT:** 80 kg
MEASUREMENTS: B129/W85/H91
BLOOD TYPE: A
LIKES: World domination
DISLIKES: Weak people, incompetent underlings
SPECIAL ABILITIES: Hypnosis

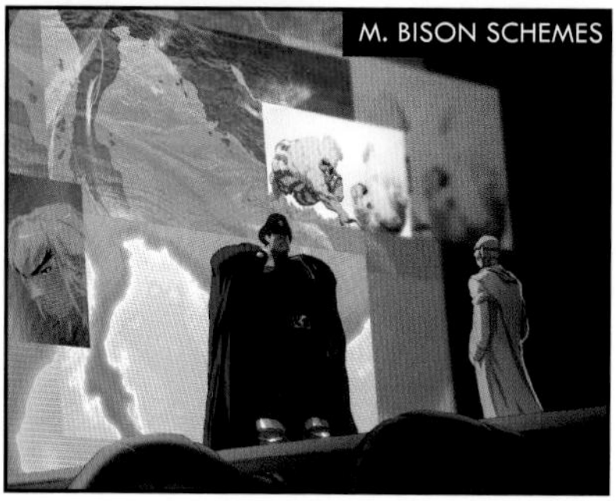
M. BISON SCHEMES

Narcotics, human experiments, arms dealing... M. Bison has had his hand in every illegal industry imaginable as the head of the criminal organization known as Shadaloo. Bison also has the frightening ability of Psycho Power at his disposal. Though he has been believed dead several times, Bison always seems to acquire a new physical body and return to plague the world. Along with Balrog, Sagat, and Vega he formed the four bosses of Shadaloo, of which he is by far the most powerful.

As the leader of Shadaloo, M. Bison controls the whole world from the shadows. He has been responsible for many dark deeds, including the death of Guile's best friend Charlie and the disappearance of Chun-Li's father. He murdered T. Hawk's father and also created and brainwashed Cammy.

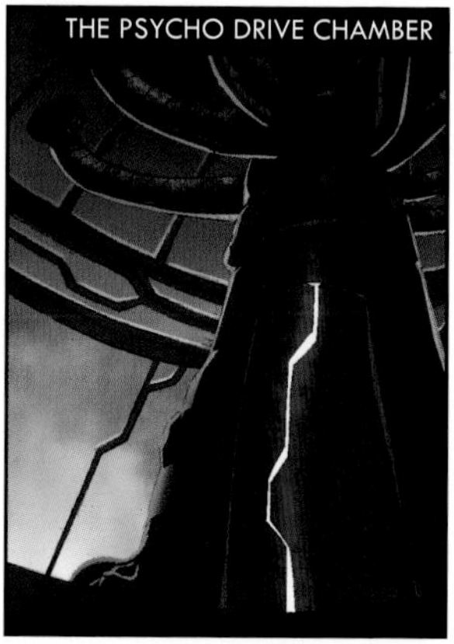
THE PSYCHO DRIVE CHAMBER

At one time, M. Bison was nothing more than a young martial artist like any other. However, his ambitions were overwhelming. In his struggle to become the best in the world of martial arts, M. Bison murdered his own master before giving in to complete chaos. M. Bison's master was the only person in the world who could manipulate the evil power known as "Psycho Power" at the time, and it is said that he passed this ability onto M. Bison and only two other students before his death.

M. Bison's entire body is imbued with Psycho Power, which allows him to hover off the ground, among other effects. Like Rose's Soul Power, Psycho Power is a spiritual energy that produces a physical effect. What makes Psycho Power different from Soul Power is the intent behind its use. When the spiritual power is gathered with evil intent, or even just used for evil purposes, it becomes what is called "Psycho Power." Bison used his knowledge of this unique energy to create one of the most powerful devices ever, the Psycho Drive.

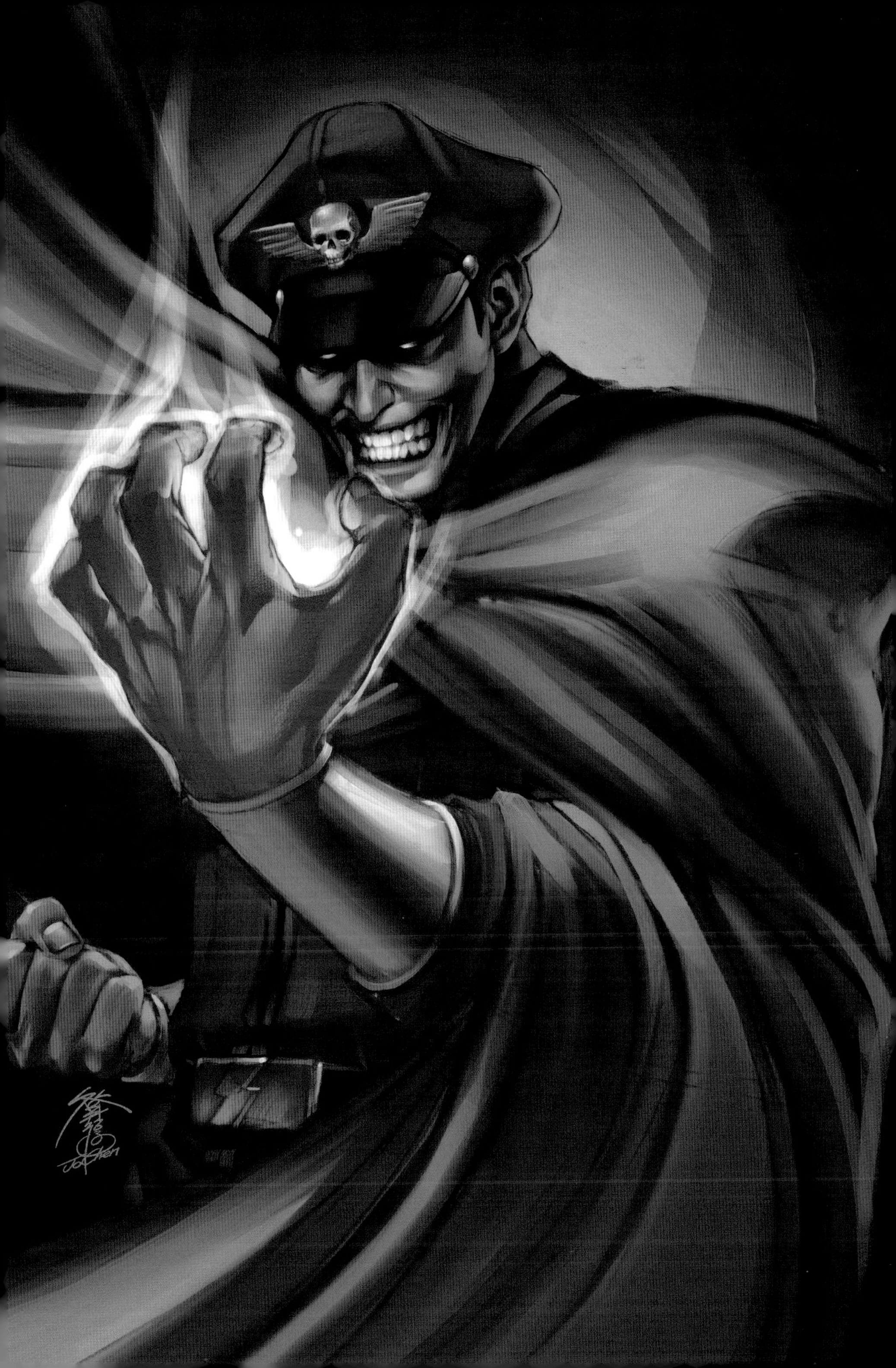

M. BISON (CONTINUED...)

King of Darkness

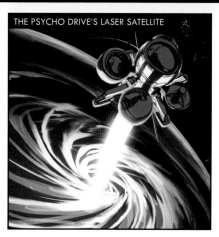

THE PSYCHO DRIVE'S LASER SATELLITE

The Psycho Drive can be used to suck the energy out of a victim being held within it and expel this energy as a powerful laser beam to terrifying effect, or it can convert Psycho Power into a light of restoration to instantly heal damage. It is said that Psycho Power will one day bring great devastation to the world.

The ultimate strategist, Bison always has a backup plan in case the worst should happen. His mastery of Psycho Power has given him the ability to transfer his spirit into and take control of a new body, should his own be destroyed. He displayed this ability after his first defeat, transferring his consciousness into the body of Rose, and remaining there until Shadaloo could create a new, permanent body for him. Since then, Bison has devoted much of Shadaloo's resources to ensuring he will never be without a backup body, resulting in the creation of Cammy as part of the Doll program, as well as Abel and Seth through the Living Incubator program. Bison also started the Street Fighter tournament as a way to gather the world's most powerful fighters for use as brainwashed Shadaloo soldiers, as well as additional potential backup bodies.

M. BISON RESURRECTED

Assuming he always has a new body to jump into, Bison could very well be immortal.

FIGHTING STYLE

Bison himself is a formidable fighter with incredible strength and deadly Psycho Power techniques. His skill and speed are far beyond normal human limits. As if that weren't enough, the force of his ultimate combat strike, the nightmarishly powerful Psycho Crusher, further augments his fighting powers.

SIGNATURE MOVES: Double Knee Press, Somersault Skull Dive, Psycho Crusher

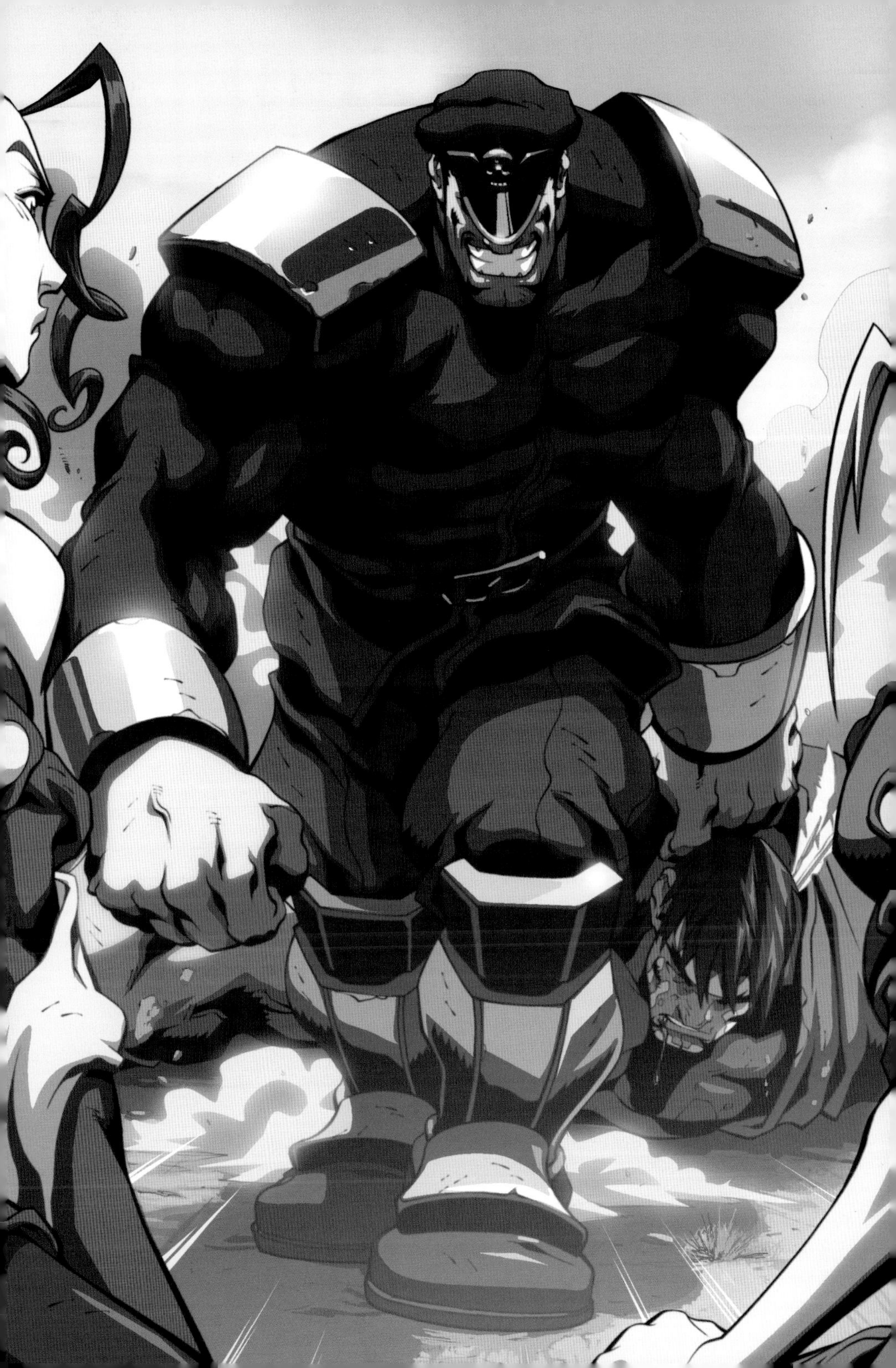

MAKI
The Heir to Bushin-ryu

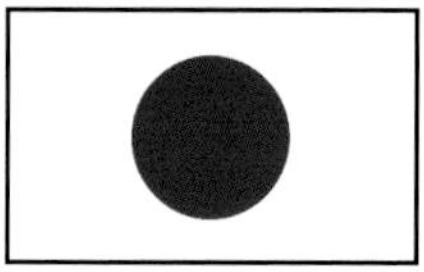

BIRTHDAY: ----------
COUNTRY OF ORIGIN: Japan
FIGHTING STYLE: Bushin-ryu Ninjutsu
HEIGHT: 160 cm   **WEIGHT:** 48 kg
MEASUREMENTS: 85B/61W/88H
BLOOD TYPE: B
LIKES: Motorcycles
DISLIKES: Waiting for anyone
SPECIAL ABILITIES: Tonfa

Maki Genryusai is a Tonfa-carrying street fighter from Japan, who practices the Bushin style of ninjutsu. Maki is the second daughter of Genryusai, 37th master of Bushin-ryu, and master to Zeku. She is also the younger sister of Rena, who is Guy's fiancée.

Maki's sister and father were once kidnapped by a new incarnation of the Mad Gear gang. With Guy nowhere to be found, Maki enlisted the aid of Metro City mayor Mike Haggar, and his friend Carlos Miyamoto. The three travelled together to Hong Kong, where they were able to rescue Maki's family and defeat the new Mad Gear gang.

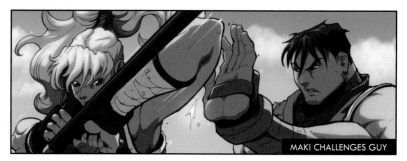

MAKI CHALLENGES GUY

Maki is intensely jealous of Guy's title as the 39th master of Bushin-ryu, feeling that as the descendant of a former master, the position should rightfully go to her. She takes every opportunity to challenge Guy in combat hoping to become the next Bushin-ryu successor, but so far has been unable to do so. After her father passed away, her resolve grew even stronger.

Maki was once the leader of a bosozoku biker gang in Japan. She is Japanese, but has dyed her hair blonde ever since her biker days.

FIGHTING STYLE
Though Maki always goes into battle with her favorite weapon, the Tonfa, it is definitely not a crutch for her. She fights using all manner of powerful kicks and knee strikes, which knock her opponents senseless. Her Tonfa is used as both an offensive and defensive weapon, spinning wildly during attacks, and giving added protection during blocks.

SIGNATURE MOVES: Genko, Haya Dash, Reppukyaku

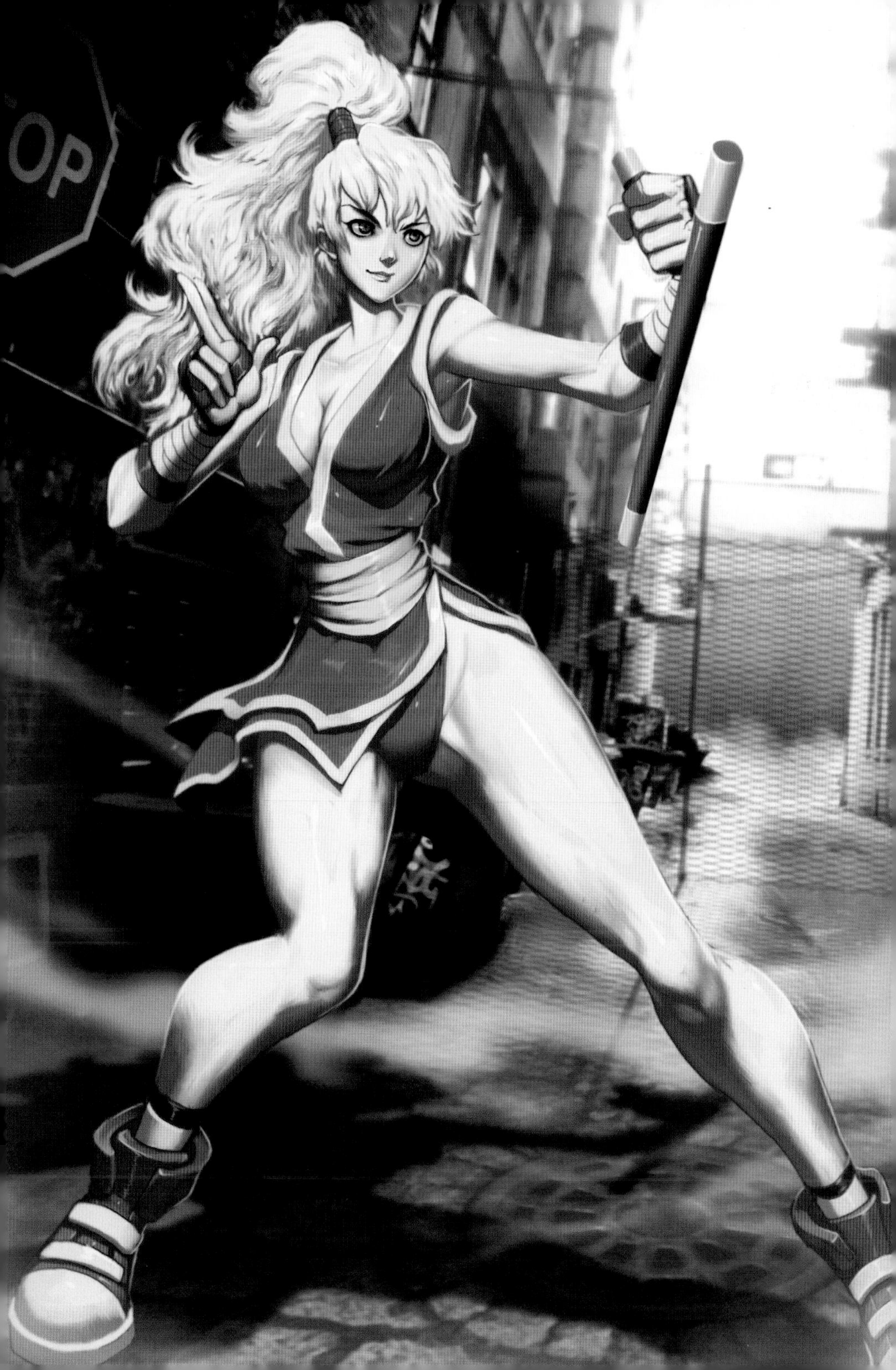
OP

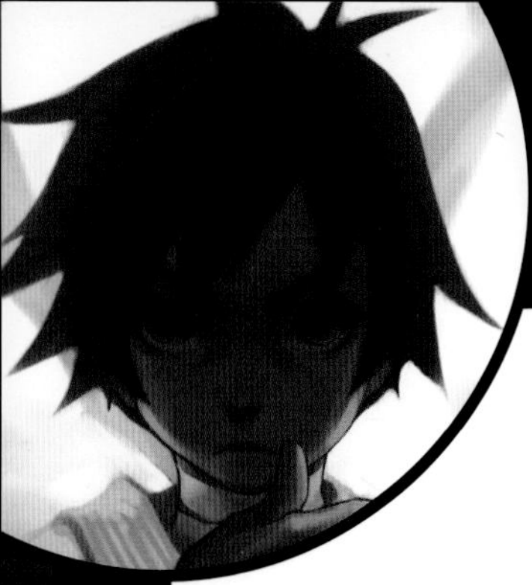

MAKOTO

The Young Sensei

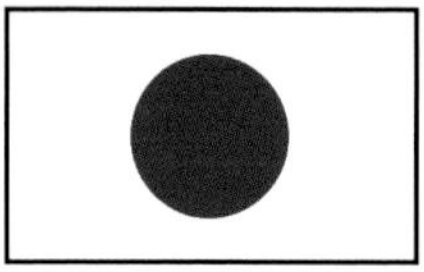

BIRTHDAY: July 1
COUNTRY OF ORIGIN: Japan
FIGHTING STYLE: Rindoukan Karate
HEIGHT: 160 cm **WEIGHT:** 56 kg
MEASUREMENTS: B80/W61/H87
BLOOD TYPE: B
LIKES: Family, Fighting
DISLIKES: Pickled ginger
SPECIAL ABILITIES: Carpentry

Makoto is a seriously passionate and rowdy karate girl. Her family ran a respected karate dojo in Tosa known as the "Rindoukan" until her father, Masaru, passed away.

Makoto's brother used his lack of karate talent as an excuse to start his career as a common businessman, leaving the family dojo closed and forgotten. Concerned over the fate of her family's dojo, Makoto traveled cross-country to promote her family's name and the dojo.

Makoto is tougher than most guys, and her speech is heavy with a Japanese dialect. She is both young and short, but the black belt around her waist speaks loudly of her abilities. She is also an expert carpenter, and spends considerable time trying to keep the Rindoukan dojo from completely falling apart.

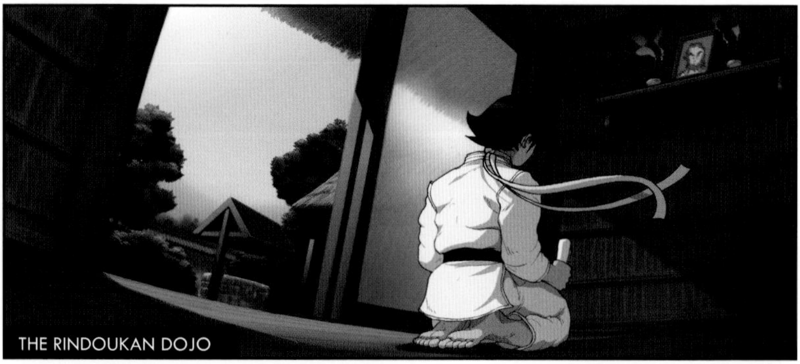

THE RINDOUKAN DOJO

FIGHTING STYLE

Makoto's fighting style is Rindoukan karate. With calmly performed special moves, rapid movements and punches or kicks that have her full body weight behind them, she has a lot more power than expected from her small body. She displays the "total victory with one hit" essence of karate. With her Tanden Renki she demonstrates emotional strength in controlling her chi.

SIGNATURE MOVES: Hayate, Oroshi, Seichusen Godanzuki

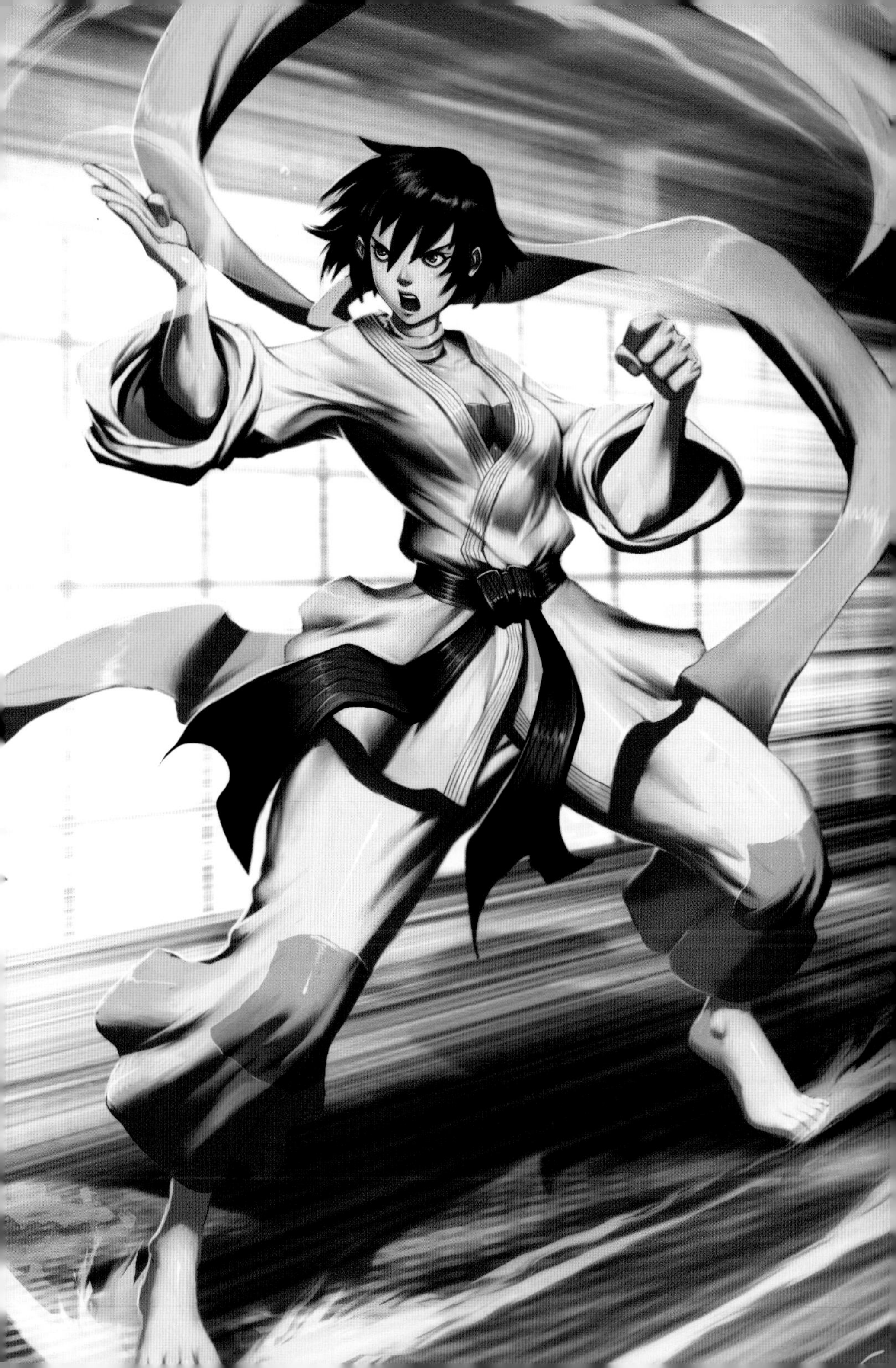

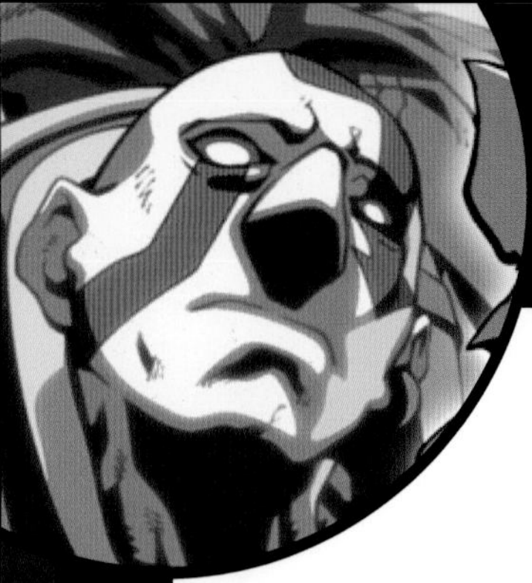

NECRO

The Living Experiment

BIRTHDAY: ---------
COUNTRY OF ORIGIN: Russia
FIGHTING STYLE: ---------
HEIGHT: --------- **WEIGHT:** ---------
MEASUREMENTS: ---------
BLOOD TYPE: ---------
LIKES: Effie
DISLIKES: Helicopters
SPECIAL ABILITIES: Love poetry

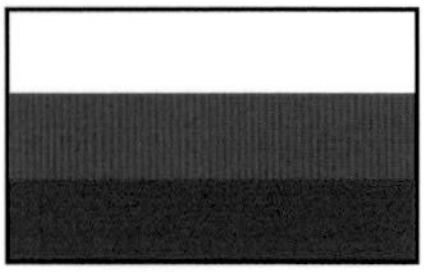

Necro is a experimentally modified Russian man who is on the run from his former masters, the Illuminati. He yearns for nothing more than freedom from his pursuers.

Illia was the third born of four brothers. After the fall of the Soviet Union, Illia left his village to seek freedom and fortune, but was captured by Gill's secret society in the vicinity of Moscow. The Illuminati modified Illia to be a humanoid weapon with rubber-like qualities and cybernetic implants, rechristening him Necro. Necro eventually was freed from his imprisonment by a girl named Effie, herself another genetic experiment. The two managed to run away together, and quickly fell in love, though they were still pursued by their former captors.

Later, the Illuminati would refine their humanoid weapon into a final incarnation – Twelve, an upgraded version of Necro meant for mass production. Necro and Effie are constantly on the run from Twelve, assigned by the Illuminati to eliminate his predecessor.

FIGHTING STYLE

Necro's fighting style involves grappling his opponents with his unpredictable and flexible rubber limbs and using the electrical current generated in his body to shock them. The cybernetic computer in his brain helps give him super human fighting abilities.

SIGNATURE MOVES: Electric Blaster, Snake Fang, Tornado Hook

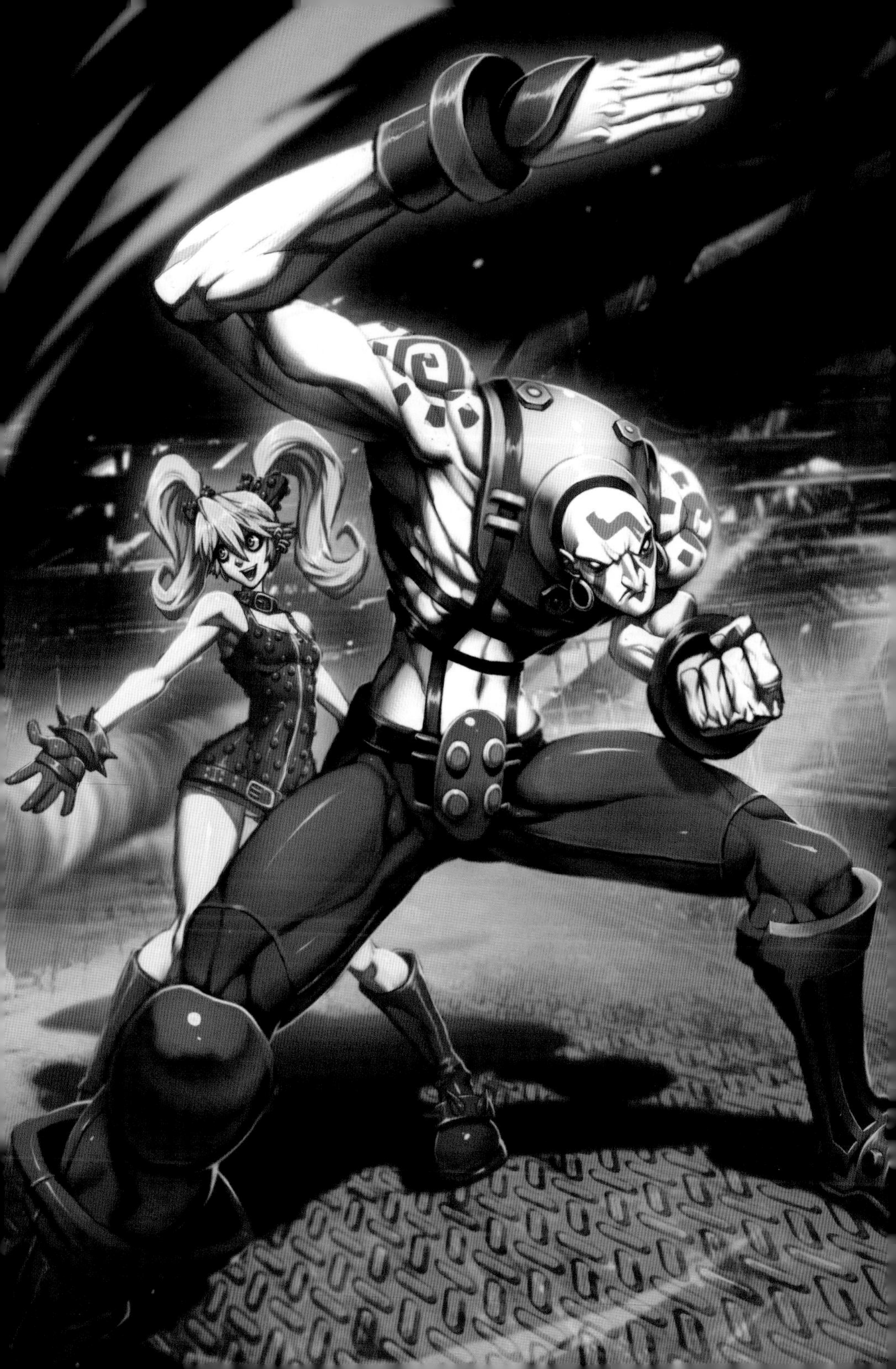

ORO
The Enlightened Hermit

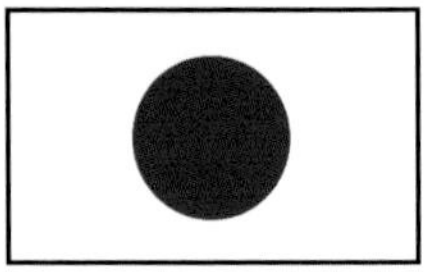

BIRTHDAY: ---------
COUNTRY OF ORIGIN: Japan
FIGHTING STYLE: Senjitsu
HEIGHT: ---------   **WEIGHT:** ---------
MEASUREMENTS: ---------
BLOOD TYPE: ---------
LIKES: Animals, pretty girls, sleeping
DISLIKES: Boredom
SPECIAL ABILITIES: Telekenisis

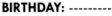

Oro is a 140-year old mystic who lives in a cave with his animal friends (including a dog and a turtle), deep within the Amazon jungle. He is outrageously young at heart and, despite his age, Oro does not feel that he has reached full enlightenment. He has trained in mysticism believing that "mystics are capable of anything," but his extreme abilities have led to a life of boredom without challenges. Knowing that no one would offer much of a challenge against his full power, Oro fights with his main arm tied behind his back.

As usual, Oro was milling about, bored out of his mind when rumors of "a secret organization" and "one who has mastered the fist" perked his interest. Hoping to find more information regarding these two items of interest, Oro set out on a new journey. Oro also wishes to find a student worthy of his attention.

Oro considers Ryu to be a potential student. Also upon meeting Akuma, Oro acted as if the two know each other from a previous encounter, but with Oro's memory being so unreliable, it's possible that the two have never met before.

FIGHTING STYLE
Oro's fighting style uses efficient movements and fluid body motion control. With athletic abilities far beyond those of a normal man, his moves are even more powerful than those of his much younger opponents. Oro has also mastered the rare ability of telekinesis, and uses it mainly to hurl huge boulders at opponents.

SIGNATURE MOVES: Nichirin Sho, Niou Riki, Oni Yanma

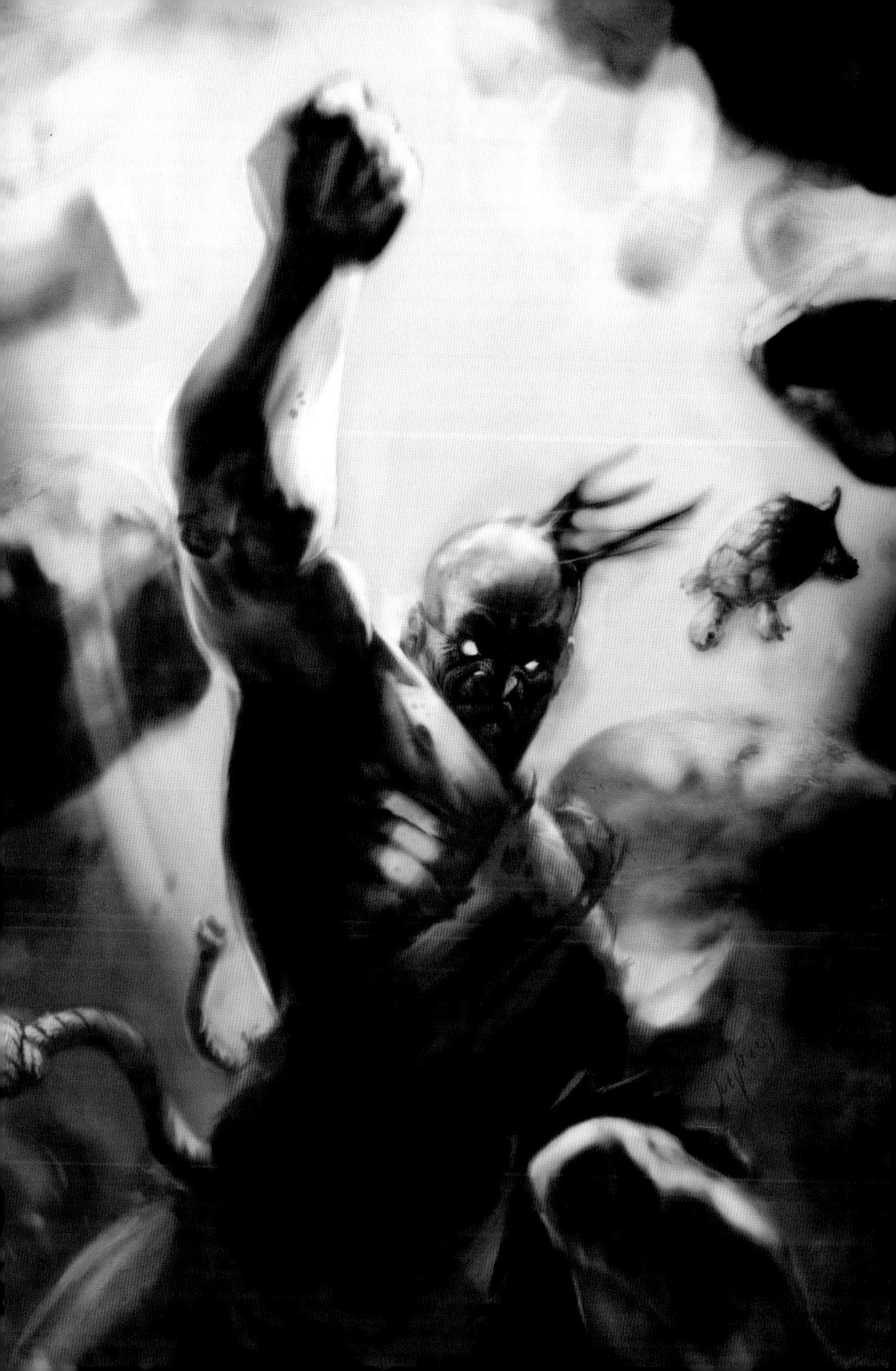

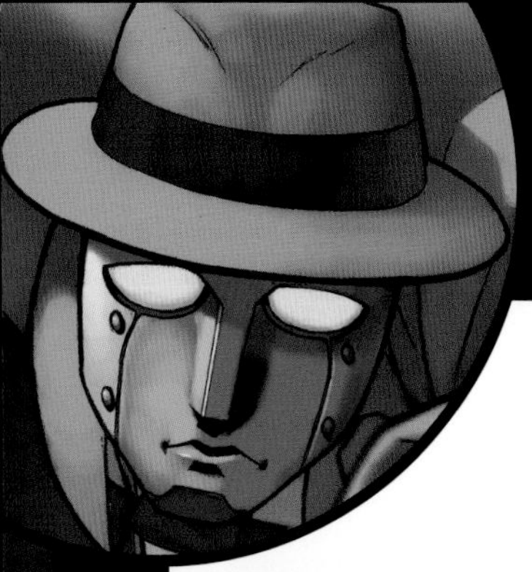

Q

The Unknown Quantity

BIRTHDAY: Unknown
COUNTRY OF ORIGIN: Unknown
FIGHTING STYLE: Unknown
HEIGHT: Unknown **WEIGHT:** Unknown
MEASUREMENTS: Unknown
BLOOD TYPE: Unknown
LIKES: Unknown
DISLIKES: Unknown
SPECIAL ABILITIES: Unknown

ORIGIN UNKNOWN

Q's existence is shrouded in mystery. His trench coat and strange iron mask are an enigma that reveals no secrets. Even the investigative powers of the CIA have uncovered little about his history or purpose. What is known is that he's been seen in crime scene photographs from inexplicable murders all over the world, seemingly defying time and space.

It is unknown why he seeks to challenge the world's greatest fighters, but Q can show up at any time, any place. Perhaps when the mystery is finally solved his true identity will become clear.

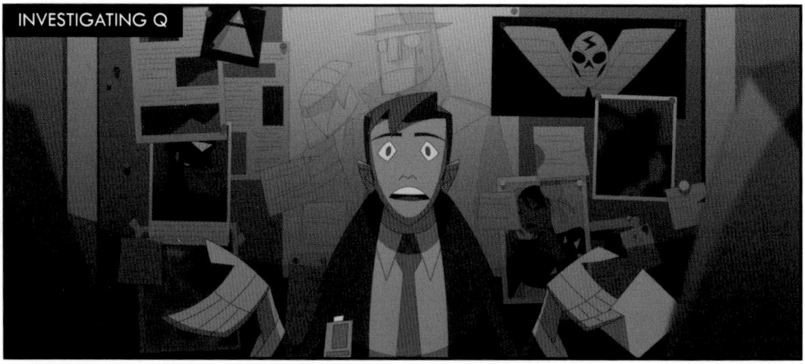

INVESTIGATING Q

FIGHTING STYLE

Q's fighting style uses the strength of his huge body with repeated crushing blows and devastating body slams. His movements are far from quick, but he can overwhelm an opponent with his long reach and determination. Much like his history, his moves come from unknown origins and are named by bystanders based on their visual appearance.

SIGNATURE MOVES: Capture & Deadly Blow, Dashing Head Attack, Total Destruction

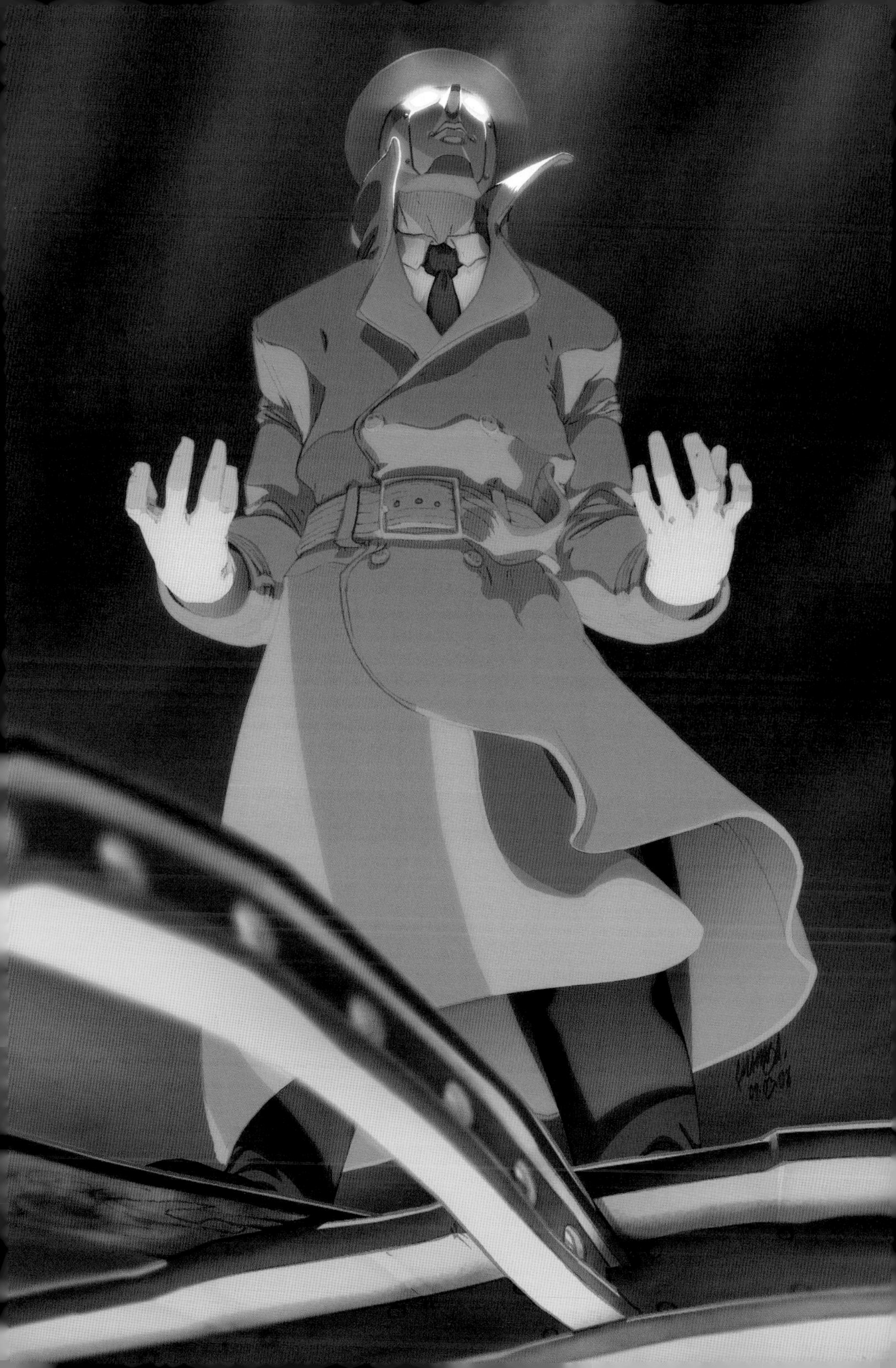

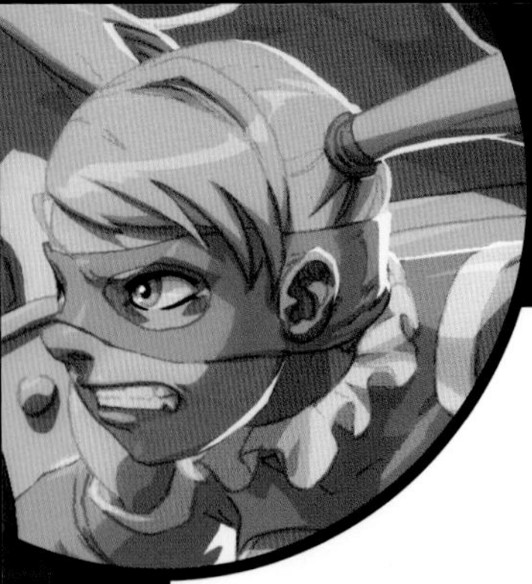

R. MIKA

Rising Star of the Ring

BIRTHDAY: ---------
COUNTRY OF ORIGIN: Japan
FIGHTING STYLE: Pro Wrestling
HEIGHT: 168 cm **WEIGHT:** 62 kg
MEASUREMENTS: B97/W72/H93
BLOOD TYPE: O
LIKES: Zangief's wrestling style
DISLIKES: Rude youngsters
SPECIAL ABILITIES: Theatrics

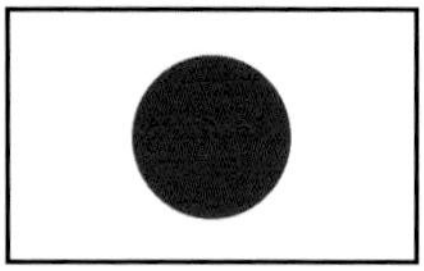

Rainbow Mika is a flamboyant young wrestler, eager to prove her fighting prowess.

Ever since she was a little girl, Mika Nanakawa dreamed of becoming a star in the ring. After graduating from junior high school, she completed her time as a trainee and proceeded to train as a student under the former professional wrestler, Yoko Harmageddon. Yoko used to be a popular wrestler, but a lower back injury forced her to retire. Yoko was instantly drawn to Mika's natural talent, and decided to whip every wrestling move she knew into her new student as a strict and disciplined trainer.

As a sort of marketing gimmick to promote her name, Mika traveled around engaging in random matches with street fighters. The mask that she wears around her eyes can sometimes make it difficult to tell what Mika is thinking or feeling, but she is a pretty emotional character with distinctive speech habits.

She admires Zangief more than anyone else and considers him to be her soul teacher. Zangief's influence has resulted in Mika preferring throw moves over any other technique. Mike trains really hard, looking forward to the day when she will stand in the ring alongside Zangief.

FIGHTING STYLE

Mika specializes in powerful wrestling maneuvers and all-out offensive attacks to achieve her many victories. She usually focuses on damaging strikes throughout a match, and saves a well-timed throw for her finishing move.

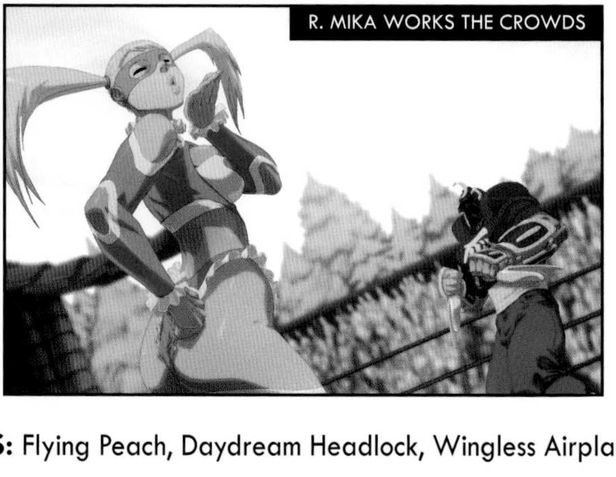
R. MIKA WORKS THE CROWDS

SIGNATURE MOVES: Flying Peach, Daydream Headlock, Wingless Airplane

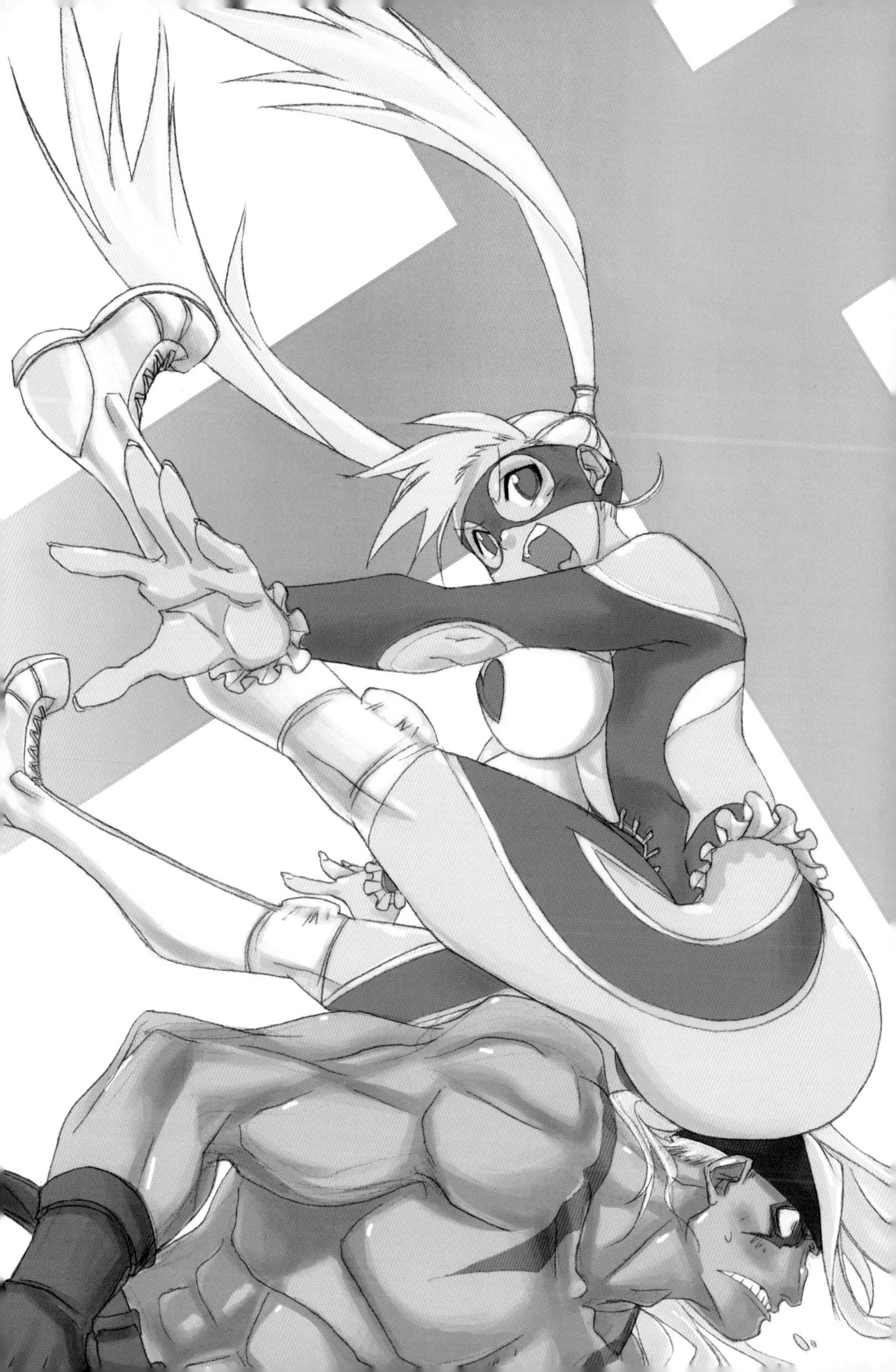

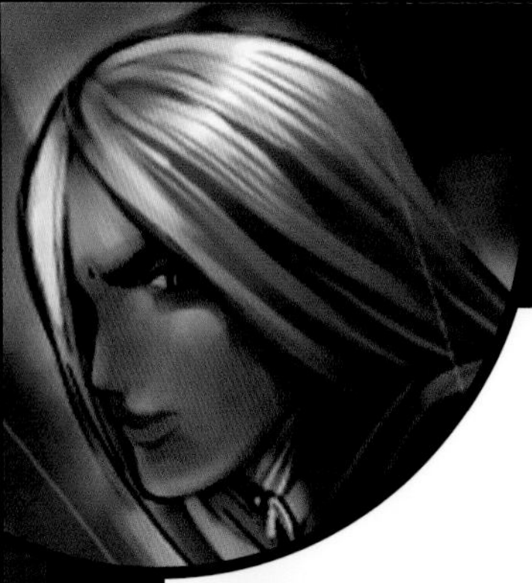

REMY

Burning Rage

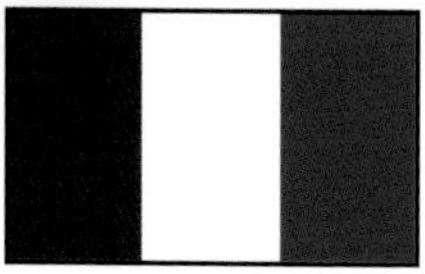

BIRTHDAY: ---------
COUNTRY OF ORIGIN: France
FIGHTING STYLE: Savate
HEIGHT: --------- **WEIGHT:** ---------
MEASUREMENTS: ---------
BLOOD TYPE: ---------
LIKES: His sister, bad moods
DISLIKES: All fighters
SPECIAL ABILITIES: Freediving

Remy is a troubled young man, torn between love and hatred. His long silver hair and smart physique give him an attractive appearance, but there is something decidedly dark about him.

Remy's deep-seated hatred towards all fighters stems from his feelings for his father, who abandoned his family to pursue the path of a fighter. On the other hand, Remy has an unnatural devotion to his late sister, whose body he keeps preserved in a frozen crystal at the bottom of the sea... and whom he speaks with often.

In the end, Remy realized that nurturing his hatred for all fighters would not change anything and resolved to let go of his past, including his sister. The symbol on his jacket is the Greek letter "Omega" symbolizing the end.

FIGHTING STYLE

Remy's fighting style uses a lot of kicks and movements that cleanly sweep his foes off their feet. Skillful legwork is his highest priority, as can be seen in his Blue Nocturne technique. Remy also uses ki-energy manipulation to deal out damage and is careful not to reveal any weak points to his opponents.

SIGNATURE MOVES: Light of Virtue, Rising Rage Flash, Cold Blue Kick

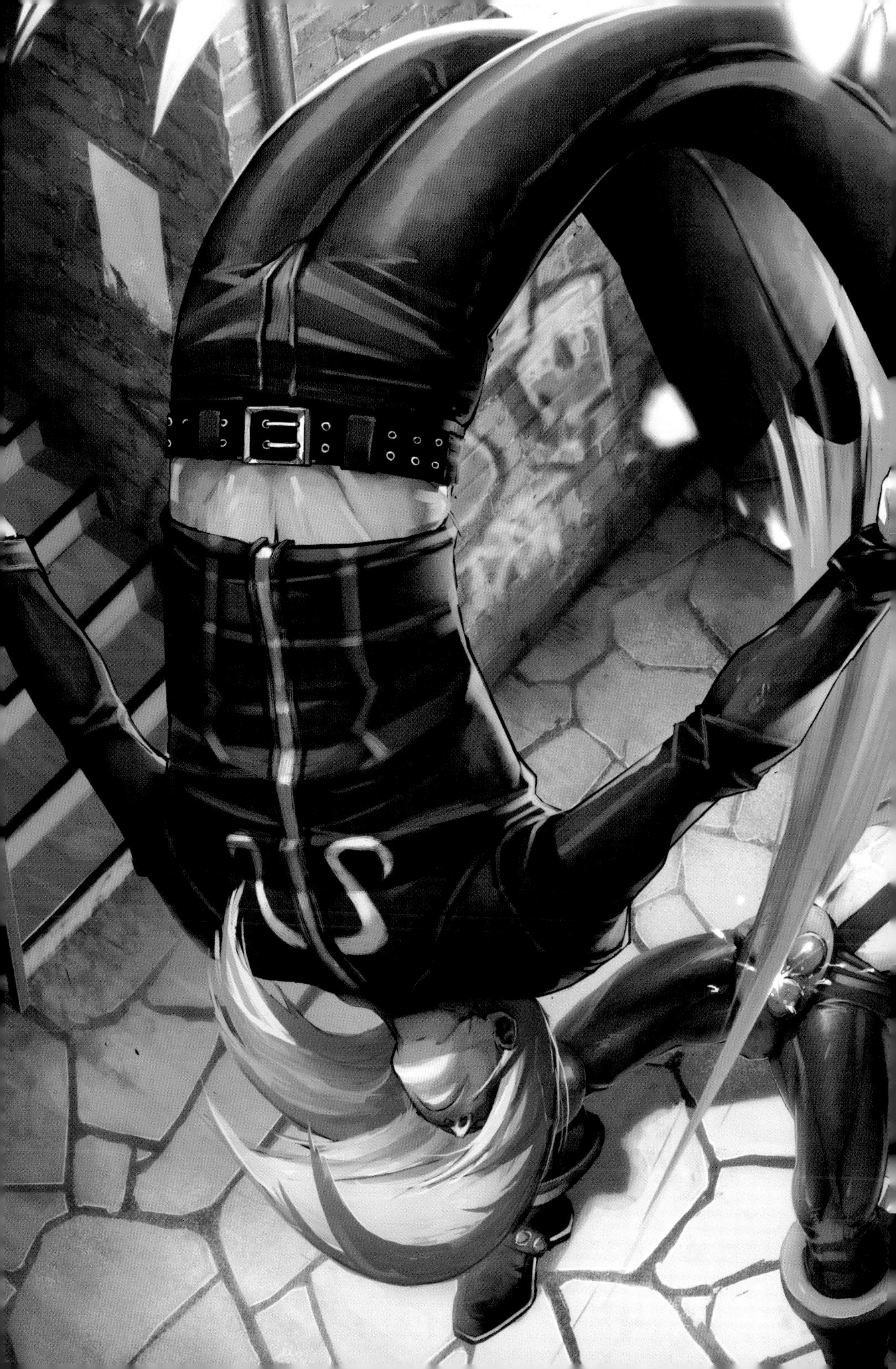

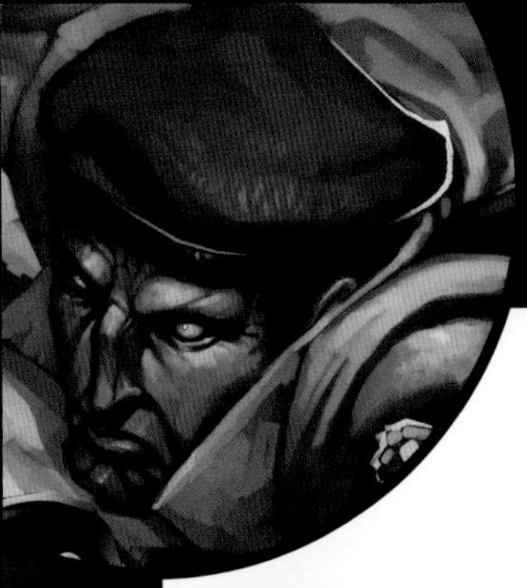

ROLENTO

The Dangerous Mercenary

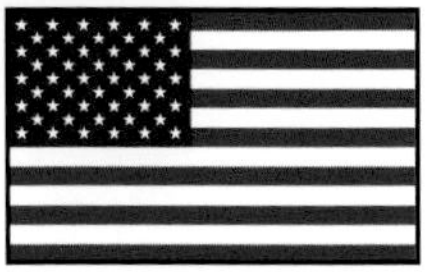

BIRTHDAY: ------------
COUNTRY OF ORIGIN: USA
FIGHTING STYLE: Weapons Expert
HEIGHT: 180 cm **WEIGHT:** 81 kg
MEASUREMENTS: B122/W86/H90
BLOOD TYPE: O
LIKES: Discipline, taking control
DISLIKES: Weaklings
SPECIAL ABILITIES: Traps, military weapons

"A nation built by soldiers, for soldiers." This is the goal of Rolento F. Shugerg, former Mad Gear member and weapons expert. Rolento belonged to the elite military unit known as the Red Berets before he got involved with the Mad Gear gang of Metro City.

Rolento remained a member of Mad Gear, thinking that the gang's goals would help him build his utopian military nation, until the group was destroyed by Metro City mayor Mike Haggar. Unlike Sodom, Rolento does not seem to have any interest in rebuilding the old Mad Gear.

Rolento has been traveling across the world in search of strong people to form the ideal national guard that any self-respecting military nation would have. Initially, Rolento had planned to recruit his former enemy, Cody, but was greatly disappointed when he saw how his old adversary had turned out.

Hoping that it would grant a quick yet considerable bump to his military might, Rolento determined that seizing control of Shadaloo would be a sound tactical decision. While Rolento is often seen as blinded and crazed by his twisted sense of ideals, his fanaticism does have its limits. He believes that M. Bison's Psycho Drive should be destroyed, deeming authority through brainwashing to be in conflict with the policies of an ideal government.

As a former soldier, Rolento is well-versed in the use of firearms and explosives. Since his days with the Red Berets, Rolento's motto has always been "Do whatever it takes to win." He believes that traps and conspiracies are all products of wisdom. He likes using his wire and knife in most of his moves, and toys with his prey using tricky movements.

Rolento and Guy have also been sworn enemies ever since Mad Gear orchestrated the Jessica Haggar kidnapping incident.

FIGHTING STYLE

Rolento's radical movements and tricky techniques make him difficult to keep track of. His weapon of choice is his staff, but when in trouble he has been known to toss a few grenades while retreating. Using weapons in fights isn't a dirty trick as far as he is concerned. The only thing that matters to him is winning.

SIGNATURE MOVES: Mekong Delta, Steel Rain, Stinger

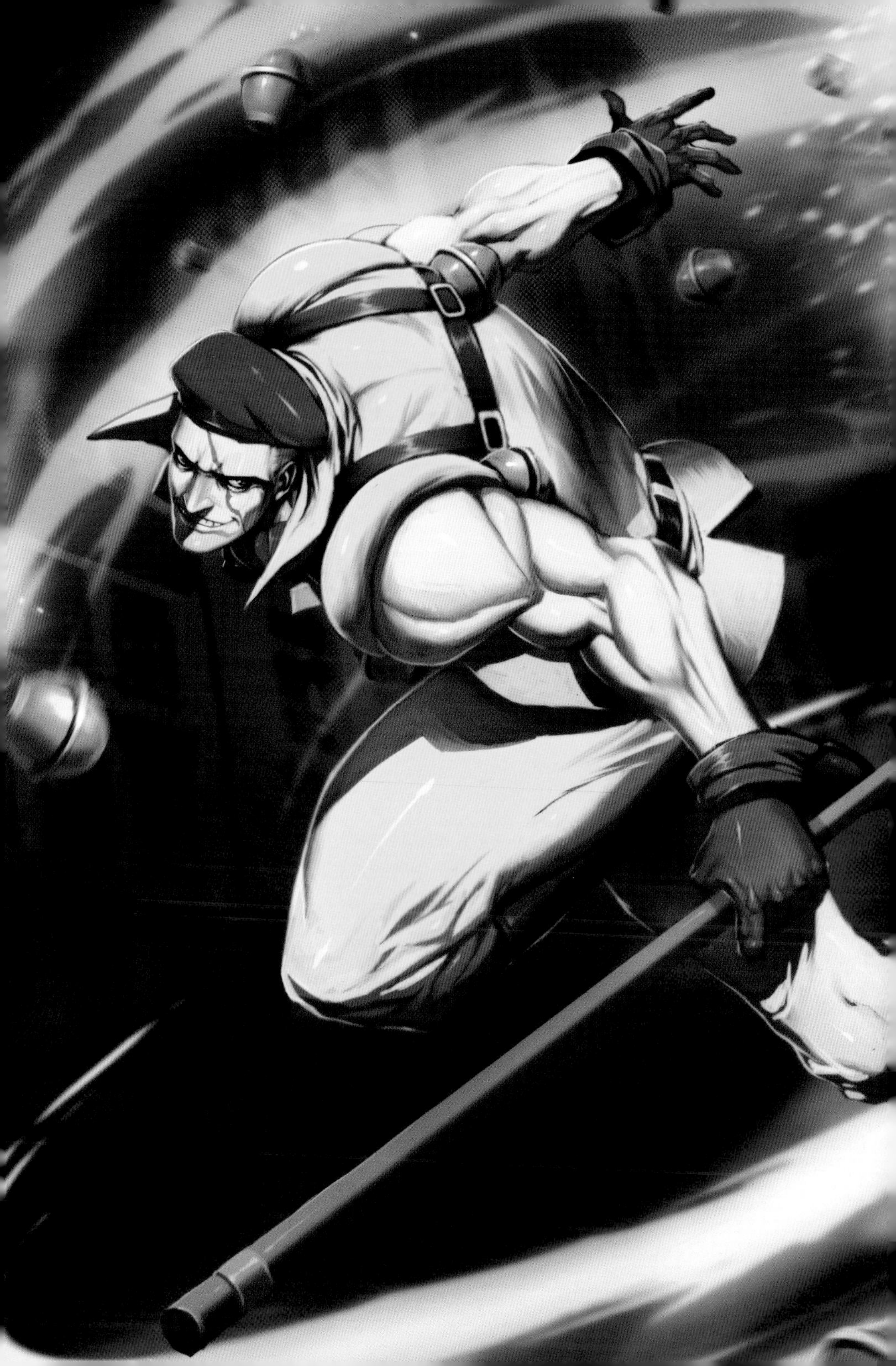

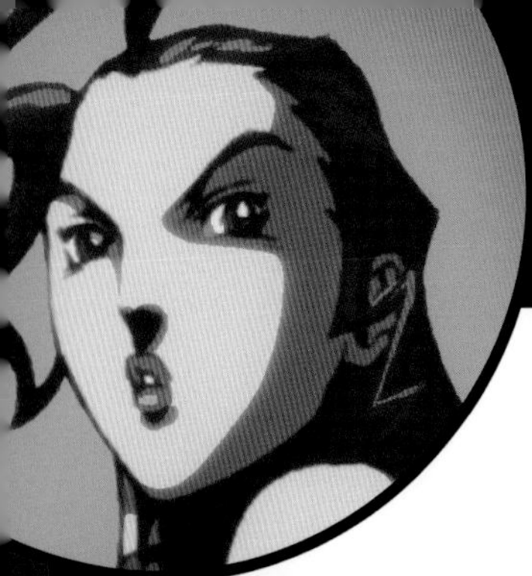

ROSE

The Dealer of Fate

BIRTHDAY: July 7
COUNTRY OF ORIGIN: Italy
FIGHTING STYLE: Soul Power
HEIGHT: 178 cm **WEIGHT:** 54 kg
MEASUREMENTS: B96/W57/H86
BLOOD TYPE: Unknown
LIKES: Sherry (wine), taking a bath
DISLIKES: UV, waking up early
SPECIAL ABILITIES: Tarot card reading

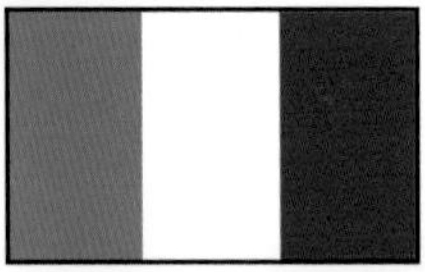

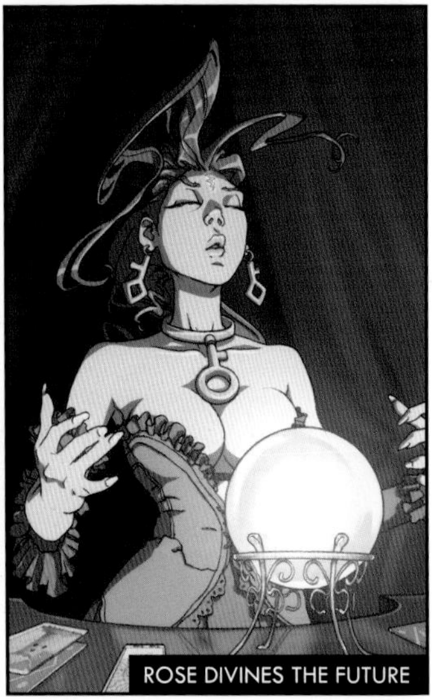

ROSE DIVINES THE FUTURE

A mysterious beauty who makes her living as a fortune teller in Genova, Italy, Rose's eerily accurate readings sometimes garner unappreciative responses.

Rose uses "Soul Power," a power that converts spiritual energy into a physical force, which she manipulates through her scarf. Believing it is her destiny to seal away the evil power known as "Psycho Power," she relentlessly pursues M. Bison, the wielder of said power. Eventually, she expanded her goals to preventing the misuse of all dark energies, putting other fighters such as Akuma on her watch list.

Rose was once M. Bison's teacher in the ways of Soul/Psycho power, and eventually learned that her soul and M. Bison's are one and the same – one soul inhabiting two bodies. During their last confrontation, Bison seemed to have been defeated. However, while his body was destroyed, his spirit survived. Bison used the soul connection he had with Rose to merge his spirit with her own, and inhabit her body after the fight. Bison maintained control of Rose, and ruled Shadaloo through her for some time, until Shadaloo scientists created a new body for him. Rose awakened later in a hospital, with no knowledge of how she got there, or her time spent as Bison's temporary vessel.

Rose's true age is unknown, but Chun-Li seems convinced that Rose is older than her.

FIGHTING STYLE

Rose's strong spirit possesses amazing abilities that she brings forth as Soul Power. Clad in a slinky long dress, her mysterious powers and smooth movements seem to effortlessly defeat opponents foolish enough to face her. Using her long scarf for defense and as a conduit for her Soul Power, it dances in such a way as to appear almost alive. Her fighting style centers around controlling the battlefield with flexible and deadly Soul Power attacks.

SIGNATURE MOVES: Soul Reflect, Soul Spark, Soul Spiral

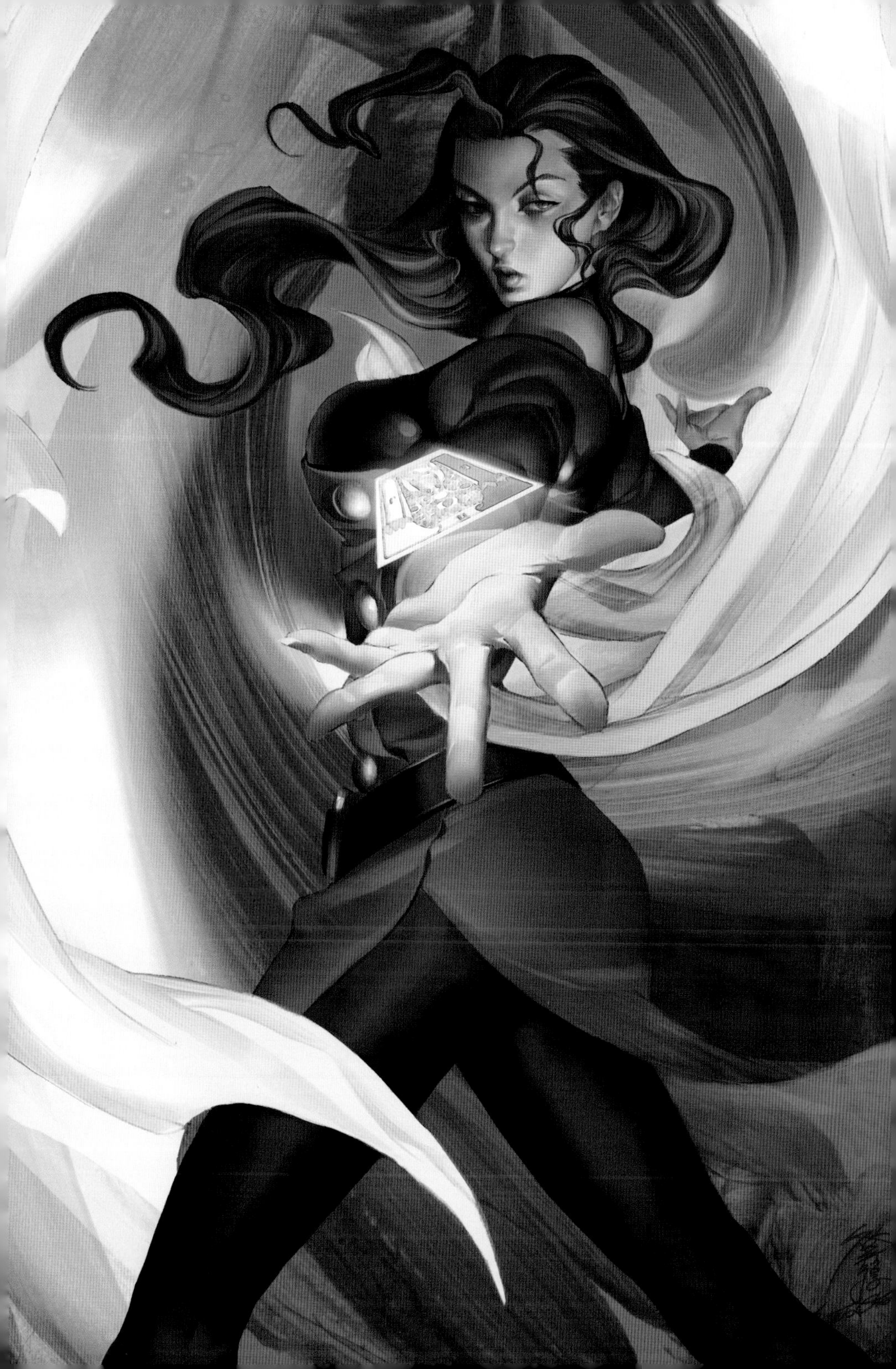

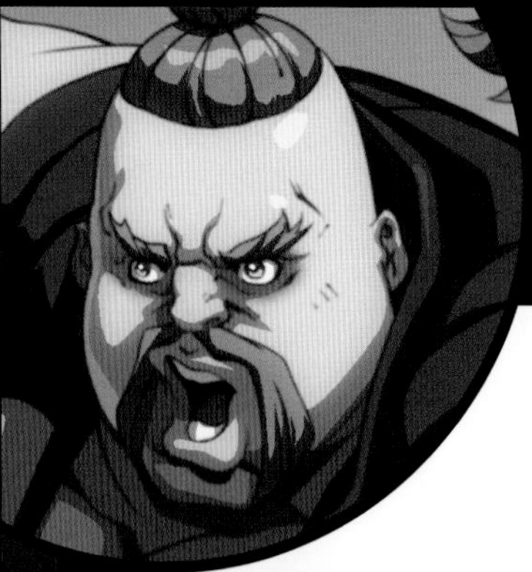

RUFUS

The Agile Giant

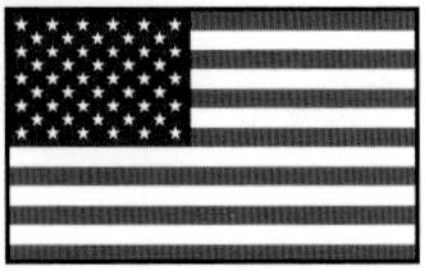

BIRTHDAY: July 30
COUNTRY OF ORIGIN: America
FIGHTING STYLE: (what he thinks is) Kung Fu
HEIGHT: 195 cm **WEIGHT:** 185 kg
MEASUREMENTS: B180/W250/H215
BLOOD TYPE: O
LIKES: Motorcycles, his girlfriend Candy
DISLIKES: Flashy people who stand out
SPECIAL ABILITIES: Karaoke

Rufus is the self-proclaimed greatest fighter in America, who battles using his own personal brand of Kung Fu. He views Ken Masters as his most worthy rival, and wishes to face him in battle... though the rivalry is decidedly one-sided.

Rufus' martial arts skills are self-taught, learned through mail order correspondence courses and watching late night Kung Fu movies. He spent some time travelling China on his bike, researching Chinese martial arts and honing his skills. His hairstyle is a tribute to the great martial artists he met in China and those he grew up watching on TV.

Rufus first met his girlfriend Candy shortly after claiming victory in a Midwestern fighting tournament. The down-on-her-luck bombshell had just been caught pulling a 'dine & dash', and found herself being chased by an angry mob. Ever the gentleman (at least when beautiful women are concerned) Rufus protected Candy from the mob, and paid off her tab with his just-won fight money. Since then, whether it's hanging at Rufus's custom motorcycle shop, riding in his chopper's sidecar, or cheering him on from ringside, Candy can always be found next to her man.

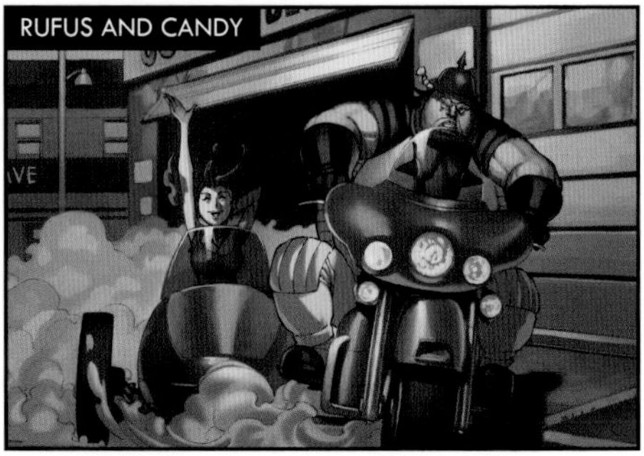
RUFUS AND CANDY

Rufus' main character flaw is that he often jumps the gun, as he has defeated many people in battle whom he mistook for Ken. He also tends to ramble on incessantly.

FIGHTING STYLE

Rufus's generous proportions and boisterous attitude often lead opponents to underestimate him. But these same opponents quickly learn that Rufus is a fast and furious fighter. His self-taught brand of Kung Fu combines rapid fire punches, aerial kicks, and moves exclusive to Rufus' unique body type like the gut-spinning Galactic Tornado.

SIGNATURE MOVES: Galactic Tornado, Messiah Kick, Snake Strike

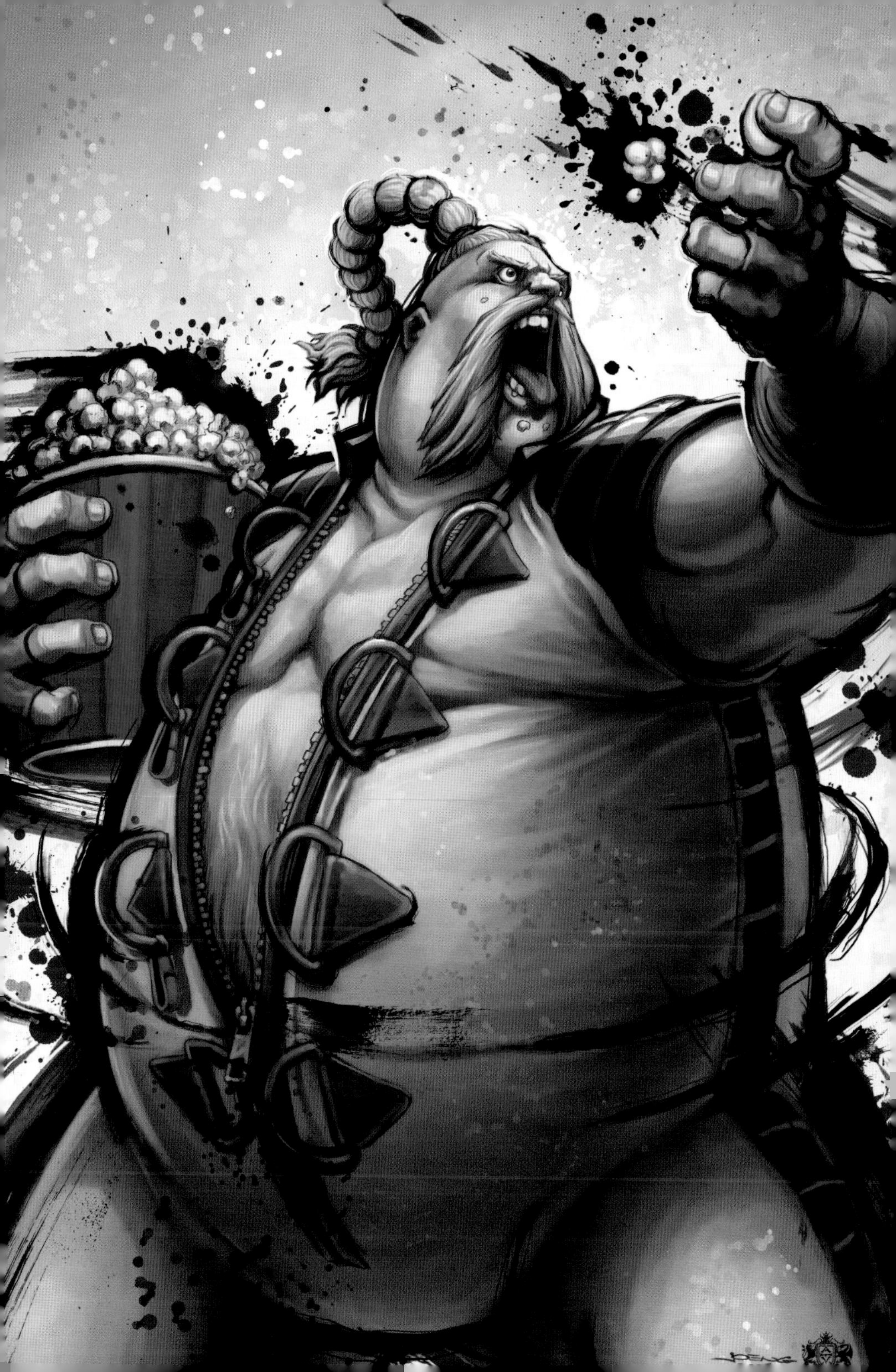

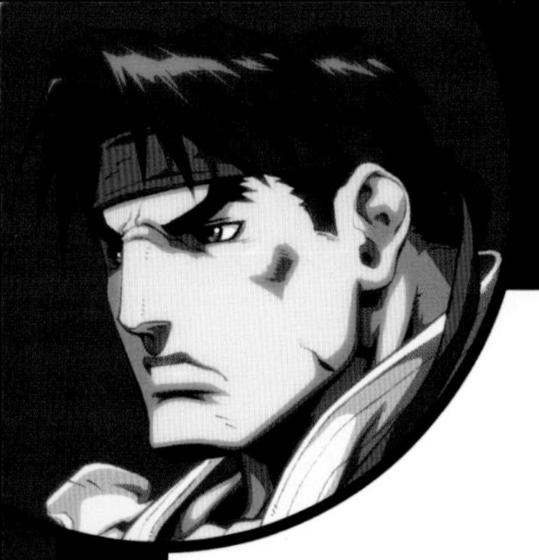

RYU

The Eternal Seeker

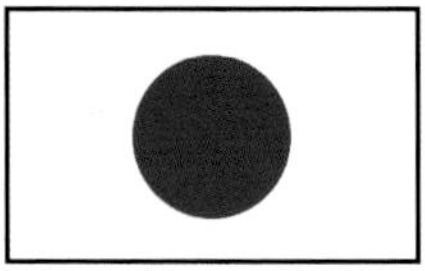

BIRTHDAY: July 21
COUNTRY OF ORIGIN: Japan
FIGHTING STYLE: Martial Arts rooted in Ansatsuken
HEIGHT: 175 cm **WEIGHT:** 68 kg
MEASUREMENTS: B112/W81/H85
BLOOD TYPE: O
LIKES: The path of the warrior in, and mizu youkan
DISLIKES: Spiders
SPECIAL ABILITIES: Can sleep anywhere, and hitchhiking

Ryu is a proud yet somewhat aloof master martial artist, who seeks nothing but to discover the path of a true martial artist. With his trademark white dougi, red headband, and bare feet, Ryu travels the world in search of new challengers, new fighting techniques, and any other knowledge that will help him reach his full potential. Many aspiring fighters idolize Ryu's strength and way of life.

Ryu trained alongside his best friend Ken under the Ansatsuken martial arts master Gouken, until Gouken was murdered by his own brother, Akuma. His time with Gouken granted Ryu an understanding of "ki", allowing him to perform ki-based attacks. But with these techniques came a great risk. When the intense desire to defeat one's enemy reaches its peak, it can be converted into a physical force known as the Satsui no Hado or "The Killing Intent". The Satsui no Hado is innately present in Ansatsuken, which means that any fighter such as Ryu who uses these moves carries the potential within them to realize its power. Ryu struggles constantly to resist the lure of this dark temptation.

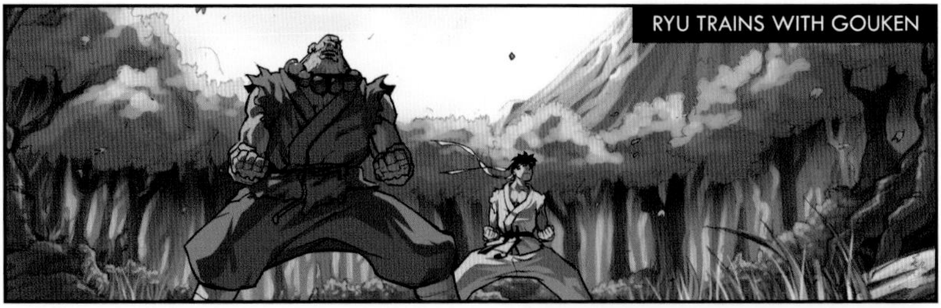
RYU TRAINS WITH GOUKEN

Ryu never stopped training, however, and managed to defeat Sagat, the Emperor of Muay Thai, in the first Street Fighter Tournament. Ryu's final Shoryuken left a permanent scar (physically and emotionally) on the previously undefeated Muay Thai master, and Sagat quickly became obsessed with defeating Ryu in a rematch. Despite having won the tournament, Ryu didn't let it go to his head, but instead began to travel the world in his pursuit of becoming a true martial artist. It was around this time that Ryu also gained a student of sorts, the schoolgirl-turned-street-fighter Sakura.

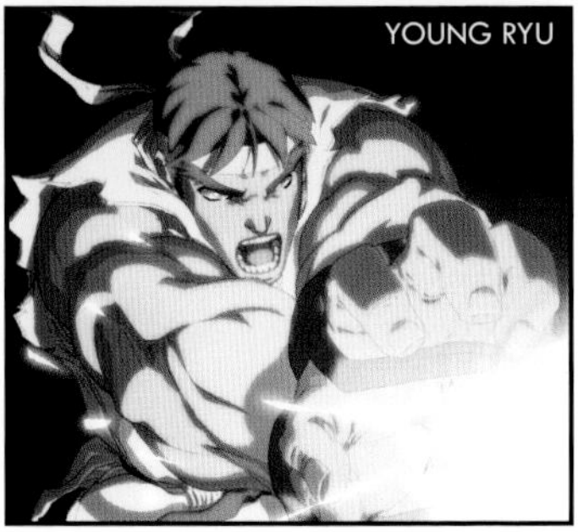
YOUNG RYU

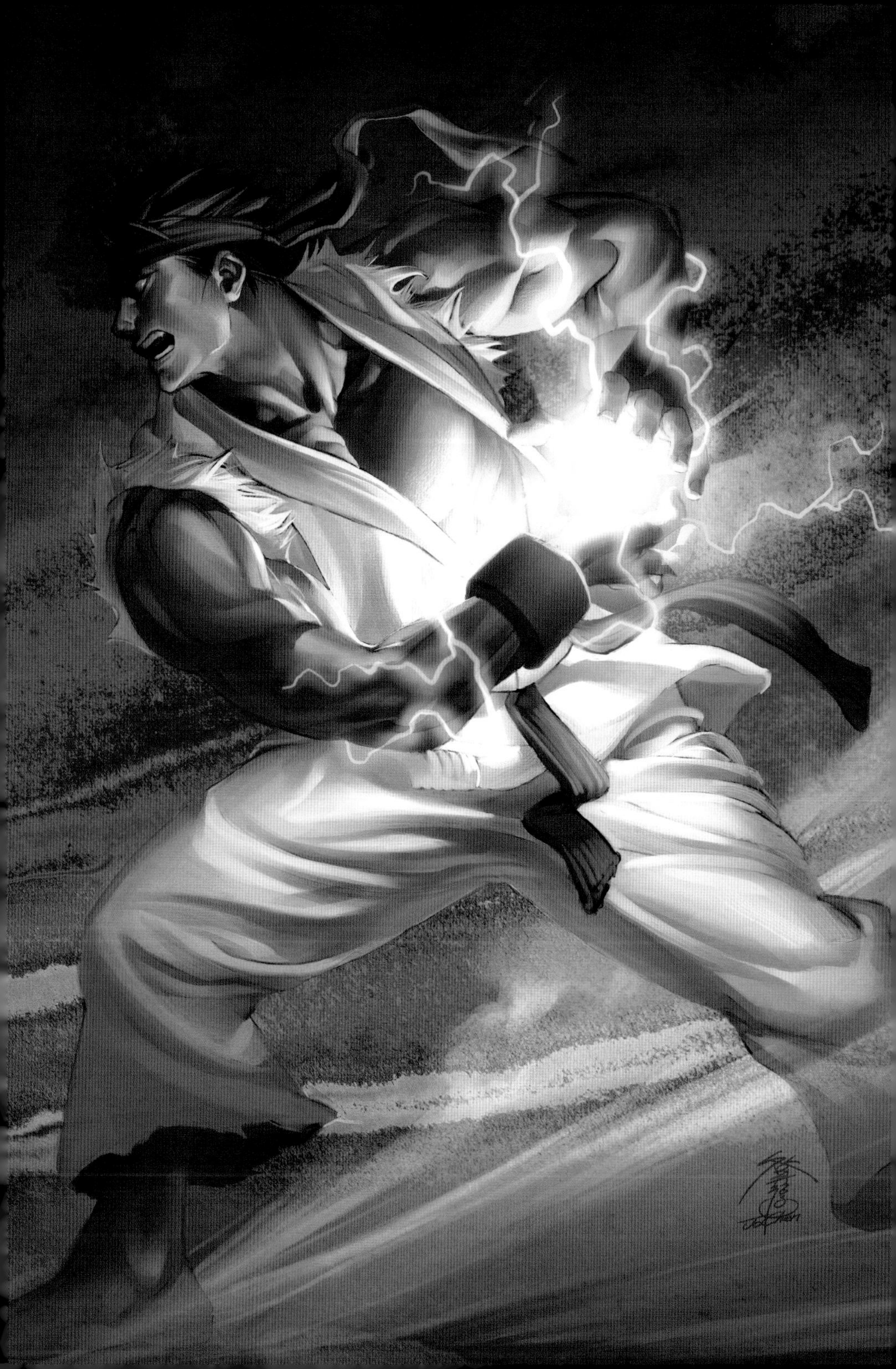

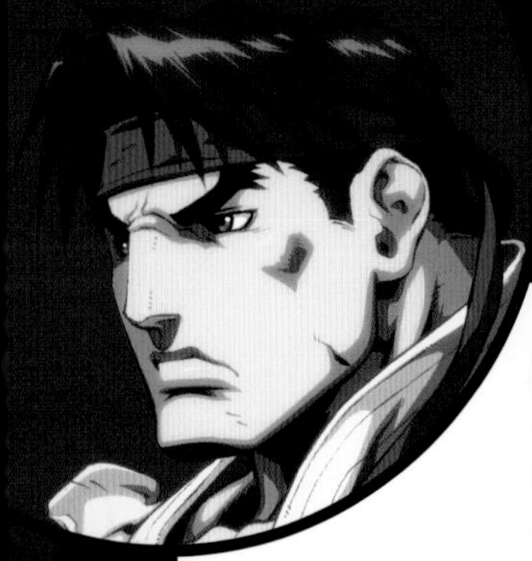

RYU (CONTINUED...)

The Eternal Seeker

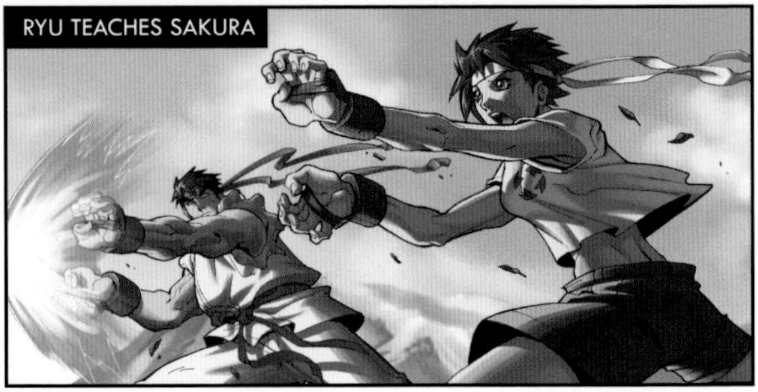

RYU TEACHES SAKURA

Upon hearing rumors of a mystery martial artist who controls something known as "Psycho Power," Ryu's interest was peaked and he left to discover what he could about this individual. This mystery man turned out to be M. Bison, leader of Shadaloo, who quickly gained an interest in Ryu. For his incredible skill and the fact that the Satsui no Hado lies dormant within him, Ryu was marked by M. Bison as a potential replacement body, eventually forcing the two into a confrontation. In this epic battle, Ryu was almost swallowed up by the power of the Satsui no Hado, but he managed to fend it off by focusing on his bond with Ken and the rest of his friends.

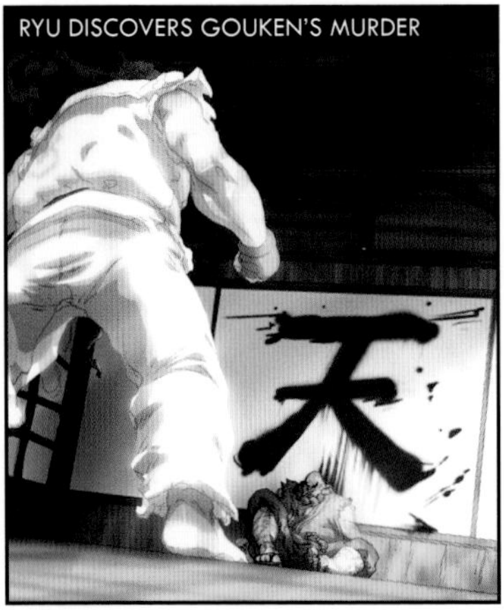

天

RYU DISCOVERS GOUKEN'S MURDER

Ryu's encounter with Shadaloo also led him to a rematch with Sagat, who had joined Shadaloo as one of Bison's four bosses. Ryu achieved another victory, but by this time Sagat had finally overcome his thirst for revenge. The two have since gained a mutual respect for each other as great martial artists.

Ryu continues to travel the world street fighting, but returns to Suzaku Palace in Japan once a year to visit his master's grave. His iconic red headband was a gift from Ken, who had previously worn it as a hair tie.

FIGHTING STYLE

Hi Ansatsuken training gave Ryu an understanding of Ki combat energy. This gave him mastery of ki-based attacks such as the Hadoken, Shoryuken and Tatsumaki Senpukyaku maneuvers. After the death of Master Gouken, Ryu strengthened his body and spirit to create an even more powerful Hadoken attack. His sense of physical combat differs slightly from Ken's. The secret of Ryu's strength comes from his honest training and unclouded understanding of martial arts.

SIGNATURE MOVES: Hadoken(aka Fireball), Tatsumaki Senpukyaku(aka Hurricane Kick), Shoryuken(aka Dragon Punch)

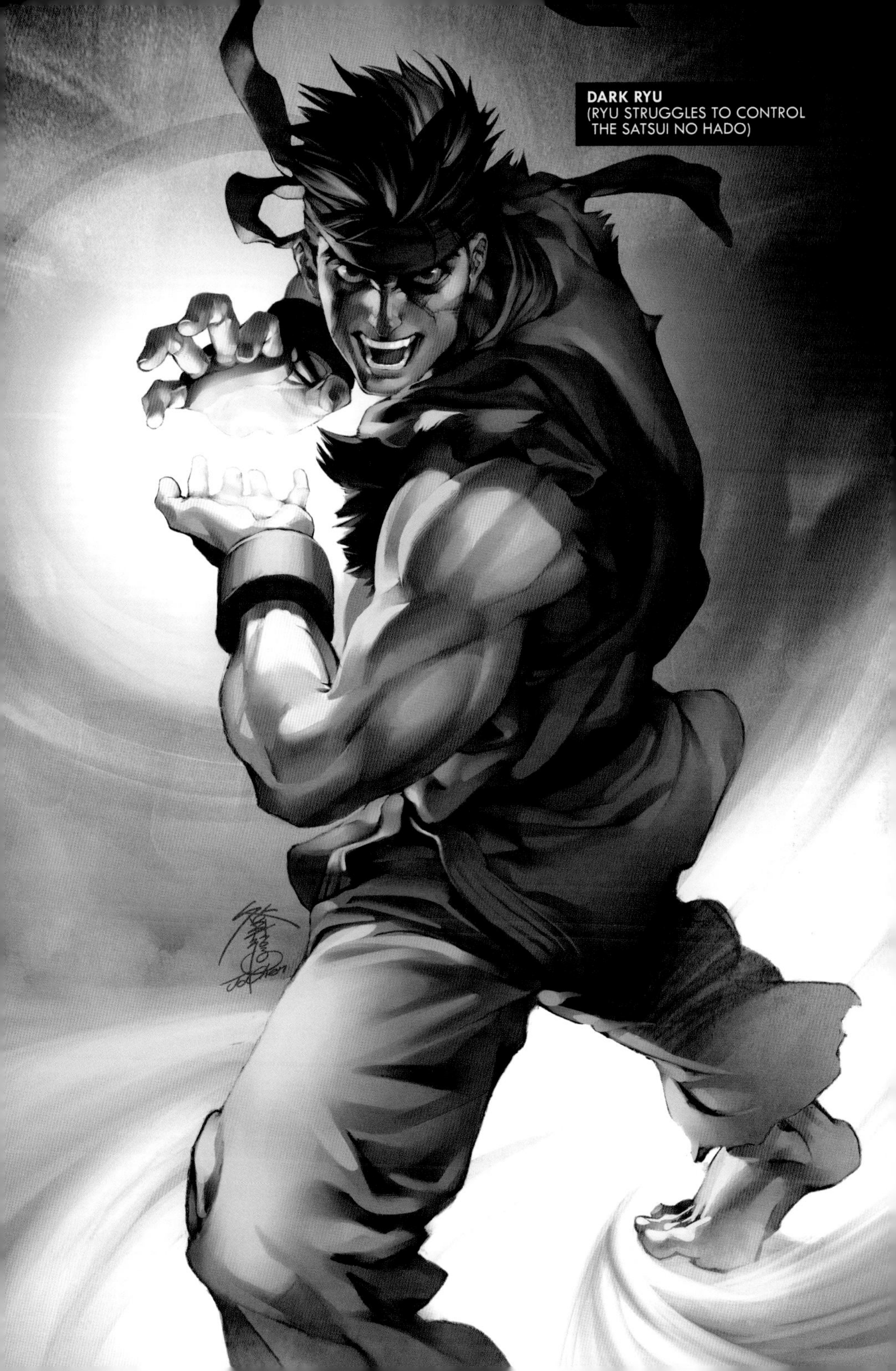

DARK RYU
(RYU STRUGGLES TO CONTROL THE SATSUI NO HADO)

SAGAT
The Fearless Emperor

BIRTHDAY: July 2
COUNTRY OF ORIGIN: Thailand
FIGHTING STYLE: Muay Thai
HEIGHT: 226 cm **WEIGHT:** 78 kg
MEASUREMENTS: B130/W86/H95
BLOOD TYPE: O
LIKES: Strong opponents
DISLIKES: Shoryuken, palliative people
SPECIAL ABILITIES: Can stay under water
for over 20 minutes

He has been known as the Emperor of Muay Thai, the Invincible Tiger, and one of the four bosses of Shadaloo. A national hero in his native Thailand, Sagat was still only a teenager when he defeated the reigning king of Muay Thai. The power of his kick is said to be peerless.

In the final match of the first Street Fighter Tournament, Sagat was defeated by Ryu's powerful Shoryuken attack. Sagat's first ever loss left a massive wound across his chest, and a deep hatred of Ryu in his soul. Sagat rededicated himself to training his body and mind with the singular goal of one day defeating Ryu. Sagat also accepted a position as one of M. Bison's four Shadaloo bosses, hoping that the resources of the criminal Shadaloo organization might help him locate Ryu for a rematch.

SAGAT IS SCARRED BY RYU

Sagat wears an eye patch, having lost the use of his right eye in a match with Go Hibiki. Go was killed by Sagat in the same match, leading Go's son Dan to later seek revenge for his father's death. Sagat also trained fellow Muay Thai fighter Adon. However, Adon would later reject Sagat, after seeing his mentor lose to Ryu.

At first Sagat's hatred of Ryu was his only motivation, but he eventually figured out that the potential for strength based in hatred is very limited. Before Sagat himself knew it, he had grown to admire Ryu's strength. Now, Sagat looks forward to a rematch with his rival not for revenge, but for the chance to see Ryu show his full potential.

FIGHTING STYLE
Through his intense training while in isolation, Sagat carefully rebuilt his fighting style, adding several powerful moves to his arsenal of attacks. Among these signature moves are the Shoryuken-styled Tiger Uppercut and the Tiger Shot projectile blast created from the rage of his burning fists.

SIGNATURE MOVES: Tiger Knee, Tiger Shot, Tiger Uppercut

サガット SAGAT

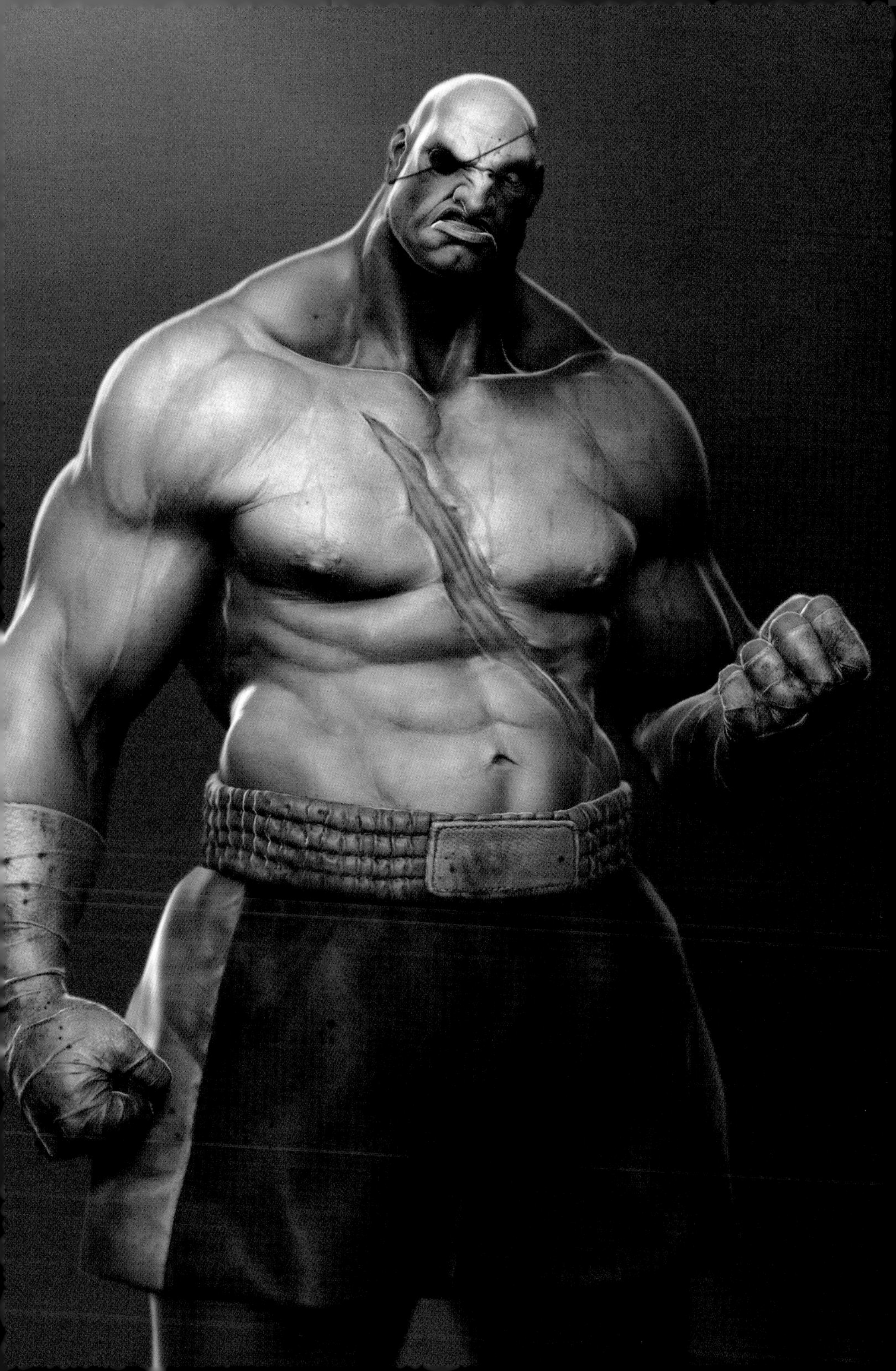

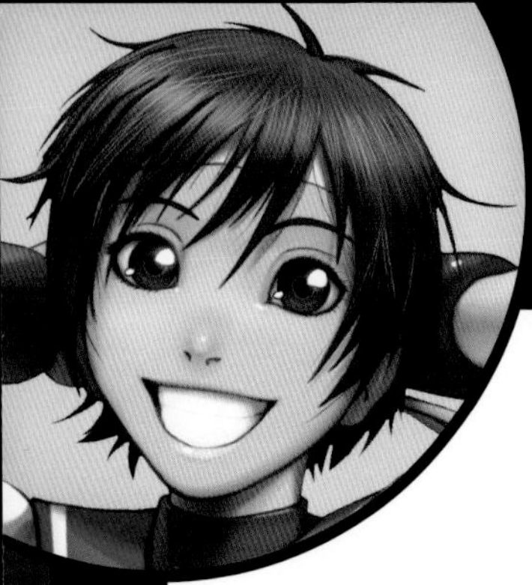

SAKURA

The Blossoming Flower

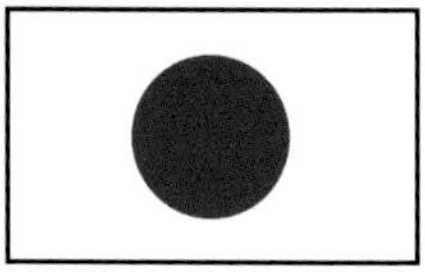

BIRTHDAY: March 15
COUNTRY OF ORIGIN: Japan
FIGHTING STYLE: Imitates Ryu
HEIGHT: 157 cm **WEIGHT:** 42 kg
MEASUREMENTS: B80/W60/H84
BLOOD TYPE: A
LIKES: Gym class, white rice
DISLIKES: Math, playing video games with her little brother
SPECIAL ABILITIES: English, cooking

Sakura is a high school student who launched herself into the world of street fighting in pursuit of Ryu. She is a cheerful girl, who can have fun no matter what she's doing, and never passes up a chance to fight someone who she thinks is stronger than her.

Sakura used to be a normal school girl living in the Setagaya district of Tokyo, until the day she saw Ryu fighting. Without even knowing his name she thought, "I need to see him again." This one thought drove Sakura into learning martial arts by imitating the moves she saw Ryu executing that day. She started wearing a white headband and red gloves to best emulate Ryu, and in the end she succeeded in meeting him again. Though her request to become his student was denied, Sakura made the decision to continue street fighting in the hopes that she could once again meet with Ryu after better understanding the true meaning of fighting.

Although they have never officially established a master-student relationship, Dan has been guiding Sakura since her early days in street fighting. Sakura's schoolmate Karin insists on treating her like a rival, and this has become a matter of some concern for Sakura.

Sakura's best friend is her schoolmate Kei, who doesn't necessarily approve of Sakura's intense interest in street fighting, but nevertheless supports her friend as best she can. Sakura is also close friends with Hinata Wakaba and Natsu Ayuhara, two girls from nearby Aoharu City.

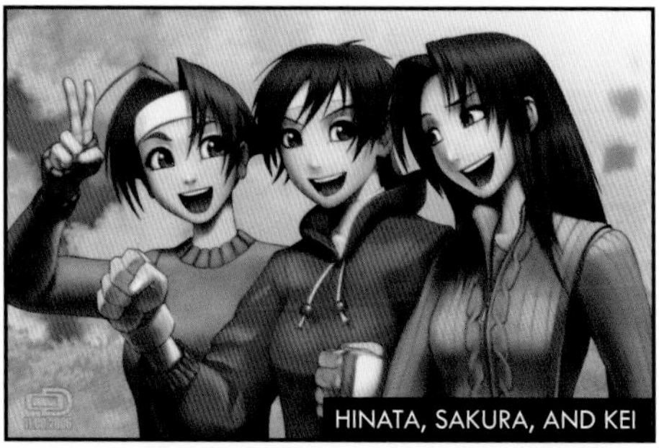

HINATA, SAKURA, AND KEI

FIGHTING STYLE

Sakura's combat style evolved as she did her best to copy Ryu and imagined that he was teaching her each and every maneuver first hand. All of her moves have similarities to Ryu's fighting style but are different to compensate for her size and speed. She may not have been formally trained but her natural talent and boundless energy make her a competent fighter nonetheless. Her use of speed and sneaky special attacks are highly effective and she can hold her own against many more experienced fighters.

SIGNATURE MOVES: Hadoken, Shouoken, Shunpukyaku

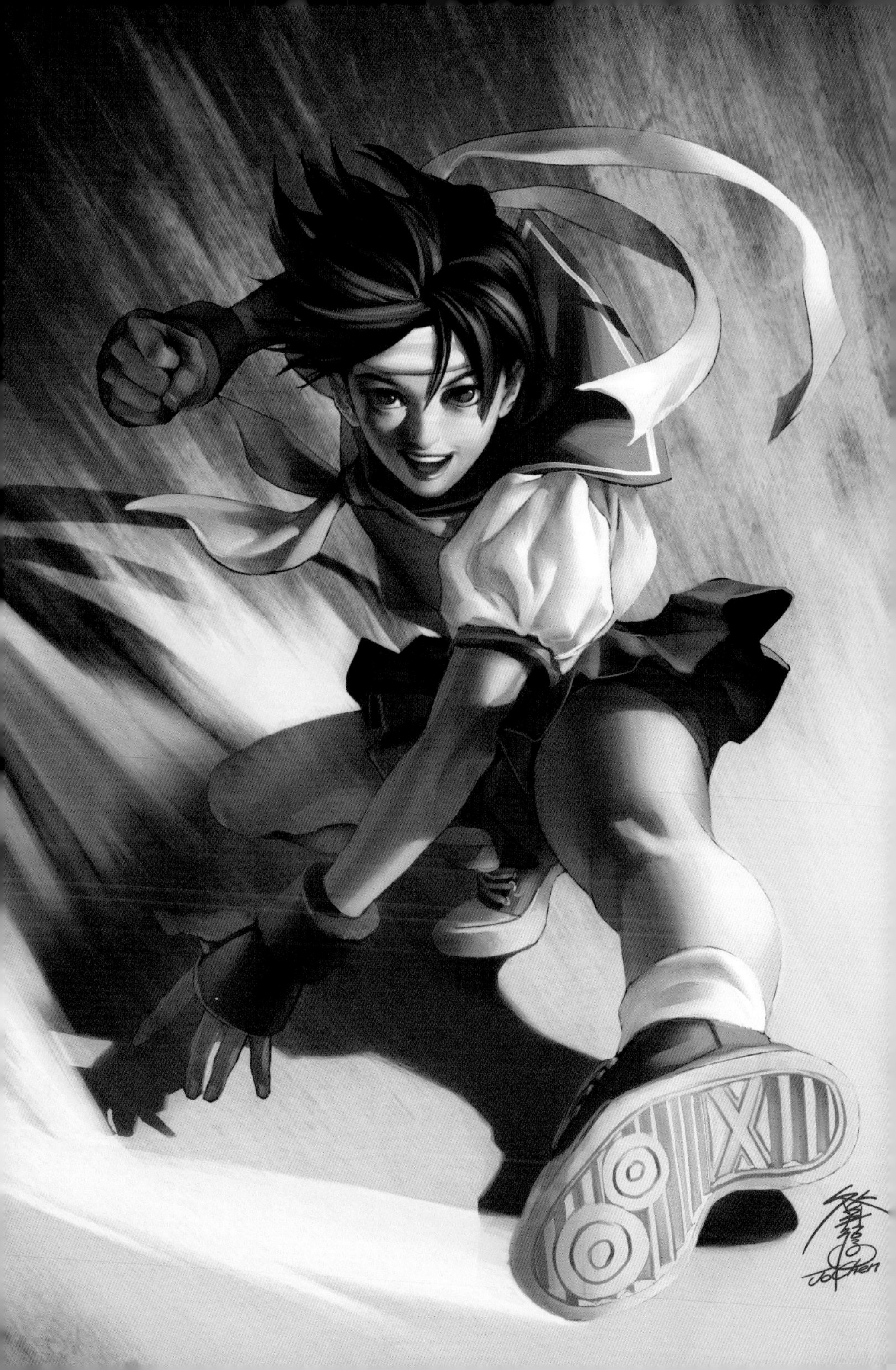

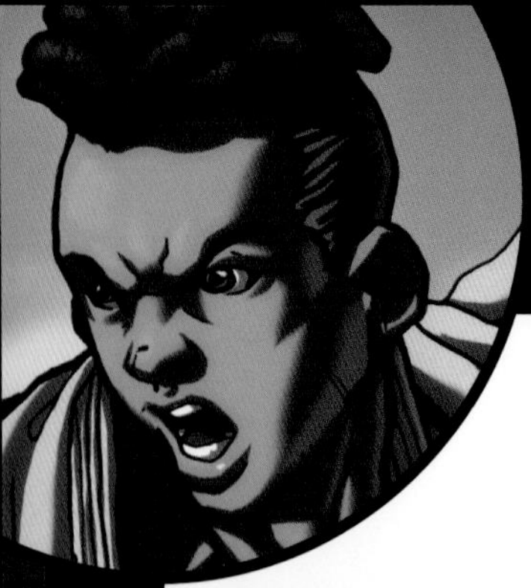

SEAN

The Cannonball Kid

BIRTHDAY: ---------
COUNTRY OF ORIGIN: Brazil
FIGHTING STYLE: Imitates Ken
HEIGHT: --------- **WEIGHT:** ---------
MEASUREMENTS: ---------
BLOOD TYPE: ---------
LIKES: Ken Masters, bubble gum
DISLIKES: Losing, being compared to Dan
SPECIAL ABILITIES: Basketball

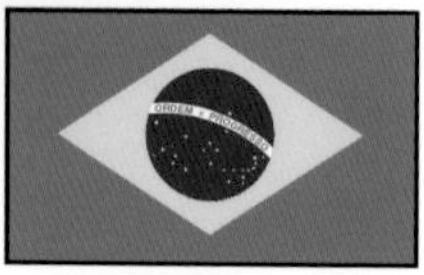

A passionate young man from Brazil, Sean Matsuda was disciplined by his Japanese grandfather, so his manners are better than most boys his age. After seeing Ken Masters fight in a tournament, Sean became a huge fan and forced his way into an apprenticeship. He calls Ken "Master" and does his best to mimic Ken's movements, but both Sean's offensive and defensive skills leave a lot to be desired.

After a year as Ken's student, Sean registered to enter his first tournament, but according to Ken he was not ready. In hopes of convincing Ken, Sean started a strict training regime. After all the hard training, he successfully won the tournament... but only in his dreams. In reality, Sean didn't even make it past the preliminaries. Despite his natural talent in the ring, Sean has a long way to go before he's mastered the fighting arts.

"Even if I lose today, I can still win tomorrow," is Sean's motto, and his dream is to one day develop his own original special move. His positive attitude and light-hearted jokes about victory and defeat aside, deep down Sean hates to lose. He excels at all sports, and is a member of his college's basketball team.

FIGHTING STYLE

Sean has copied elements of Ken's fighting style out of admiration for the seasoned warrior, but always adds his own twists to them. Although his techniques and power could never reach those of Ken's, he uses them as the basis for his own original moves that take advantage of his naturally flexible body. A skilled blocker, Sean often uses defensive techniques to wait for the opportune moment to strike.

SIGNATURE MOVES: Dragon Smash, Hado Burst, Tornado

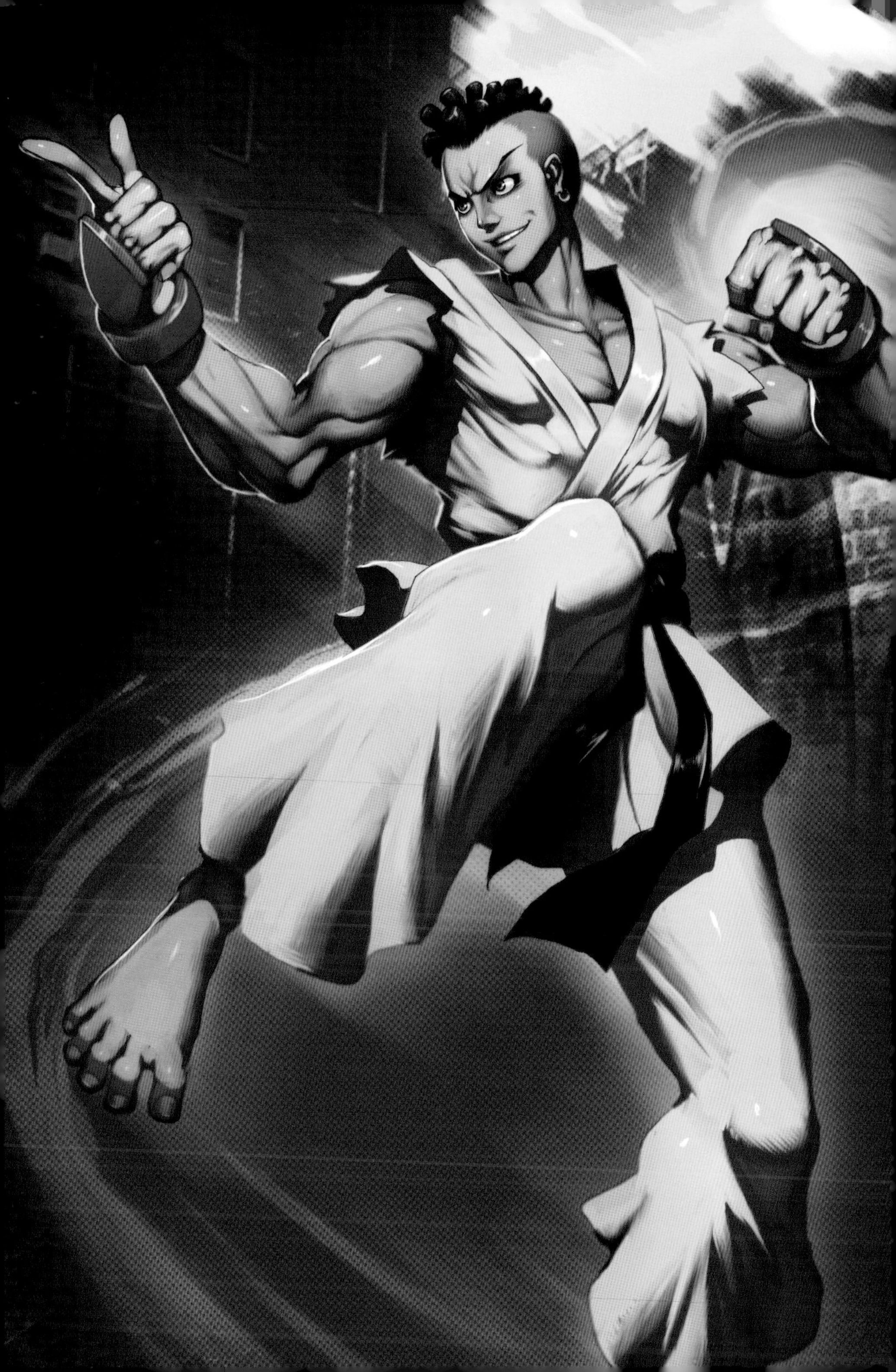

SETH
Master of Puppets

BIRTHDAY: Unknown
COUNTRY OF ORIGIN: Unknown
FIGHTING STYLE: Move duplication
HEIGHT: 198 cm   **WEIGHT:** 85 kg
MEASUREMENTS: B130/W85/H89
BLOOD TYPE: Unknown
LIKES: Plotting
DISLIKES: Needy, clingy people
SPECIAL ABILITIES: Modding things

Seth is the CEO of S.I.N. (Shadaloo Intimidation Network), the division of Shadaloo responsible for developing weapons. Having altered his own body cybernetically, Seth is able to learn and use any fighting style he sees.

Seth was created through the Living Incubator program as one of 26 potential replacement bodies for M. Bison. These bodies were devised from not only M. Bison's own cells, but also a mixture of other particularly promising genetic material. Upon his creation, Seth was not given a name but only a number, Fifteen.

THE LIVING INCUBATOR PROGRAM

Not one to waste resources and have his backup bodies just laying around, Bison placed Fifteen in charge of S.I.N., where he went on to develop the Tanden Engine. The engine granted Fifteen the ability to register data of other fighters' moves and to freely use these moves. Initially, Seth installed this new technology only in himself, but Bison was impressed enough to include the device in all of his Living Incubator bodies.

Fifteen also developed the powerful device known as BLECE (Boiling Liquid Expanding Cell Explosion). The BLECE is able to draw out and absorb the "ki" found in all living things and amplify this energy. This amplified energy resonates with living cells, forcing the liquid inside the cells to explode. This causes massive physical damage (and typically death) to any target within range of the device. The more ki that exists in a living being, the more powerful the BLECE effect will be. This effect could potentially be used to turn any fighter who is adept in the use of ki into a sort of living bomb.

セス SETH

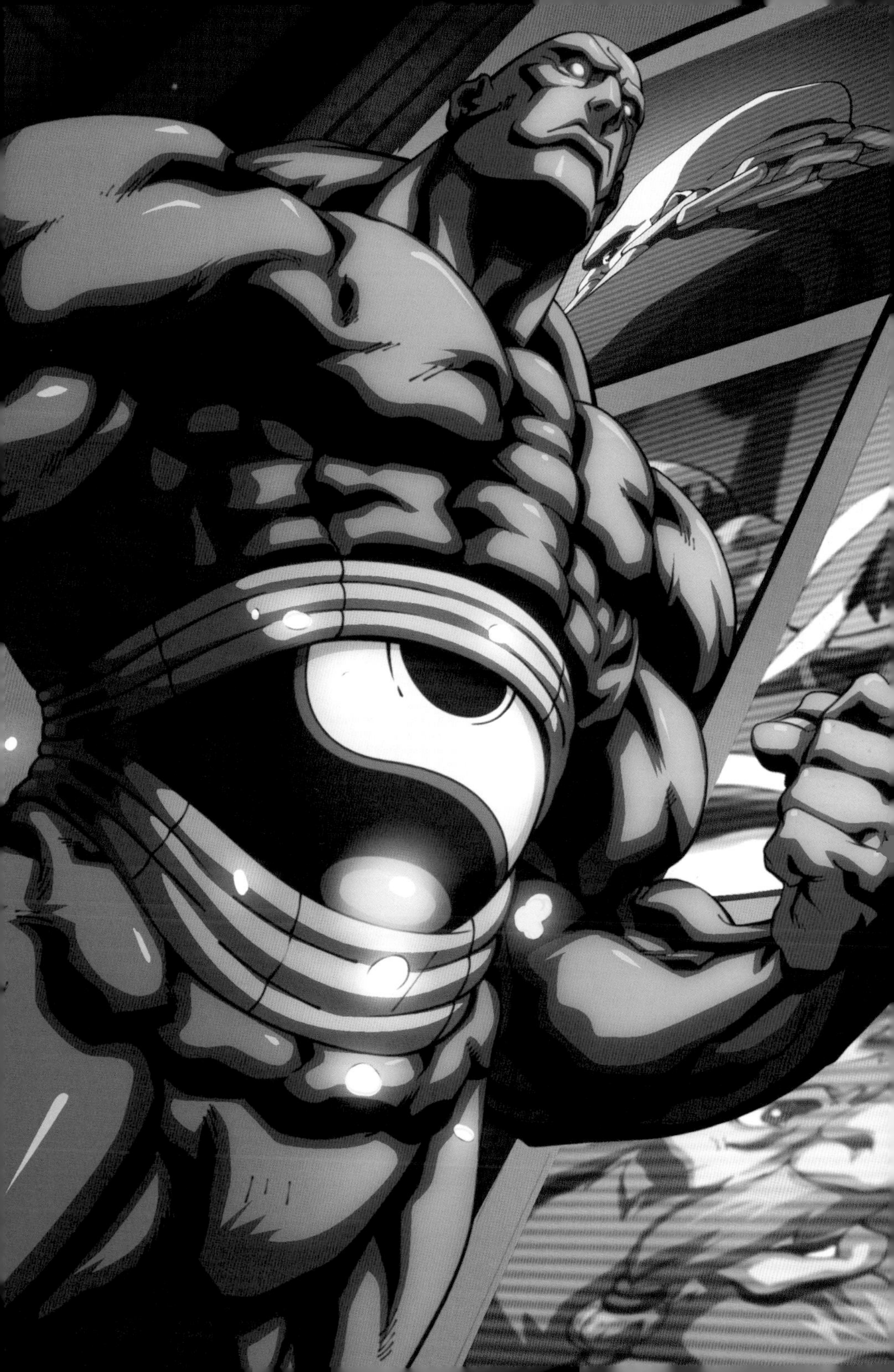

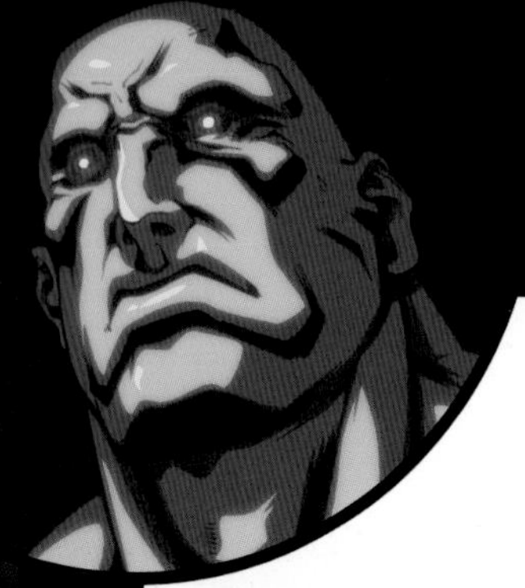

SETH (CONTINUED...)

Master of Puppets

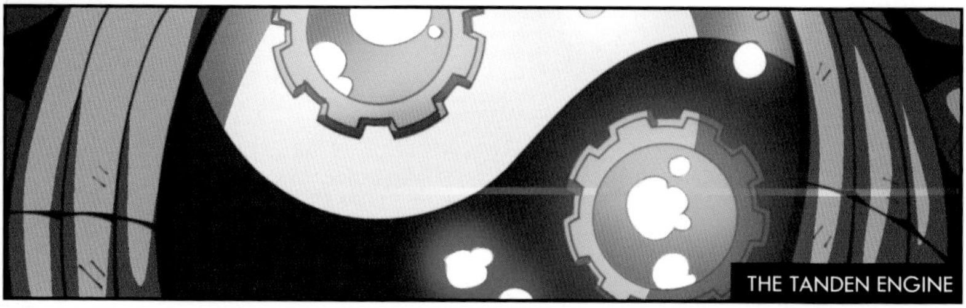

THE TANDEN ENGINE

Fifteen eventually grew tired of being Bison's puppet. With the power of the BLECE device at his command, Fifteen renamed himself Seth, rebelled against Bison, and separated S.I.N. from the rest of Shadaloo. But his newfound independence wasn't enough, as Seth vowed to eventually take all that Bison had, and more.

Seth also later created the Feng Shui Engine, a miniature version of the Tanden Engine technology, which acts as the fighter Juri's left eye. It does not allow her to record and learn fight data, but does enhance her existing abilities. Seth is quite aware that Juri intends to betray him, but keeps her as a lackey anyway. He feels she is still useful and not a real threat to his plans.

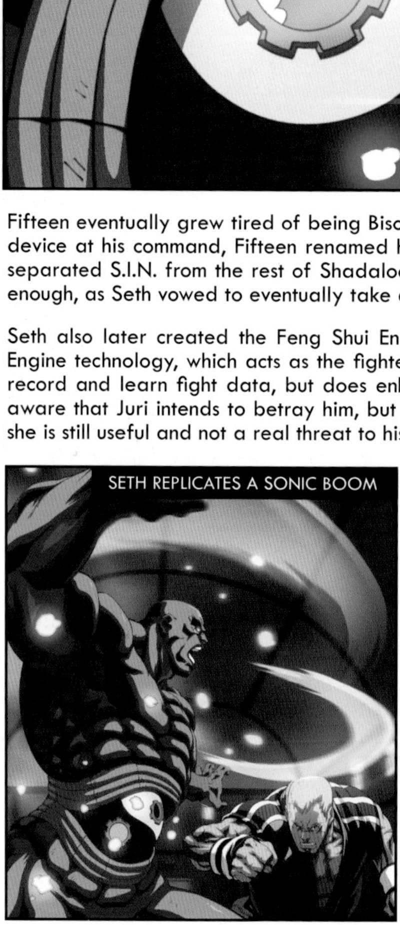

SETH REPLICATES A SONIC BOOM

The mercenary Abel was another product of the Living Incubator project, making him and Seth genetic brothers of a sort.

FIGHTING STYLE

Thanks to his Tanden Engine, Seth's fighting style is really more of a fighting database which combines the most powerful attacks of the world's greatest fighters. His repertoire includes Ryu's Shoryuken, Guile's Sonic Boom , Zangief's Piledriver, Chun-Li's Yosokyaku, Dhalsim's stretching and teleportation powers, and many more leveraged techniques. He also has the unique ability to create an artificial gravity well, sucking his opponents in and leaving them open for multiple strikes.

SIGNATURE MOVES: Tanden Storm, Tanden Stream, Tanden Typhoon

THE BLECE DEVICE
(BOILING LIQUID EXPANDING CELL EXPLOSION)

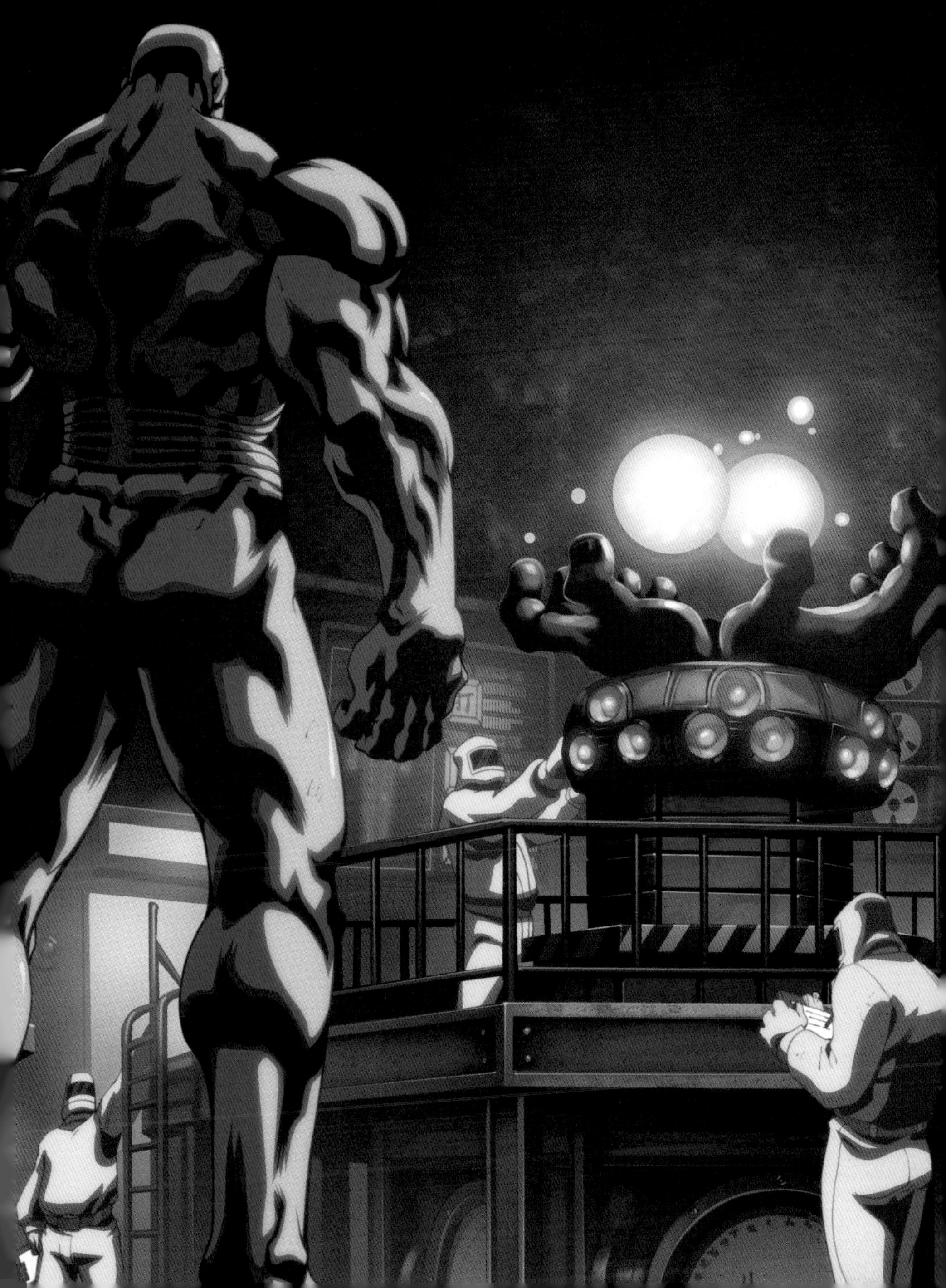

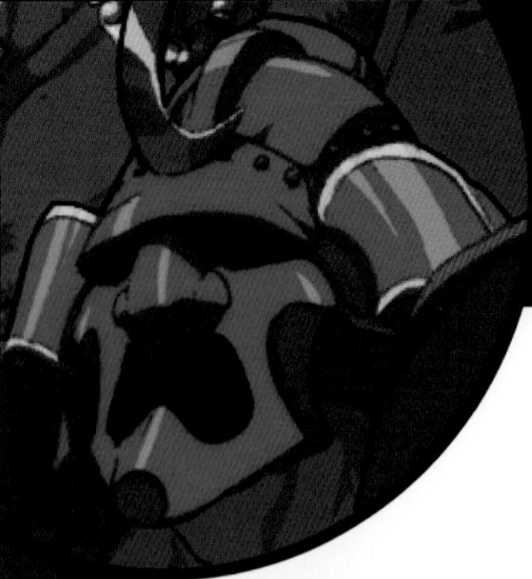

SODOM

The Otaku Fighter

BIRTHDAY: ---------
COUNTRY OF ORIGIN: America
FIGHTING STYLE: Self-taught martial arts
HEIGHT: 206 cm **WEIGHT:** 108 kg
MEASUREMENTS: B148/W98/H103
BLOOD TYPE: A
LIKES: Japanese spirituality and goods
DISLIKES: Guy
SPECIAL ABILITIES: Water performances, driving big trucks

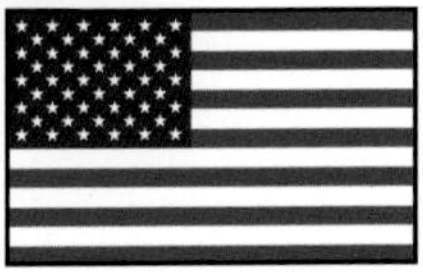

Sodom is a Japan-loving man who is traveling in search of strong people to assist him in rebuilding the Mad Gear gang. Sodom has wanted to know everything about Japan ever since he watched a television show called "Shogun". Pursuing his Japanism, Sodom wanders the world, exploring the Wabi-sabi state of mind.

When Jessica Haggar was kidnapped, Sodom encountered Guy for the first time, and was deeply wounded by Guy's suggestion that he holds many misconceptions of Japan. Guy's words drove Sodom to travel to Japan and study Japanese martial arts, where he acquired a new weapon (the jitte). Despite taking the long trip, Sodom seems to have only deepened his misconceptions of Japan.

Besides being a member multiple incarnations of Mad Gear, Sodom is also an underground wrestler and promoter of this sport. In the underground wrestling ring, Sodom was undefeated. When he wields the blade known as "Muramasa," he is called "Shogun" and feared by many. Guy was the first opponent to defeat Sodom, destroying his perfect record.

Sodom is very keen on recruiting Japanese fighters into his new Mad Gear, attempting to sway E. Honda, and even his rival Guy into joining. He even went so far as to rename another team he was a member of as "Maddo Gia", so that it would sound like a Japanese mispronunciation of "Mad Gear" when spoken aloud. Sodom's outfit is a strange collection of blue jeans, body armor, and a Samurai kabuto and mask. He speaks Japanese, albeit a little awkwardly. A giant convoy parked in the Arizona desert is Sodom's beloved vehicle.

Sodom is convinced that certain Japanese "unlucky words" can inflict spiritual damage on his enemies and has incorporated these words into the names of his moves.

FIGHTING STYLE

Sodom struggles with offensive and defensive techniques, trying to find harmony within himself and within the heart of his opponent. In the heat of battle he sometimes babbles near complete nonsense in Japanese. When victorious against a foe he happily gives a little street performance for any audience who may be present.

SIGNATURE MOVES: Jigoku Scrape, Butsumetsu Buster, Daikyou Burning

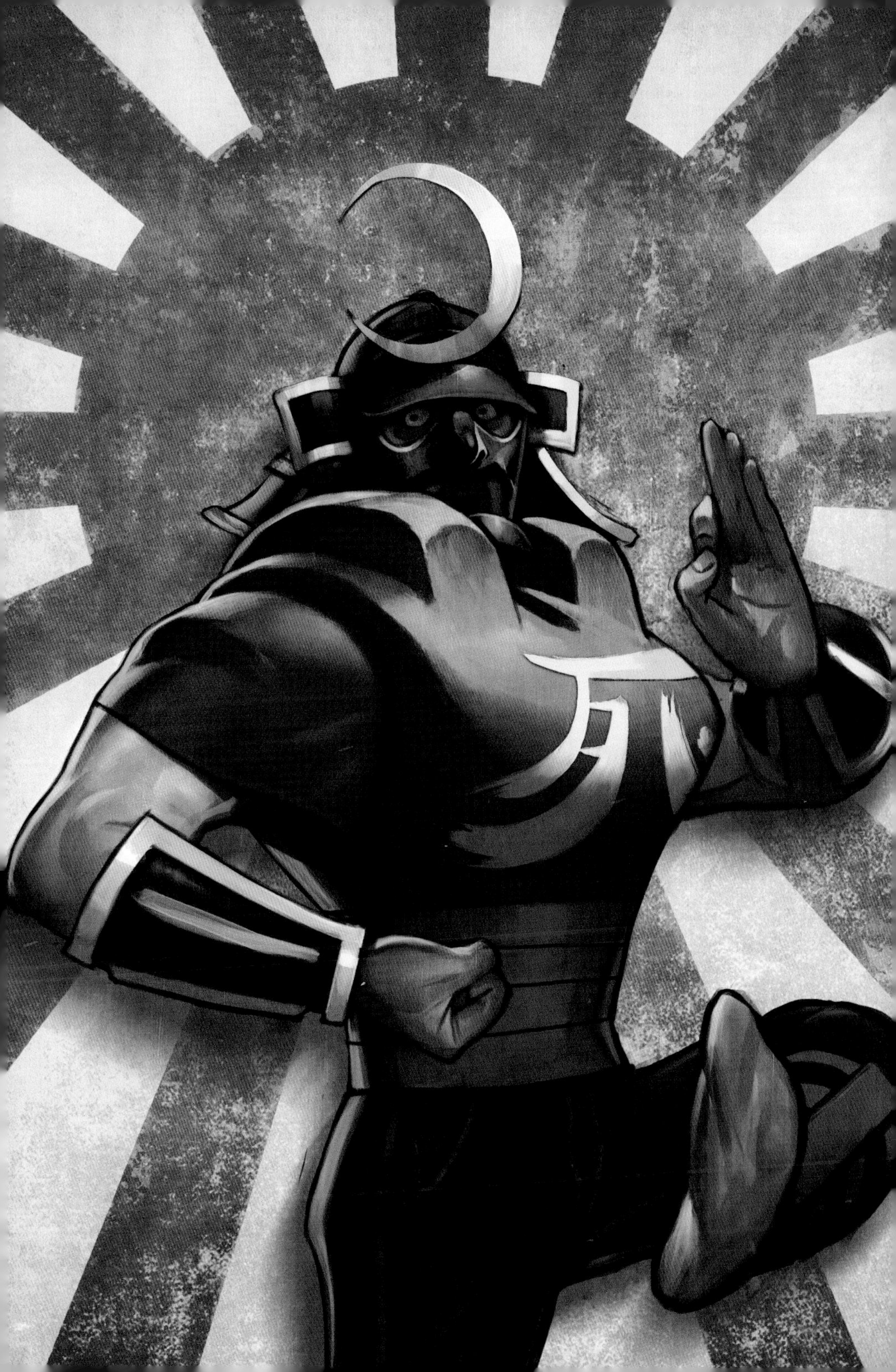

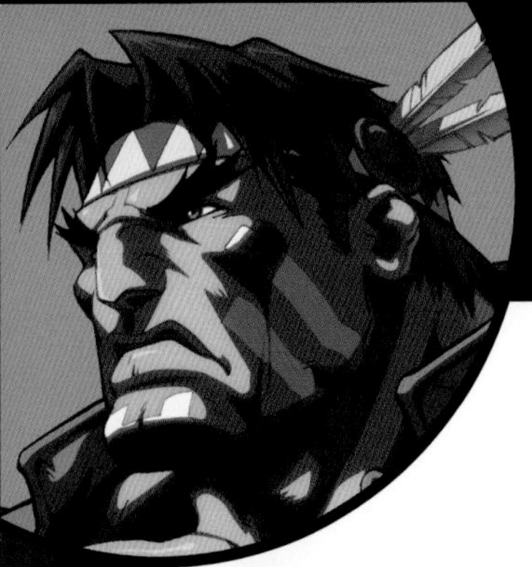

T. HAWK

The Honorable Warrior

BIRTHDAY: July 21
COUNTRY OF ORIGIN: Mexico
FIGHTING STYLE: Thunder Foot Martial Arts
HEIGHT: 230 cm **WEIGHT:** 162 kg
MEASUREMENTS: B114/W98/H112
BLOOD TYPE: O
LIKES: Animals, and hair accessories
DISLIKES: Lies
SPECIAL ABILITIES: Wood carving, talking to birds of prey

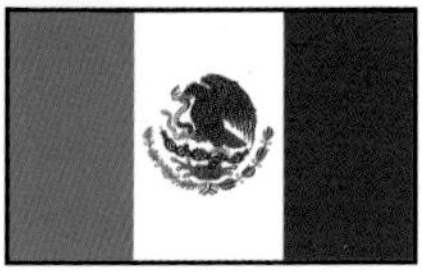

The Native American warrior Thunder Hawk is the hero of the Thunderfoot tribe. He has a very gentle personality, and always treats animals with a deep respect. T. Hawk pursues Shadaloo in hopes of finding his missing lover, Julia.

In recent years, a number of residents of the Thunderfoot village had gone missing and T. Hawk was convinced that all of the disappearances were connected in some way. As the best warrior of the village, T. Hawk left the village to find the source of the disappearances. Finding out that Shadaloo was behind it all, and that Julia had been brainwashed into becoming the Shadaloo Doll Juli, T. Hawk sets his sights on M. Bison. The doll known as Noembelu is also another kidnapped member of the Thunderfoot tribe.

After his father, Arroyo Hawk, was murdered by Bison, T. Hawk and his tribe were driven away from the lands they called home. Despite these hardships T. Hawk continues to fight on, hoping to one day recover his homeland and also free Julia and Noembelu from Shadaloo's control.

T. Hawk was childhood friends with Mexican wrestler El Fuerte, having lived for a brief time in the same village. The two lost touch when they were separated, but found each other again as adults.

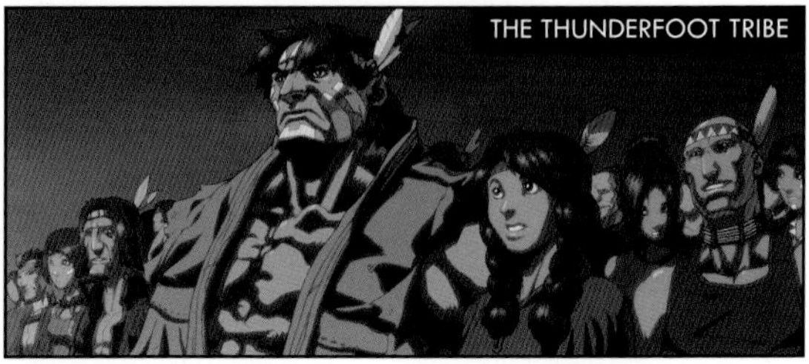
THE THUNDERFOOT TRIBE

FIGHTING STYLE

In battle, T. Hawk uses his powerful physique and crushing blows to overpower his enemies. His Condor Dive showcases more dexterity than many would expect from the giant warrior. In comparison, his destructive Mexican Typhoon move utilizes incredible strength as he swings his foe by the head and smashes them into the ground.

SIGNATURE MOVES: Condor Dive, Mexican Typhoon, Tomahawk Buster

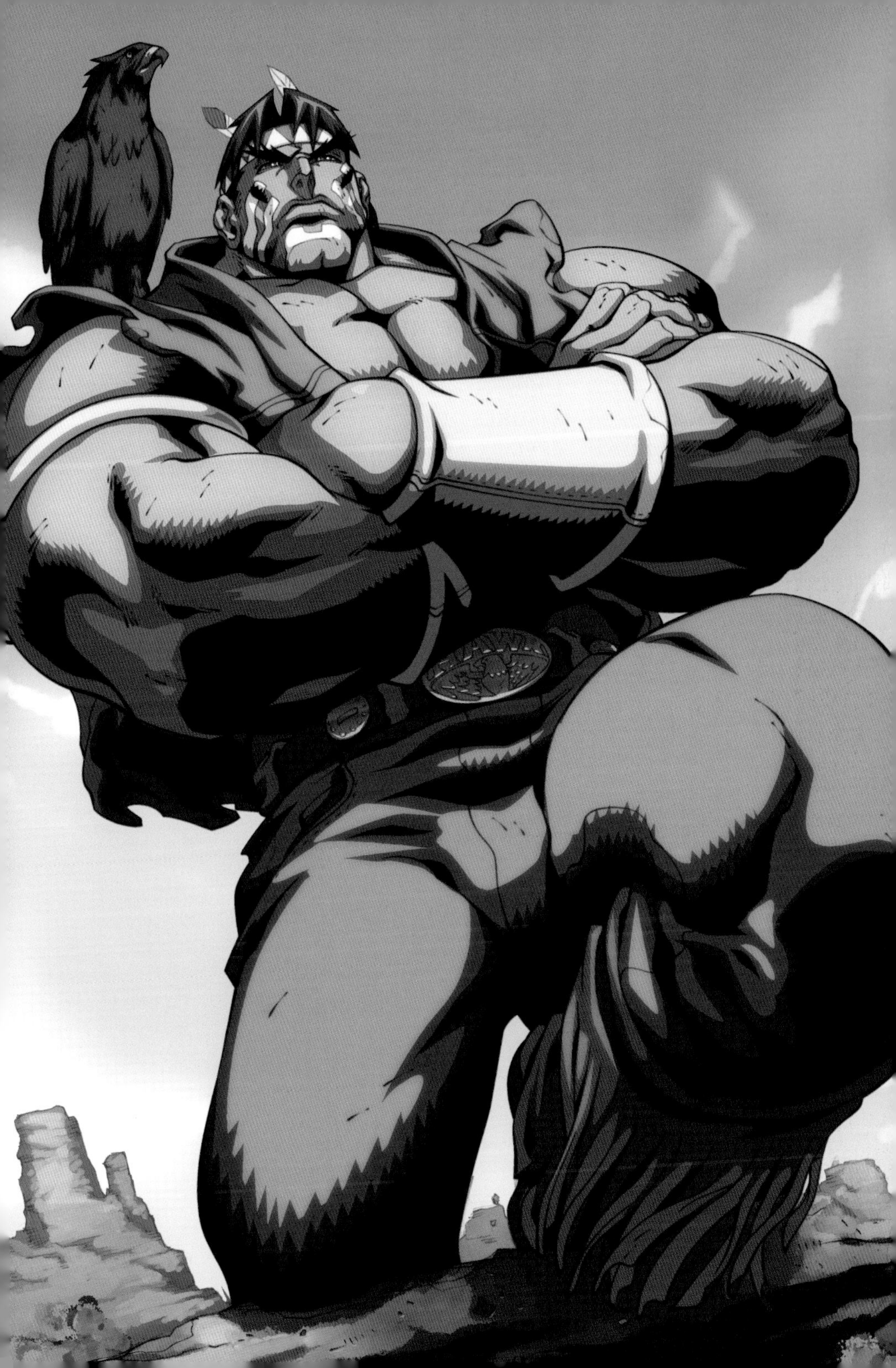

TWELVE
The Ultimate Weapon

BIRTHDAY: N/A
COUNTRY OF ORIGIN: N/A
FIGHTING STYLE: Hyper adaptation
HEIGHT: --------- **WEIGHT:** ---------
MEASUREMENTS: ---------
BLOOD TYPE: N/A
LIKES: N/A
DISLIKES: N/A
SPECIAL ABILITIES: Shapeshifting

Twelve is one of the extreme humanoid weapons that Gill's Illuminati organization developed. It is the finalized mass production model created using modification methods that have been improved upon since the days of Necro. Twelve's assigned mission is to capture Necro and Effie, who have escaped from the clutches of the Illuminati.

The flexible nature of its physical body goes beyond that of the traditional "rubber man." With its limbs stretching and bending at will, and the additional capability of taking on the form of his opponent, there is still much that remains unknown about Twelve's true potential. Twelve is able to regenerate any damage it suffers, but the very process that makes it whole again also rewrites any memories of pain and pleasure it had experienced.

Twelve speaks only in binary code. Unbeknownst to the scientists who created it, Twelve has started to develop a sense of self-awareness.

URIEN PLANS TO PUT TWELVE INTO FULL PRODUCTION

FIGHTING STYLE

With its protein body, Twelve's unique combat style is based on constantly changing forms to become the optimal weapon for any given situation. It also has the ability to copy every aspect of an opponent including appearance and abilities, giving it unimaginable power.

SIGNATURE MOVES: A.X.E., D.R.A., N.D.L., X.C.O.P.Y.

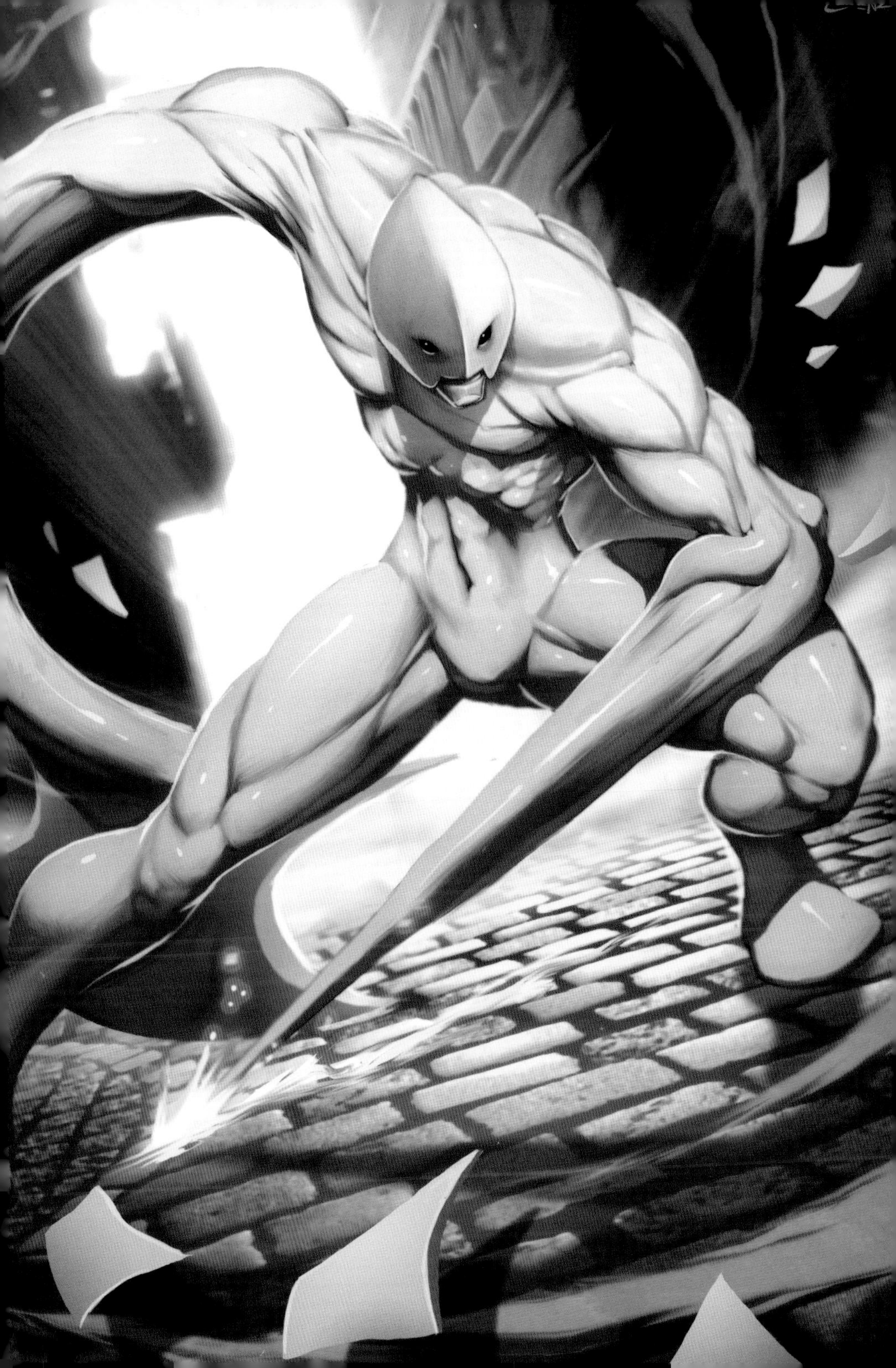

URIEN
The Dark Horse Destroyer

BIRTHDAY: Unknown

COUNTRY OF ORIGIN: Unknown

FIGHTING STYLE: Illuminati secret techniques

HEIGHT: --------- **WEIGHT:** ---------

MEASUREMENTS: ---------

BLOOD TYPE: ---------

LIKES: Suits

DISLIKES: Gill

SPECIAL ABILITIES: Genetic research

Urien is Gill's younger brother, and a member of the secret society known as the Illuminati.

Like Gill, Urien had been selected as a presidential candidate by the Illuminati, and has been receiving special education since he was 6 years old. Deemed emotionally unstable, Urien was forced into the vice president position while Gill was ushered into the illustrious position of president. Having lost the prize to his older brother, Urien could not hide his rage and envy. Eventually Urien was able to seemingly defeat his brother in combat and took the title of president for himself. His excitement was short-lived, however, and Urien received quite a shock when he found out that Gill had already been elevated to the position of Emperor of the Illuminati, outranking the president.

Despite having wrestled the Illuminati presidency away from his older brother, Urien would never know peace as long as Gill loomed over him as the Emperor. Obsessed with his desire to overthrow Gill and take the reins of global control, Urien has set out to challenge his brother once again.

Unlike Presidents of the past, Urien does not seem to have any desire to "preserve and pass on" the Illuminati's teachings, going so far as to destroy the collection of brains known as "the inheritance of the society". Urien also advocates a belief known as the Human Reconstruction Theory, which surmises that genetically enhanced healing powers hold the key to immortality. It is this theory that has driven the Illuminati's living weapon experiments like Twelve and Necro. This theory grants the power to restore physical damage on the cellular level. If the Illuminati were to find a way to eliminate the side effect of memory loss, immortality could very well be made a reality.

FIGHTING STYLE
With his muscular body giving him power and speed, Urien's fighting style is built around the secret and ancient arts kept by the Illuminati. There are supposedly 66 secret techniques known to the organization, and Urien has mastered a particularly potent one called Aegis Reflector. With an array of energy projectiles, dashing moves and long reaching attacks at his disposal, Urien's power is equal to that of Gill, even though their abilities are quite different.

SIGNATURE MOVES: Metallic Sphere, Aegis Reflector, Temporal Thunder

ユリアン URIEN

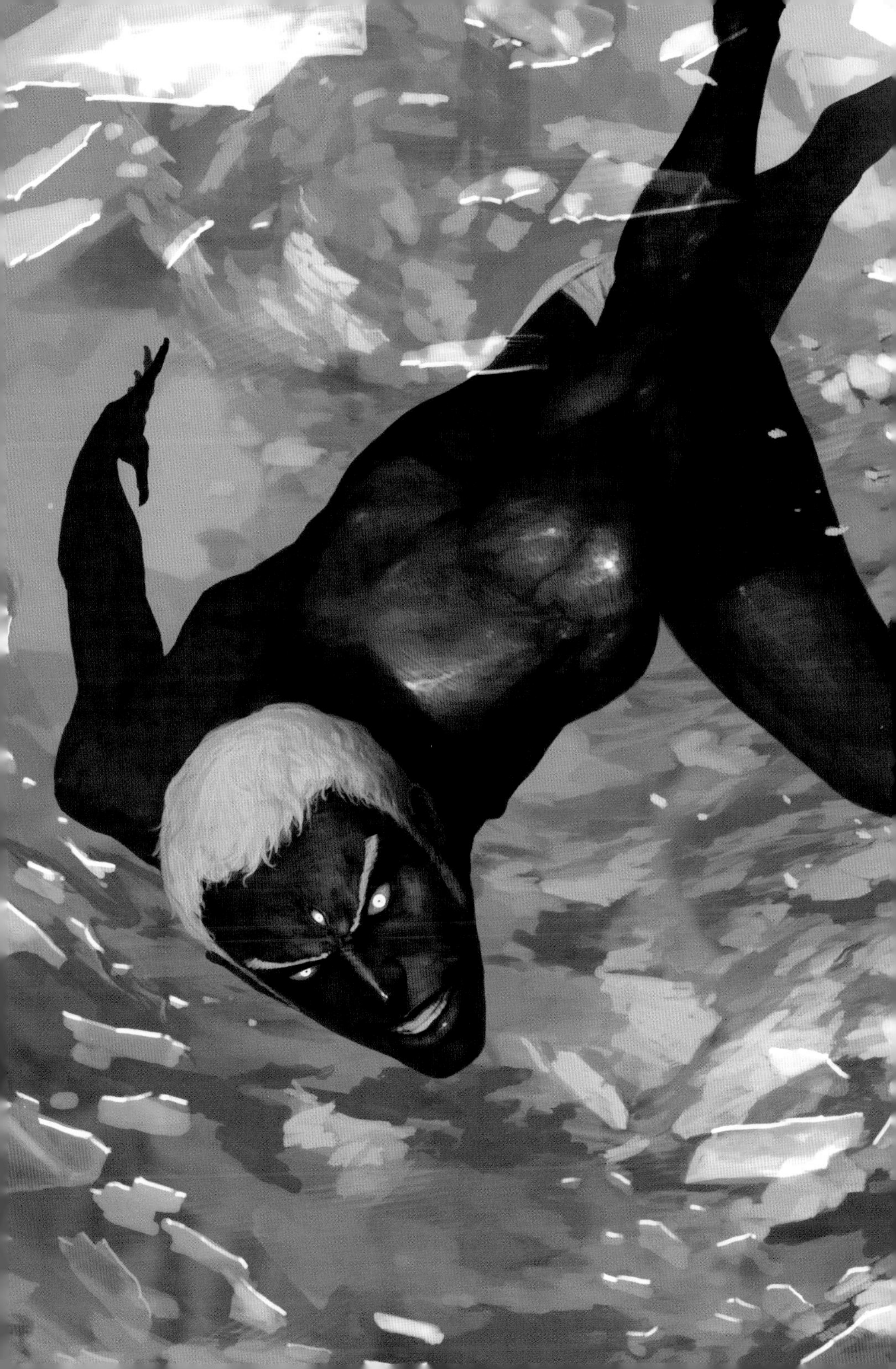

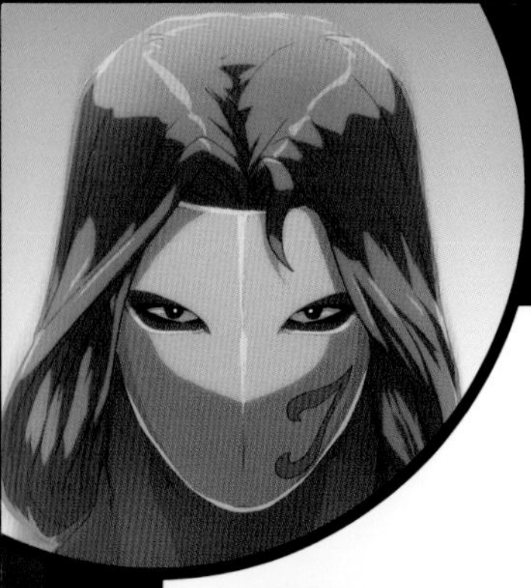

VEGA

Wielder of the Claw

BIRTHDAY: January 27
COUNTRY OF ORIGIN: Spain
FIGHTING STYLE: Spanish Ninjutsu
HEIGHT: 186 cm **WEIGHT:** 72 kg
MEASUREMENTS: B121/W73/H83
BLOOD TYPE: O
LIKES: Beautiful things, and himself
DISLIKES: Ugly things, blood splatter splashback
SPECIAL ABILITIES: Narcissism, sticking to walls

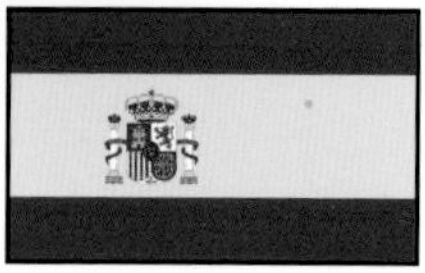

Vega is a born narcissist who believes he is the epitome of beauty, and that beauty is the truest form of strength. He is driven to annihilate everyone and everything in the world that does not meet his beauty requirements. The claws he wears are to ensure that he does not need to come in direct contact with his prey, and the mask is to protect his face from the blood spray. He is also one of the four Shadaloo bosses, having been a part of the organization since its early days. When he was young, Vega learned Ninjutsu from a Japanese acquaintance, which is how he acquired his superhuman speed and destructive abilities.

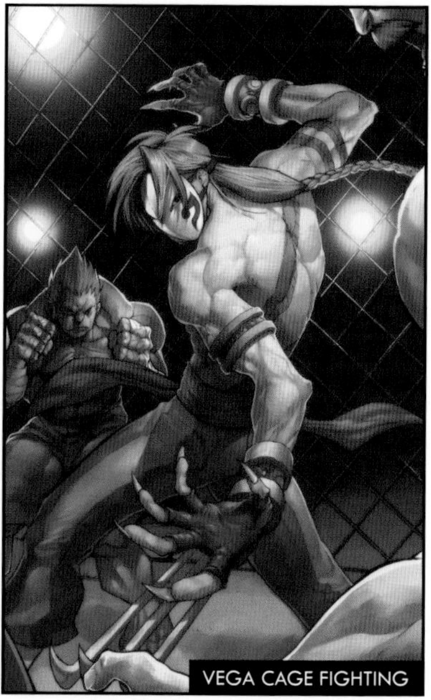
VEGA CAGE FIGHTING

Vega was born the only child of a beautiful noblewoman from a fallen house and an ugly but wealthy man. His twisted thoughts, obsessions, and value system regarding beauty were all handed down to him from his mother. He was powerfully affected by his father's murder of his mother, and it is said that this trauma is the reason Vega insists on maiming his defeated opponents.

Vega has shown a personal interest in Cammy, perhaps out of respect for her own physical beauty. He has at times ignored M. Bison's orders to kill or capture her, and on occasion even helped Cammy put a crimp in Bison's plans. Conversely, Vega appears to harbor an intense jealousy for Chun-Li's beauty.

FIGHTING STYLE

Vega is a cunning fighter who specializes in elaborate aerial maneuvers and acrobatics to unnerve his opponent's concentration. Having trained in Ninjutsu since childhood, he's merged it with other speed-oriented fighting techniques to create a beauty, power and perfection that is all his own.

SIGNATURE MOVES: Barcelona Attack, Izuna Drop, Sky High Claw

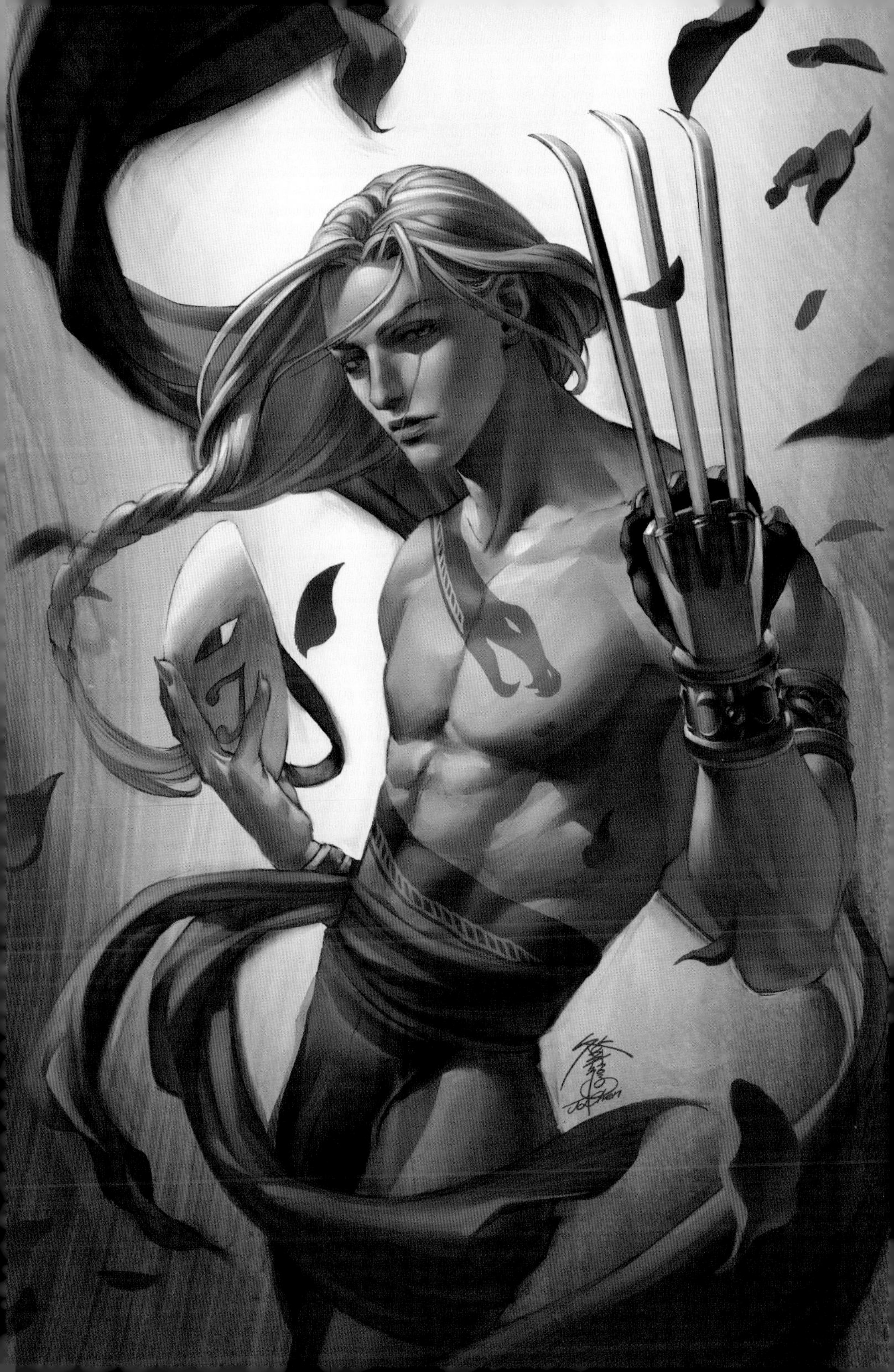

YANG
The Blue Dragon

BIRTHDAY: ---------
COUNTRY OF ORIGIN: China
FIGHTING STYLE: Kung Fu
HEIGHT: ---------   **WEIGHT:** ---------
MEASUREMENTS: ---------
BLOOD TYPE: ---------
LIKES: His hair, Hoimei
DISLIKES: Coming in second
SPECIAL ABILITIES: Hairstyling

Yun and Yang are twin brothers who were named by the eight kingpins of the Hong Kong underground. The twins are trusted and respected as the young leaders of the city, known to many as the "Twin Dragons," with Yun being the white dragon and Yang being the blue dragon. They both learned Chinese martial arts from their grandfather, and thus their fighting styles are very similar.

Of the two brothers, Yang is the one who sports the pointed hairstyle. Yang is the calm, insightful type, and is a meticulous planner. He always keeps an eye on the big picture, and helps his brother out when necessary. In combat, Yang never loses sight of himself and tends to draw his opponent into his own pace. While his brother Yun burns with a sense of duty, believing that he and his brother are meant to protect their community, Yang is overwhelmed by his desire to test his skills against his brother's.

Although he has feelings for a childhood friend named Hoimei, Yang knows she has a crush on his brother and has refrained from letting her know of his true feelings. Burying his feelings for Hoimei seems to have left Yang vulnerable to the advances of Hoimei's younger sister Shaomei, as a relationship between the two has developed.

Yun and Yang can often be seen hanging out at a local restaurant called Shoryuken, where Hoimei and Shaomei both work. Yang also has a white pet cat.

FIGHTING STYLE
Like Yun, Yang learned various styles of Kung Fu from his grandfather and then carefully developed his own fighting style. He fights with a calm nature and deep insight and his techniques surge out toward his opponent with a flurry of blows. His style is slightly different from Yun's, though it's hard to judge which of the two has a superior technique.

SIGNATURE MOVES: Byakko Soushoda, Senkyutai, Seiei Enbu

ヤン YANG

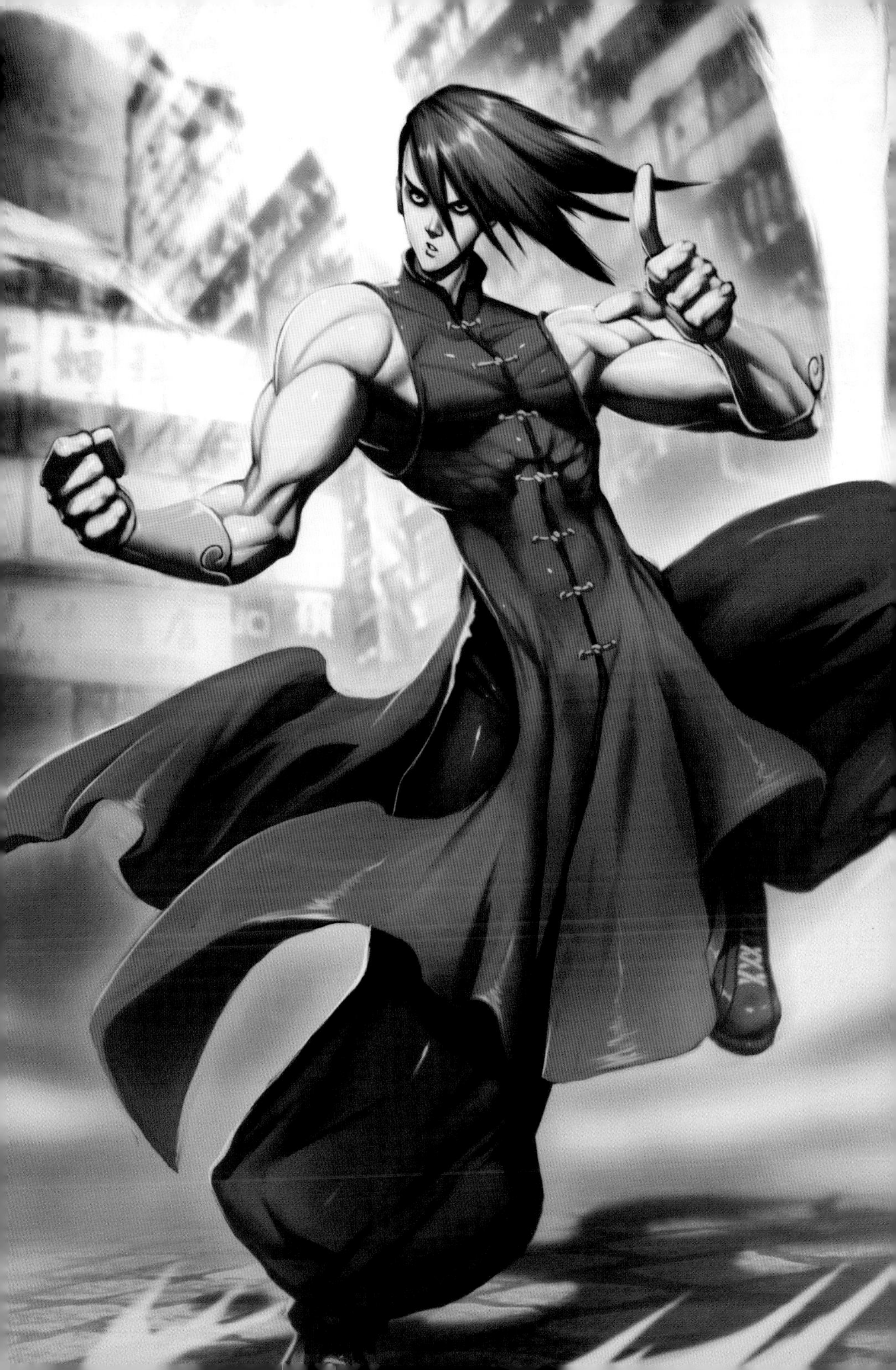

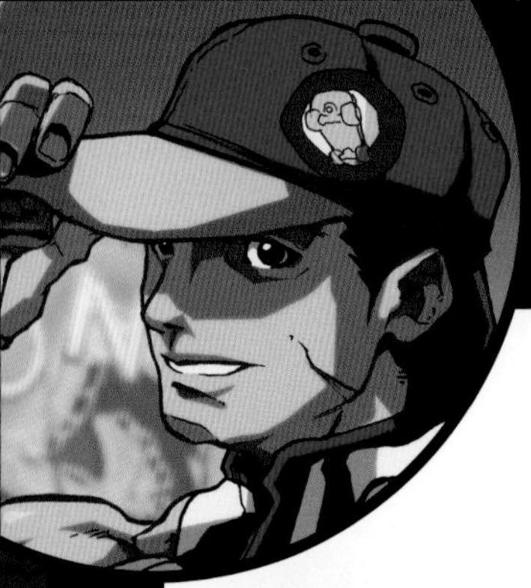

YUN

The White Dragon

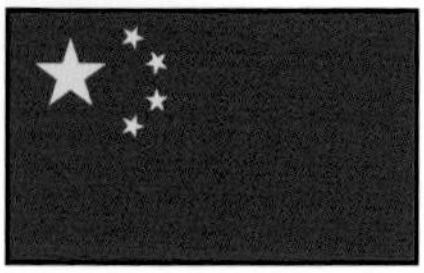

BIRTHDAY: ---------
COUNTRY OF ORIGIN: China
FIGHTING STYLE: Kung Fu
HEIGHT: 171 cm **WEIGHT:** 62 kg
MEASUREMENTS: 104B/79W/85H
BLOOD TYPE: B
LIKES: Kung Fu movies
DISLIKES: Crime
SPECIAL ABILITIES: Skateboarding

Twin brother to Yang, Yun is the brother with a long braid who wears a ball cap. He is quite the cheerful rascal, with a sharp wit and even sharper intuition. Yun fights like a fickle breeze, moving and turning on a moment's whim. He is not nearly as serious as his twin brother, and his "fight first, ask questions later" attitude tends to get him in trouble with Yang.

Realizing that the hand of evil was curling its claws around his beloved city of Hong Kong, Yun was quick to decide that the best defense was a good offense, and pledged to infiltrate the source of the evil.

Though his senses seem finely tuned to the needs of Hong Kong, Yun is more than a little dense when it comes to matters of the heart, and he is oblivious to the emotional turmoil of Hoimei and Yang, despite the fact that their turmoil is centered around himself.

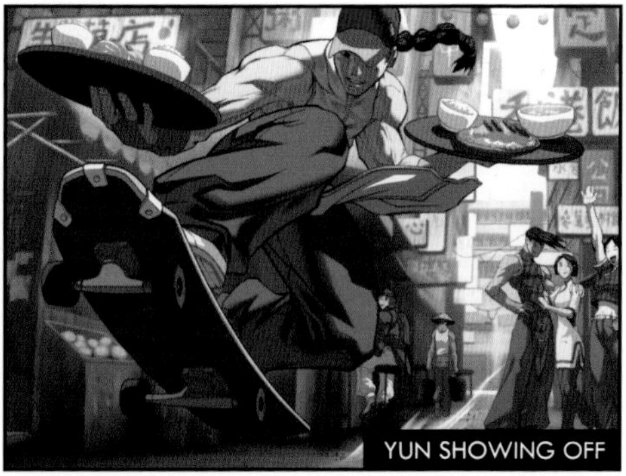

YUN SHOWING OFF

Yun and Yang are also known as the "Lee Brothers", named after their uncle, a well-known Chinese martial artist named Lee.

Yun's personal dream is to one day star in a film with famous Hong Kong movie star Fei Long.

FIGHTING STYLE

Yun's fighting style is Kung Fu. Using his keen intuition, he ignores what he sees and cuts into his opponents with a flurry of continuous attacks. His absolute confidence leads him to taunt his enemies with brazen phrases such as, "You didn't think you could win, did you?"

SIGNATURE MOVES: Geneijin, Tetsuzanko, Zesshou Hohou

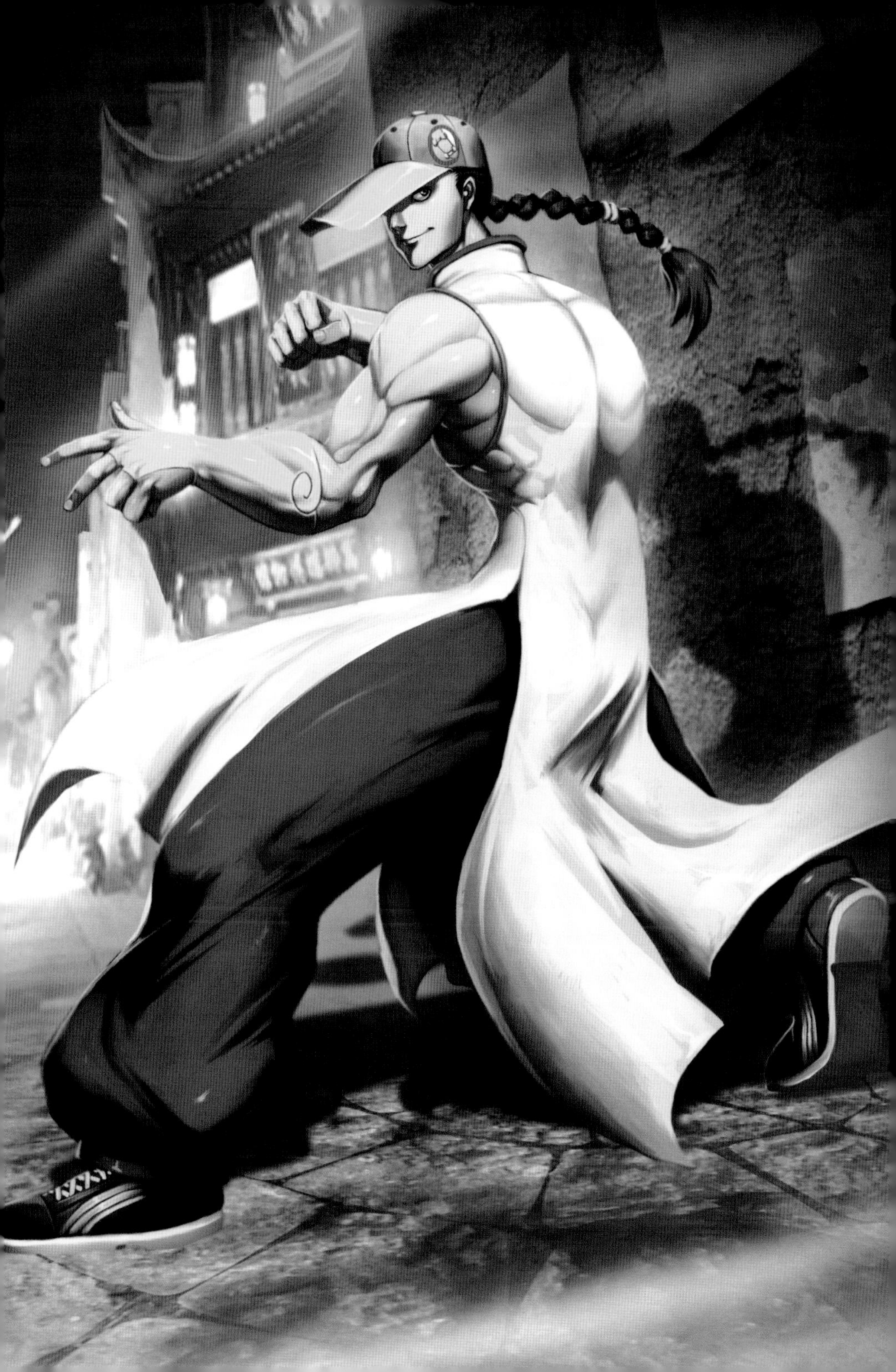

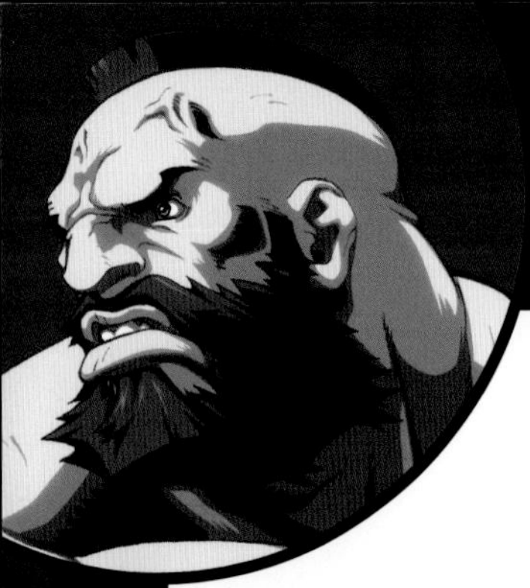

ZANGIEF

The Red Cyclone

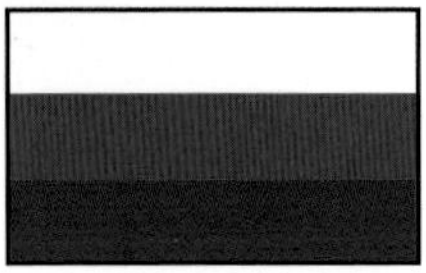

BIRTHDAY: June 1
COUNTRY OF ORIGIN: Russia
FIGHTING STYLE: Mix of Russian and American wrestling
HEIGHT: 214 cm **WEIGHT:** 115 kg
MEASUREMENTS: B163/W128/H150
BLOOD TYPE: A
LIKES: Wrestling, Cossack dancing
DISLIKES: Ranged attacks like the Hadoken, beautiful women of marriageable age
SPECIAL ABILITIES: Vodka shots, cold resistance

Zangief is a Russian professional wrestler of superhuman strength who loves his country more than anything else in the world. His flamboyant appearance is complete with a mohawk, a densely hairy chest, and bright red undies. People call him the Red Cyclone, and he quite likes the name. His unique fighting style is a blend of Russian and American professional wrestling.

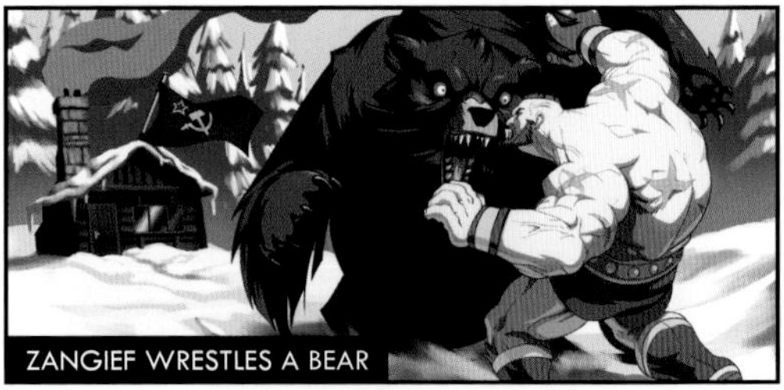
ZANGIEF WRESTLES A BEAR

Zangief was an undefeated fighter in the underground wrestling world until his winning streak got him kicked out. With nothing else to do, Zangief was living alone in the mountains when he was approached by the General Secretary of Russia, who acknowledged his great strength. He praised the way Zangief had dedicated himself to fighting, and Zangief made a promise to show the world the full might of Russia. In order to further enhance his body, Zangief accepted the General Secretary's offer to fund his training, but a shortage in funds forced Zangief to live in a small shed in the mountains and train with the local bears. When he believed himself ready, Zangief began challenging the strongest warriors of the world.

Zangief believes that muscular beauty like his own is true beauty, and loathes Vega for his pursuit of a beauty that is in direct conflict of this belief. Zangief also sees All American Champion Ken Masters as a rival, and their fight continues the age old battle between Russia and the USA.

R. Mika, a young fellow wrestler, admires Zangief, and the two have a master-student relationship. Zangief is also good friends with sumo wrestler E. Honda.

FIGHTING STYLE

Zangief looks to legitimize his wrestling abilities by crushing his opponents with sheer power. Although his gigantic size hampers his maneuverability, he can perform devastating one-hit attacks and powerful throws that specialize in doing maximum damage. Since all of his attacks involve up close grapples and strikes, Zangief is at a distinct weakness against projectile attacks.

SIGNATURE MOVES: Atomic Suplex, Double Lariat, Screw Pile Driver

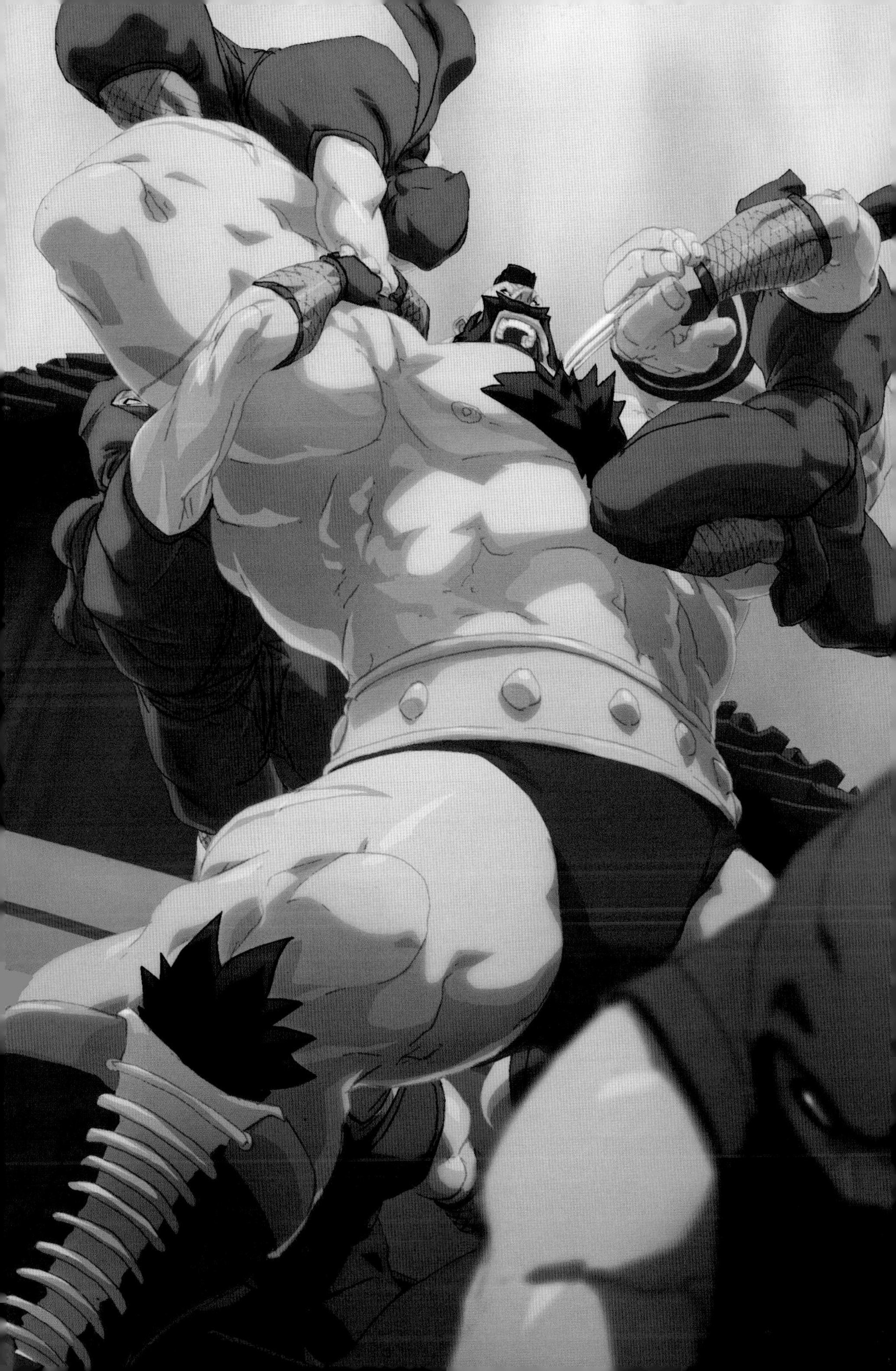

AGNI
Agni is a god of India with mastery over fire. Dhalsim's ability to manipulate artificial fire is due to the divine gifts of this deity.

AMY
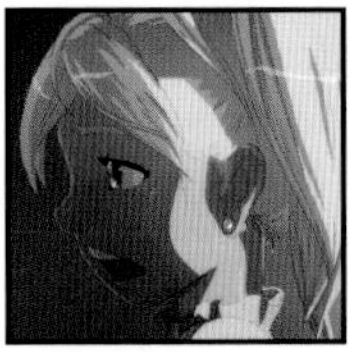

Guile and Julia's daughter. Amy is a pretty young girl with long ponytails who, together with her mother, pursues her father in order to bring him back to his family life. Amy is a penpal to Dhalsim's son, Dhatta.

ANNA
One of the Judgment Gals. Anna is a blonde, Russian girl who wears a long coat and a furry hat.

APRILE
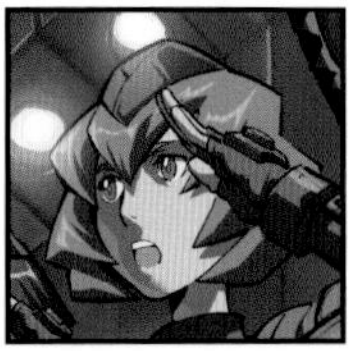

A member of M. Bison's personal guard, the Dolls. Originally hailing from Italy, her name is the Italian word for April. Aprile's younger brother Maggio has been searching for her, but is unaware that his sister is now a part of Shadaloo.

ARROYO HAWK
T. Hawk's father. When their tribe was attacked by Shadaloo, Arroyo and his son were the only survivors. They fled from their holy land and lived quietly together until M. Bison returned to murder Arroyo while T. Hawk was elsewhere.

BELLAMACHA
The pet parrot owned by Dee Jay's manager Rick.

C.I.A.
The Central Intelligence Agency. The CIA is a civilian intelligence agency that provides national security information to the United States government. C. Viper is secretly a member of this agency.

C.W.A.
The Capcom Wrestling Association. The CWA is a wrestling federation formed through the merger of several smaller wrestling leagues. Mike Haggar is a former CWA wrestler.

CANDY
The bombshell-blonde, cowboy-hat-clad girlfriend of Rufus. Whether feeding him cheese burgers, riding in his motorcycle's sidecar or cheering him on from ringside, Candy is always close to her man.

CARLOS MIYAMOTO
A swordsman who grew up in South America, where he learned various types of martial arts. He is a good friend of Metro City mayor Mike Haggar, and assisted in the rescue of Maki's father and sister from Mad Gear.

CHAIRMAN
This man oversees the meetings of a secret Illuminati society. Historically, even within the secret society itself, the presidents and chairmen have been the only ones who have been made aware of the existence of their emperor. The current chairman is an elderly man with a white beard. Representing the opinion of the entire committee, the chairman officially designated Urien as the new president and revealed the existence of their emperor to him.

CHUN-LI'S FATHER
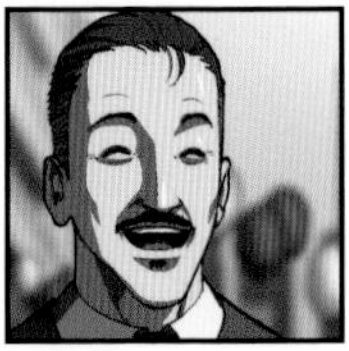

The man who Chun-Li has spent many years trying to find. He was a part of the ICPO's narcotics investigative unit until he was pulled into an incident involving Shadaloo, and disappeared without a trace. Her father's disappearance was the reason Chun-Li got into street fighting. Chun-Li's father was a master Chinese martial artist and was also the one who trained Chun-Li. He was also a good friend of Gen, and the kick called Genden Ansatsu Shuu that Chun-Li uses was passed from Gen to her father before Chun-Li learned it. Though his body has never been found, Chun-Li's father is presumed dead.

COLONEL KEITH WOLFMAN

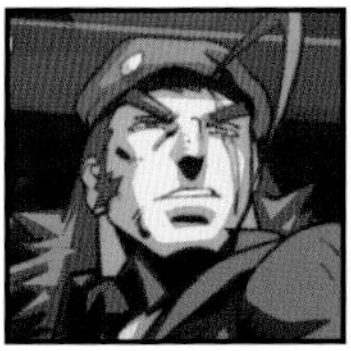

Colonel Wolfman is an instructor for Delta Red. He saved Cammy's life, taking her in and naming her Cammy at a time when she couldn't even remember her name. Keith feels badly for Cammy, who lost her memory due to the unnatural modifications she was put through, and he does everything he can to protect her from being used by the military as a human weapon. The Colonel sports a scar across his left eye from an unnamed battle.

COMMANDER W. WATSON

Commander Watson holds the highest rank in Delta Red, though he is rarely seen.

DEAN

A former street fighter who once teamed up with Guy and Mike Haggar to take down the Skull Cross Gang. His ability to use electric attacks have led to rumors that he is not completely human.

DECAPRE

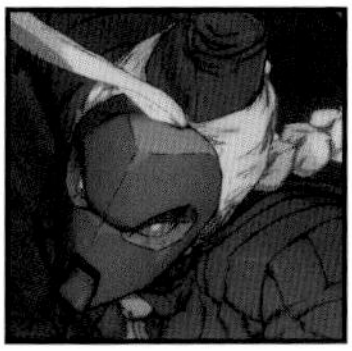

A member of M. Bison's personal guard, the Dolls. Decapre hails from Russia, and her name is based on the Russian word for December.

DELTA RED

The SIS Special Operations Unit that Cammy is a part of. Only the most elite of soldiers are selected to join Delta Red, and each team is made up of four to five members. The Delta Red logo is an upside down red triangle. Members include Cammy, Colonel Wolfman, Lita Luwanda, Matthew McCoy and George Ginzu

DHATTA

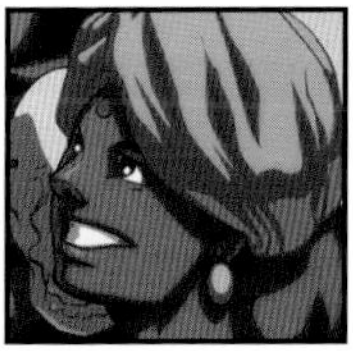

Dhalsim' and Sally's young son. Dhatta is not a yoga master like his parents, and thus eats like any growing boy. At one time Dhalsim street fought for money just to pay for Dhatta's impressive food bills. Dhatta is penpals with Guile's daughter, Amy.

DOCTOR KURE

An Illuminati scientist. Doctor Kure's duties include the maintenance of Twelve and the other humanoid weapons, based on the Human Reconstruction Theory that Urien preaches.

DOLLS

M. Bison's elite personal guard. The Dolls are made up of brainwashed young women from around the world. Although anyone under Bison's mind control is considered a 'Doll' (including Cammy in her Killer Bee days), the term is most often associated with a group of twelve girls. Each of these girls is named after a calendar month in their respective languages. The Dolls include Enero, Février, März, Aprile, Satsuki, Juni, Juli, Santamu, Xiayu, Jianyu, Noembelu, and Decapre.

DON

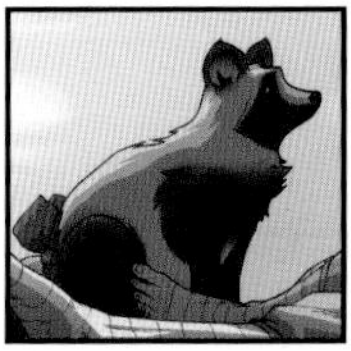

Don the tanuki is Ibuki's pet and shows up with her just about everywhere. There is a red ribbon tied to Don's tail.

EFFIE

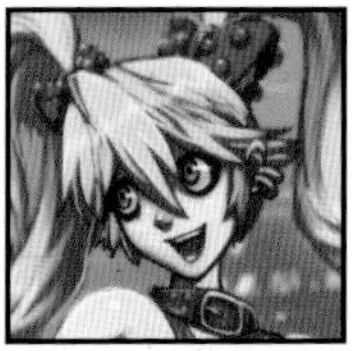

Effie is the little girl who came to Necro's aid, rescuing him from his imprisonment. Though she is physically quite cute, her blank stare and the deep bags under her eyes give her a rather frightening look. Effie and Necro ended up falling in love and are currently on the road together, like a pair of happy runaways. Like Necro, Effie is a modified human, and her very existence is supposed to be a secret. Effie is also one of the Judgment Girls.

ELIZA

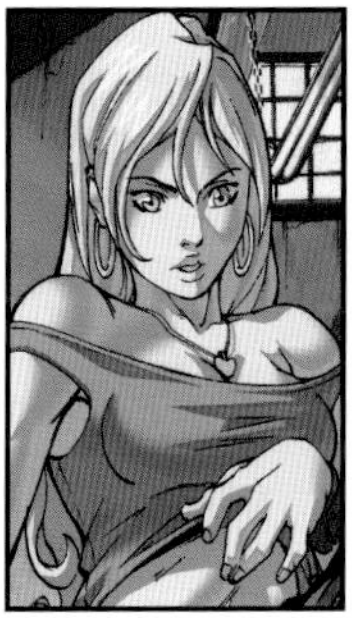

Ken's wife, and the mother of their child, who leaves quite an impression with her sexy clothes, blond hair, and incredible beauty. Eliza met Ken in the U.S.A. and the two spent many days happily in love. One day, Ken was inspired to visit his old friend Ryu in Japan, and he left Eliza's side. Refusing to give up on their relationship, Eliza followed Ken everywhere, and the two were eventually brought together again.

She would prefer that her husband refrain from dangerous activities, but she still supports his decision to participate in competitive tournaments. She has no problem showing her affections toward Ken in front of others, kissing his cheeks and loving on him with general abandon. Eliza is the younger sister of Guile's wife, Julia.

ENERO

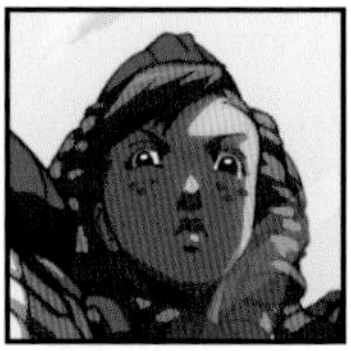

A member of M. Bison's personal guard, the Dolls. Enero hails from Spain, and her name is based on the Spanish word for January.

ENJO

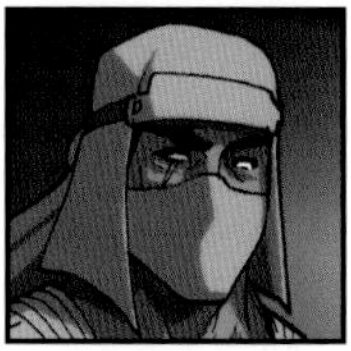

A member of Ibuki's clan and a resident of the Glade of Ninjas. He dresses like the archetypical ninja.

FAIR LIBRA

One of the Judgment Gals. Fair Libra is a tall black girl from America who wears a t-shirt, shorts, and rollerblades.

FEVRIER

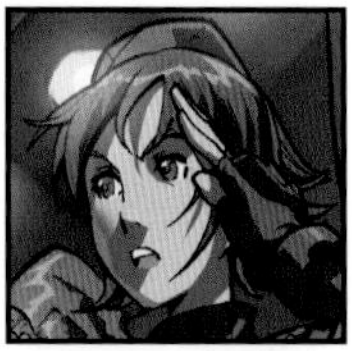

A member of M. Bison's personal guard, the Dolls. Février is from France, and her name is the French word for February.

FRENCH MERCENARY

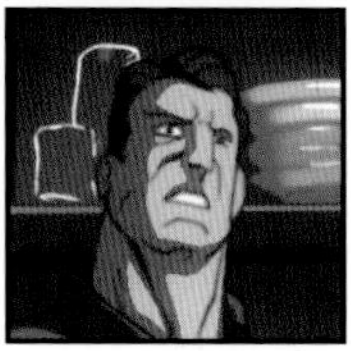

Abel's adoptive father. He took the amnesiac Abel into his mercenary unit as a favor to his friend Charlie Nash, teaching Abel everything he knew about combat and special ops training. He was later killed in a car accident.

GEKI

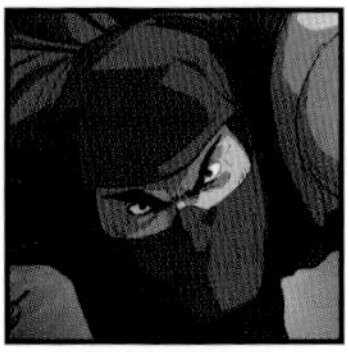

Geki is a fighter from Japan. He got into street fighting in order to show people the might of ninjas. He specializes in the use of shurikens and claws.

GENDA

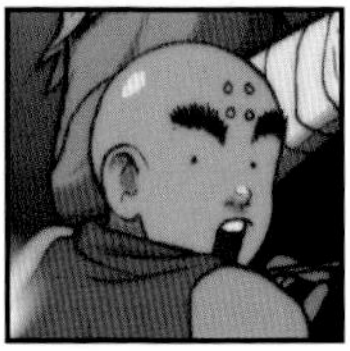

A young man who lives in the Glade of Ninjas. He can be recognized by his shaved head.

GENRYUSAI

The 37th master of Bushin-Ryu, and predecessor to Zeku. Genryusai is father to Maki and Guy's fiancée, Rena. He also aided in the Bushin-Ryu training of Guy.

GEORGE GINZU

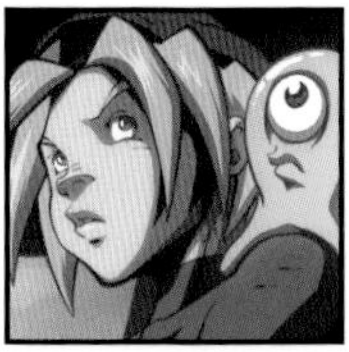

George is a rather short man who belongs to the same Delta Red squad as Cammy. George is the team's computer expert.

GO HIBIKI

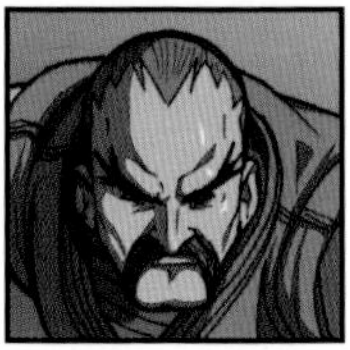

Dan's father. Go stood toe to toe against Sagat and managed to render one of Sagat's eyes useless before being defeated. Go eventually passed away from his wounds, and his death became the reason Dan hates Sagat. While Dan is something of a joke as a martial artist, his father was actually quite skilled. Go's most striking features are his mustache and his long nose, which makes his face reminiscent of a Japanese tengu mask.

GOUTETSU

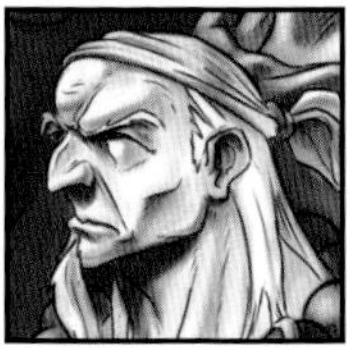

The master of the two brothers, Gouken and Akuma. 20 years prior to the Street Fighter tournament, Goutetsu was murdered by Akuma, who had been consumed by the power of the Satsui no Hado. He is the first known victim to be killed by the might of Akuma's Shungokusatsu.

GUNLOC

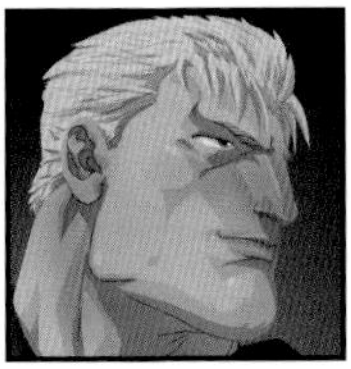

A professional wrestler who was trained by Mike Haggar. Gunloc is rumored to be related to a famous American street fighter who is quite particular about his haircut.

H.W.A.

The Huge Wrestling Army. Poison started this organization to ensure Hugo would always have opponents to fight. Since its foundation, the HWA has grown to over 50 members.

HATONOYAMA

One of E. Honda's sumo students.

HINATA WAKABA

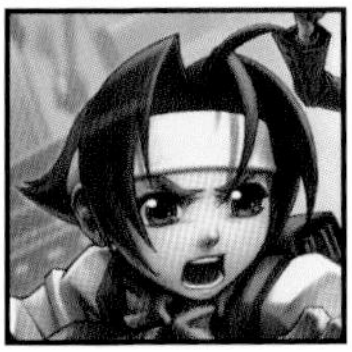

A first-year student at Taiyo High School, and a good friend of Sakura's.

HOIMEI

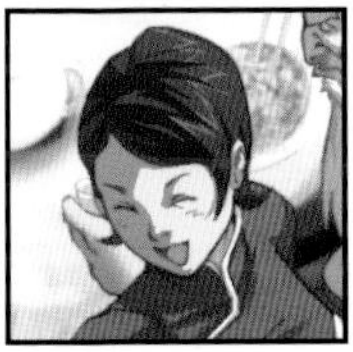

A cute, short-haired girl, who has a shy younger sister named Shaomei. Hoimei works at her father's food stall, Shoryuken. She is a childhood friend of Yun and Yang's, and though her competitive personality results in constant squabbles with the brothers, she does care about them quite deeply. Out of her concern for the brothers, who always seem to be doing something dangerous, Hoimei tends to speak rather sharply at them even though she does not mean to. She is aware that Yang is harboring feelings for her, but she has a crush on Yun and is unable to be herself in front of him.

I.C.P.O.

The International Criminal Police Organization, also known as Interpol. The ICPO facilitates cooperation between police organizations around the world. Chun-Li is a member of the ICPO, as was her father.

ILLIA

The real name of Necro.

ILLUMINATI

The elite and secret society lead by Gill. The Illuminati are a millennia old group who controls events, governments, and people, with the intent of building the perfect world by the year 2200. The Illuminati are responsible for the creation of Twelve, the modification of Necro and Effie, and the mysterious G-File. They were also the hosts of the third Street Fighter Tournament.

ISHIZAKI

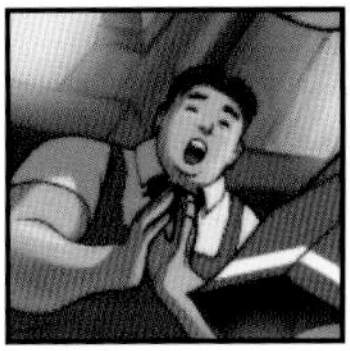

Karin's assistant. Ishizaki personally sees to the needs of the super princess, Karin. He wears an apron over his well-kept suit and bow tie, but is a little overweight.

JESSICA HAGGAR

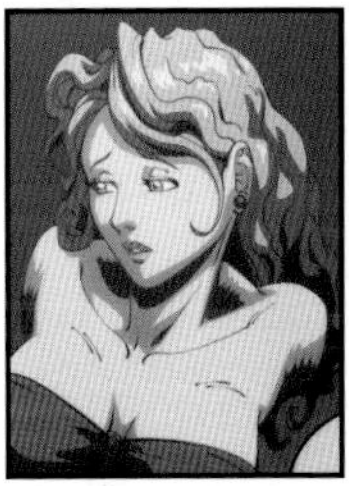

Mike Haggar's daughter and girlfriend of Cody. Jessica and Cody have apparently grown apart during Cody's prison days. Jessica was once kidnapped by the Mad Gear gang.

JIANYU

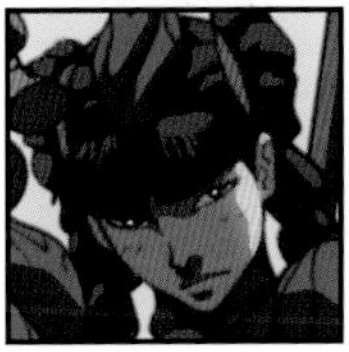

A member of M. Bison's personal guard, the Dolls. Jianyu is from China, and her name is based on the Mandarin word for October.

JIMMY

The real name of Blanka. It is used only by his mother and by Dan.

JUDGMENT GIRLS
A group of young women who decide the winner of street fights after a double K.O. or a tie after a time out. The Judgment Girls include Anna, Effie, Fair Libra, Julia, Lilly, Rifa, Toli and Tonfa.

JULIA
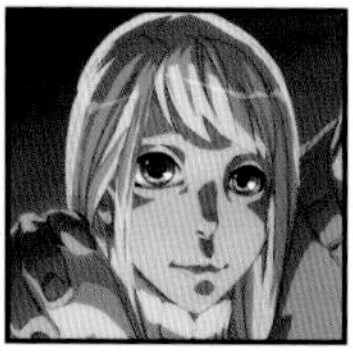
Guile's wife, and the mother of their daughter Amy. Julia loves her husband, but hates his dangerous military career. She wishes Guile would settle down into a desk job and spend more time with his family. Julia is the older sister of Ken's wife Eliza.

JULIA(2)
The real name of Shadaloo Doll Juli.

JULIA(3)
One of the Judgment Gals. Julia is from England, and she looks very refined with her blond hair and riding clothes.

JULIAN
A female CIA agent. Julian discovered that the mysterious man known as Q was the common link in all of the strange incidents the CIA was investigating.

JOE
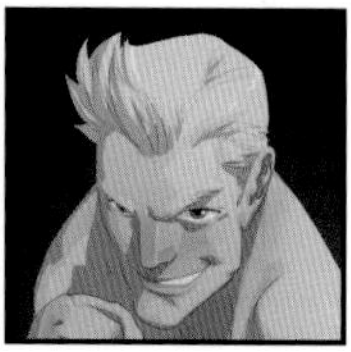
A fighter representing America. Joe is an underground martial arts champion who uses street fighting as a way to train. His favorite move is the Rolling Sobat.

KEI CHITOSE
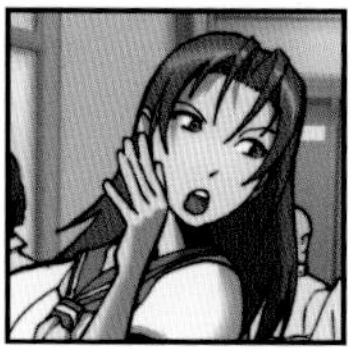
Kei is a high school girl and friends with Sakura. In contrast to Sakura's short hair style, Kei has long hair. She doesn't necessarily approve of Sakura's intense interest in street fighting, but does show up for her matches.

KOLIN
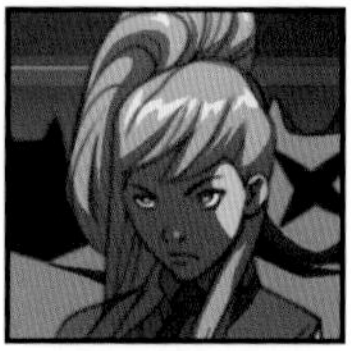
Gill's personal secretary. This blonde beauty is definitely not the friendly, approachable type.

KODAL
An elephant that Dhalsim can be seen riding sometimes. Kodal is Dhalsim's friend and mode of transportation.

LAUREN
The daughter of C. Viper.

LEE
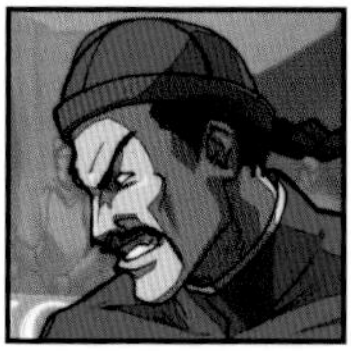
A fighter representing China. Lee is a master of Chinese martial arts, and though he is willing to grant a match to opponents who he deems worthy, he never guarantees that they will live to regret challenging him. At first glance, Lee looks like your average chubby chef of Chinese cuisine, but he's definitely quicker than he looks. Lee is also the uncle of twin brothers Yun and Yang, who have been nicknamed the "Lee Brothers" due to Lee's infamy.

LILLY
One of the Judgment Gals. Lilly is from India.

LITA LUWANDA
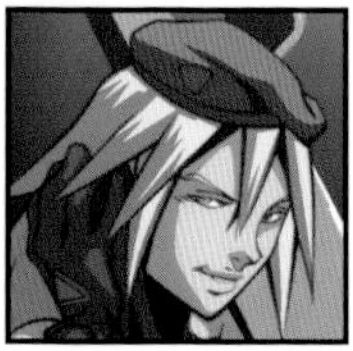
One of Cammy's Delta Red teammates. Lita's long blond hair is her most striking feature. Lita is the team's melee weapons expert.

LUCIA
A female police officer and head of the Metro City Special Crimes Unit. Lucia once teamed up with Mike Haggar and Guy to take down the Skull Cross Gang.

MAD GEAR
A street gang originally operating out of Metro City. There have been many iterations of Mad Gear over the years, some more competent than others, but all definitely on the wrong side of the law. Past members of Mad Gear include Hugo, Poison, Rolento, and Sodom.

MAGGIO
Little brother to the Doll Aprile. He knows his sister is missing, but is not aware that she is now a part of Shadaloo.

MARU NO UMI
One of E. Honda's sumo students.

MARZ
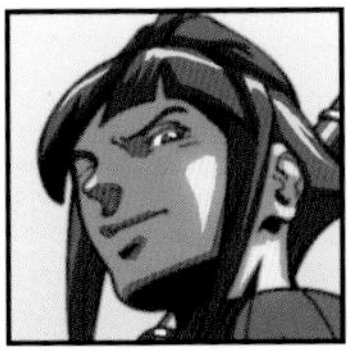
A member of M. Bison's personal guard, the Dolls. März is from Germany, and her name means "March" in German.

MASARU
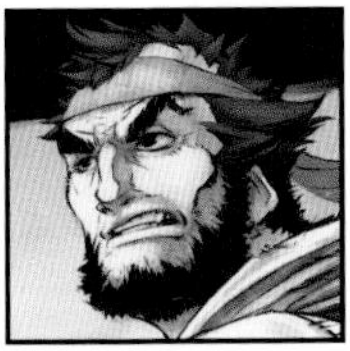
Makoto's father, now deceased. Masaru was the owner of Rindoukan before Makoto.

MATTHEW MCCOY
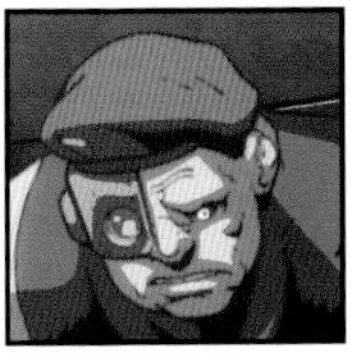
One of Cammy's Delta Red teammates. He is physically imposing and sports a cybernetic eye. Matthew is the team's ranged weapons expert.

MAYA
The real name of C. Viper.

MEL
Ken and Eliza's son. Mel is the apple of Ken's eye and Ken would forgive his son for anything, including a direct hit to a certain sensitive area of the body. Though Mel is an innocent boy, it is true that he is the one responsible for turning Ken into a soft mushy man of fatherhood, and thus negatively impacting Ken's relationship with his best friend, Ryu. Mel has blond hair and striking blue eyes just like his mother.

MIKE
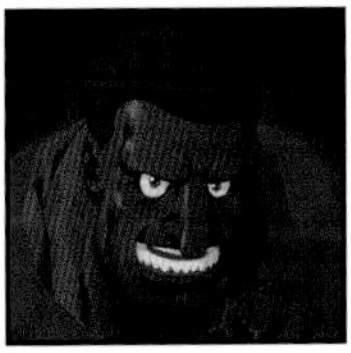
A street fighter who comes from America. Mike used to be a champion class professional boxer, but left the world of boxing behind when he accidentally killed his opponent in a boxing match.

MIKE HAGGAR
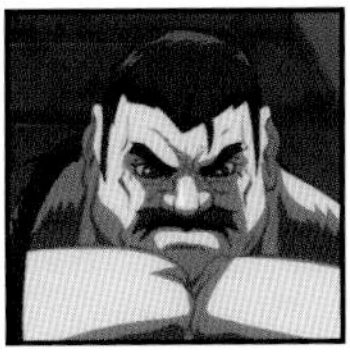
Mayor Mike "Macho" Haggar of Metro City detests all forms of evil and believes in justice. He is a former professional wrestler who turned to politics in hopes of cleaning up the crime-ridden Metro City.

Haggar famously teamed up with Cody and Guy when Haggar's daughter, Jessica, needed to be rescued from the Mad Gear gang. He later joined another rescue mission with Carlos Miyamoto and Maki, to rescue Maki's sister and father from a new Mad Gear iteration. He also teamed up with Dean and Lucia to stop the Skull Cross Gang.

NARUMI
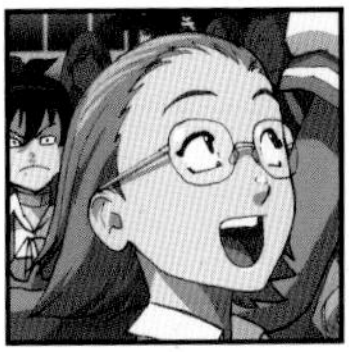
A girl with glasses who Elena befriends at her high school in Japan. Elena calls this petite and shy girl by the endearing nickname "Naruchan." When Elena's time in Japan was finished, she, Narumi, and a few of their schoolmates took a trip to Elena's homeland in Africa.

NATSU AYUHARA
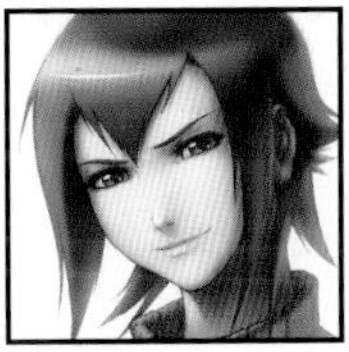
Natsu is a student and volleyball player at Gorin High School. She is a good friend of Sakura.

NOEMBELU
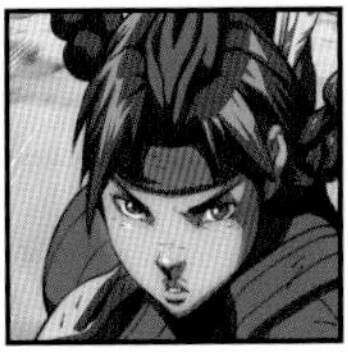
A member of M. Bison's personal guard, the Dolls. She is a Latin American woman named from the Latin word for November.

OCCHAN
The old man who runs a food stall in Hong Kong. He is the father of Shaomei and Hoimei, and is also acquainted with Yun and Yang.

ORTH K GOTCH

Dudley's longtime butler. He has a distinctively curled moustache.

PATRICIA

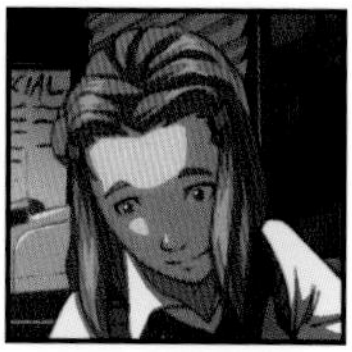

Tom's only daughter. Patricia is a cute, 14-year old strawberry blonde girl. Patricia's nickname is "Pat," and she calls Alex "Alec."

POISON

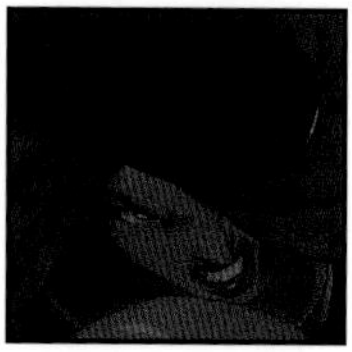

A former member of the Mad Gear gang, and Hugo's wrestling manager. Poison is like a big sister to Hugo, and covers for Hugo's awkwardness with a quick wit and solid organization skills. Hugo and Poison do squabble every now and then, but it is obvious that they are a good match for each other. Poison came up with the idea for the "H.W.A."(Huge Wrestling Army) when she noticed the list of willing opponents for Hugo was getting shorter and shorter. Poison and Hugo are always trying to find members for their new team, and the two can be very persuasive talent scouts.

Though she may seem like a dynamite babe, anyone who knows the real Poison will tell you she's anything but lady-like.

RAION

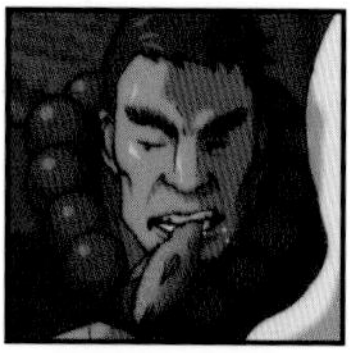

A ninja who lives in the Glade of Ninjas. Being big and muscular, the carpenter look suits Raion quite well.

RENA

Guy's fiancée, and the older sister of Maki.

RETSU

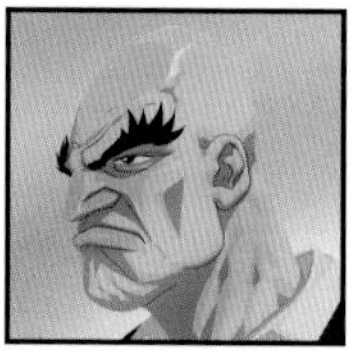

An older fighter hailing from Japan. A monk at the Shorinji temple, Retsu was an instructor of Shorinji Kempo until he was exiled from the temple for his unwillingness to let go of his personal conflicts. His most notable feature is his shiny bald head.

RICHARD BURGMAN

The public relations officer for the CIA. In his report regarding Q, he states that the CIA is unable to make any official comment on the existence of the subject known as "Q."

RICK

Rick has been acting as Dee Jay's manager for a while, but is constantly troubled by Dee Jay's carefree ways. Rick has a pet parrot named Bellamacha.

RIFA

One of the Judgment Gals. Rifa is a Chinese girl who wears the blue China dress with a red floral pattern. She does not wear a hair accessory of any kind.

S.I.N.

The Shadaloo Intimidation Network. S.I.N. is the weapons development arm of Shadaloo, and is responsible for technologies such as the Tanden Engine and the BLECE device. Seth is the CEO of S.I.N.

SABU

The dog owned by Guile's daughter, Amy.

SALLY

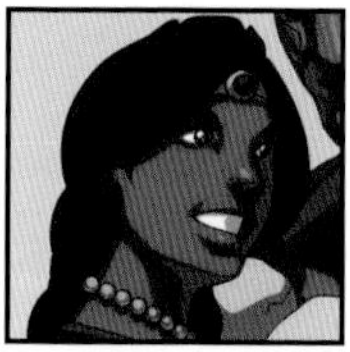

Dhalsim's wife, and mother to their son, Dhatta. A beautiful young woman, some would say Sally is out of Dhalsim's league. Sally studies yoga like her husband, and her special abilities include being able to regulate the amount of food she needs to consume.

SAMANTHA

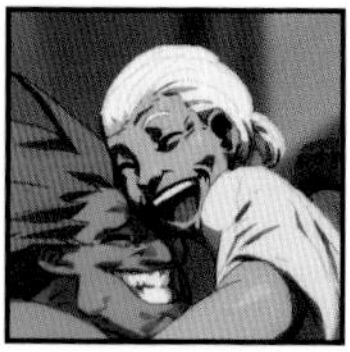

Blanka's mother. A warm and loving individual with a big heart who accepts her child despite his mutated and inhuman form.

SANJOU

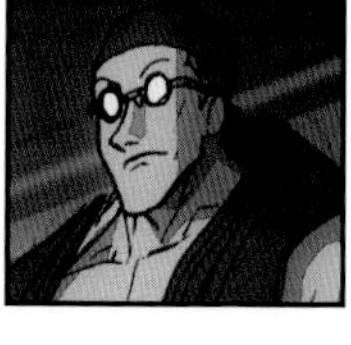

A tall ninja who lives in the Glade of Ninjas. Sanjou is usually dressed like a scholar.

SANTAMU

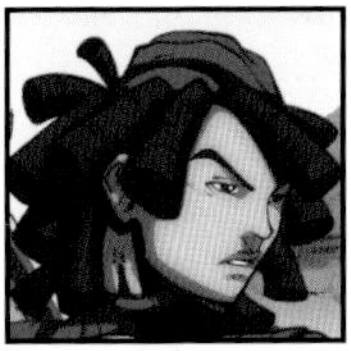

A member of M. Bison's personal guard, the Dolls. Santamu hails from Vietnam, and her name is based on the Vietnamese word for August.

SARAI KUROSAWA

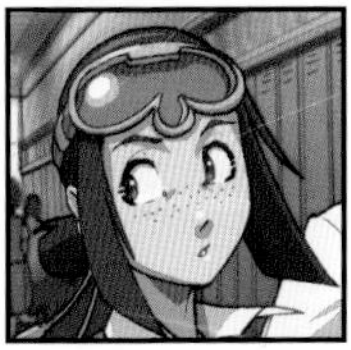

A freckled young girl who lives in the same town and attends the same school as Ibuki, with whom she is good friends.

SATSUKI

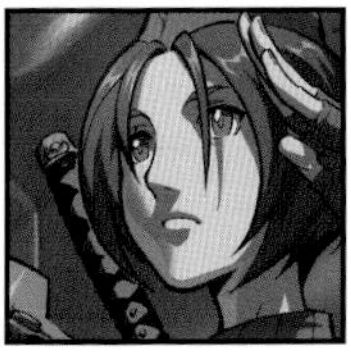

A member of M. Bison's personal guard, the Dolls. She originally hails from Japan, and her name means "May" in Japanese.

SENPAI

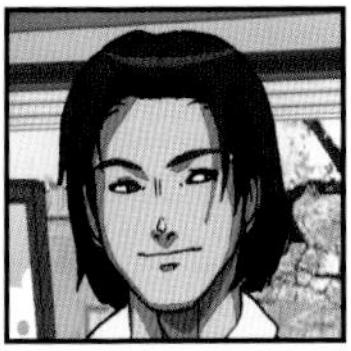

A student who attends the same college as Ibuki. He is a member of the "Ninjutsu Research Club" at the college. Though he is quite attractive, Senpai's personality is a little unusual.

SHADALOO

The most powerful criminal organization on earth, lead by M. Bison. Shadaloo's ultimate goal is to control the entire world. Shadaloo hosted the second Street Fighter Tournament.

SHAOMEI

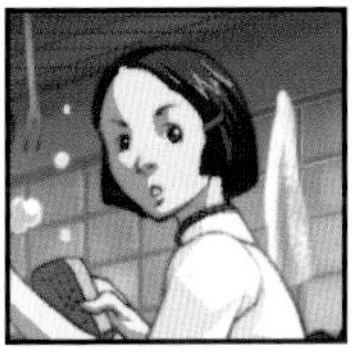

Hoimei's younger sister. Shaomei works at the Shoryuken food stall with her sister. When compared to her older sister, Shaomei is quiet and shy, but does get along very well with Yun and Yang. Shaomei has a small crush on Yang. Although she has noticed that Yang seems to have feelings for her sister Hoimei, Shaomei has no intention of giving up just yet. She may be the shyer of the two sisters, but Shaomei is capable of some surprisingly bold actions.

SHIBAZAKI

The young butler serving Karin Kanzuki's household. His distinguishing features include his slicked back hair and his glasses. Shibazaki's main duty is to act at Karin's right arm.

SKULL CROSS GANG

A Metro City gang that formed to fill the void left from the fall of Mad Gear.

TOLI

One of the Judgment Gals. Originally from China, Toli wears a dark blue China dress similar to the one that Tonfa wears. Toli's bangs are parted to the sides.

TOM

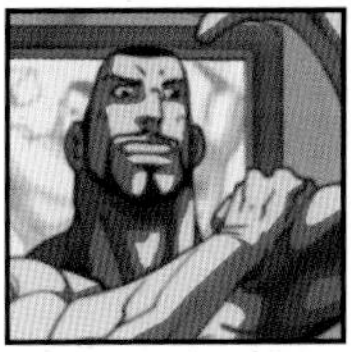

A friend of Alex's father, who acts as Alex's trainer. Tom lives with his daughter, Patricia, and Alex. He serves as a father figure for Alex, and is also the kind of martial artist Alex hopes to be one day. Tom is a veteran, and currently travels between bases as an eminent combat instructor for the U.S. military. One day, Tom was sent to the hospital after having a street fight with a blond man (Gill), and this incident led to Alex's departure. In the end, however, Tom recovered from his wounds and was there to welcome Alex upon his return.

TONFA

One of the Judgment Gals. Originally from China, Tonfa wears a white China dress and a floral hair accessory. She is one of the more popular members of the Judgment Gals.

TSUKUSHI KUSAGANO

Tsukushi is Sakura's little brother. Unlike his big sister, who loves to do anything involving physical activity, Tsukushi prefers to spend his time at home playing video games.

U.S. AIR FORCE

The aerial and space warfare division of the United States armed forces. Charlie Nash and Guile are both U.S. Air Force officers.

XIAYU

A member of M. Bison's personal guard, the Dolls. Xiayu is from China, and her name is based on the Mandarin word for September.

YOKO HARMAGEDDON

Yoko is R. Mika's trainer, and is also the one who gave her the ring name "Rainbow Mika." Yoko is a former professional wrestler, who retired due to a back injury. She can often be seen riding a scooter.

YASUHANADA

One of E. Honda's sumo students.

YUTA

A boy who lives in the Glade of Ninjas. He wears a cloth on his head and is about the same age as Ibuki.

ZEKU

The 38th master of Bushin-Ryu, and predecessor to Guy. Zeku is a middle aged man with unkempt hair and a green dougi. Guy was still just a young hooligan when Zeku found him, but Zeku saw a natural talent in Guy and decided to pass the Bushin style down to him. Just before Guy left for America, Zeku told him to "overcome all" before disappearing without a trace.

ADDITIONAL NOTES

- Numbers that appear in the characters' basic stats in this book (height, weight, measurements) may change in the future.

- Some characters have portions of their basic stats missing, noted by a dashed line (Adon for example has no birthday). This indicates information that has never been officially established in any Street Fighter game or sourcebook as of the writing of this encyclopedia.

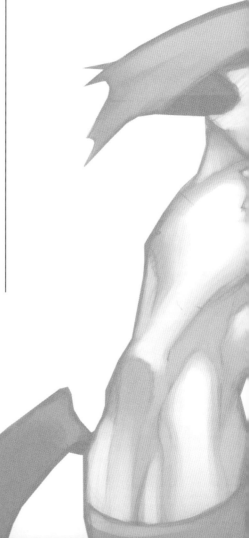

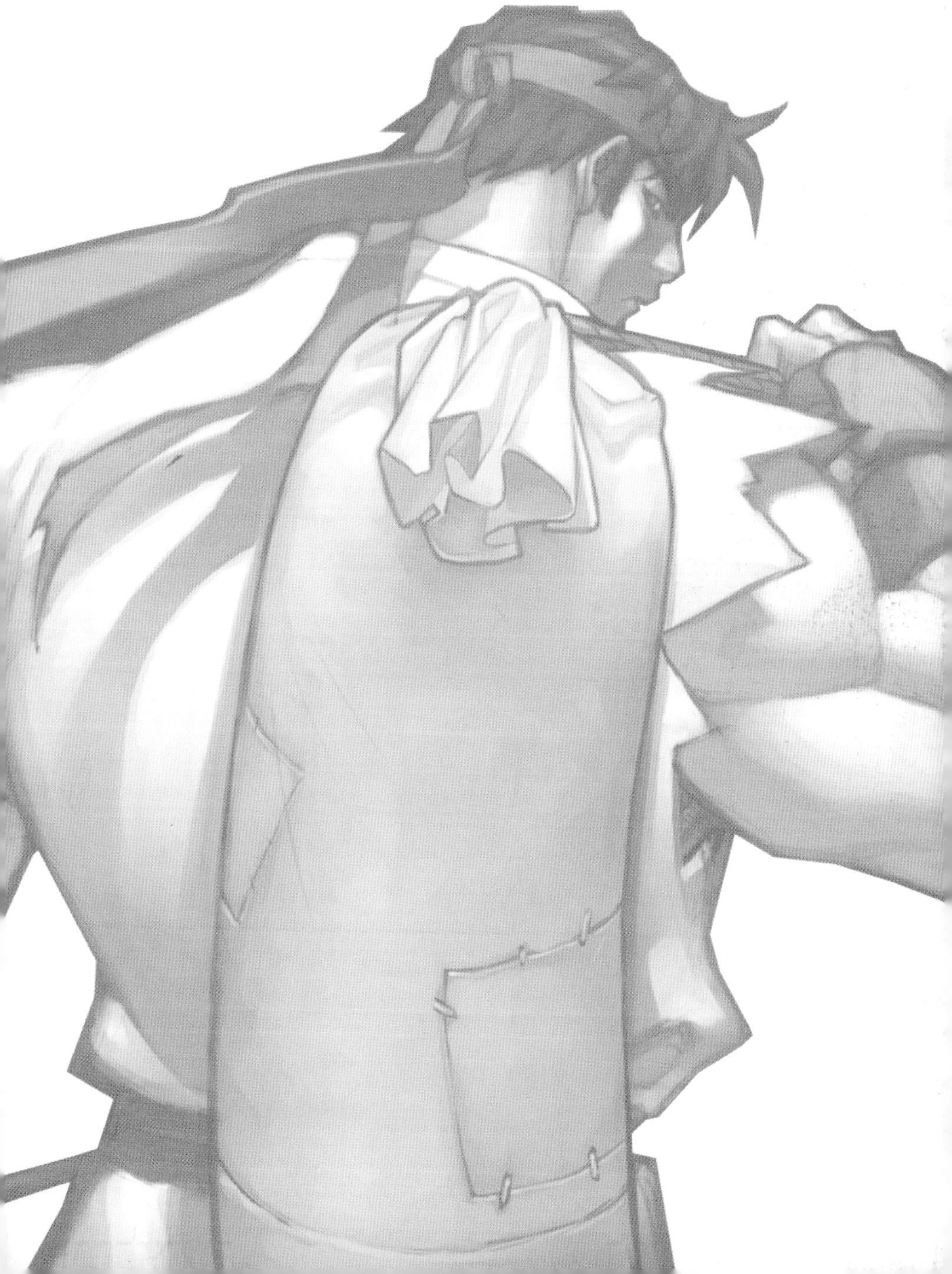

GRAPHIC NOVELS

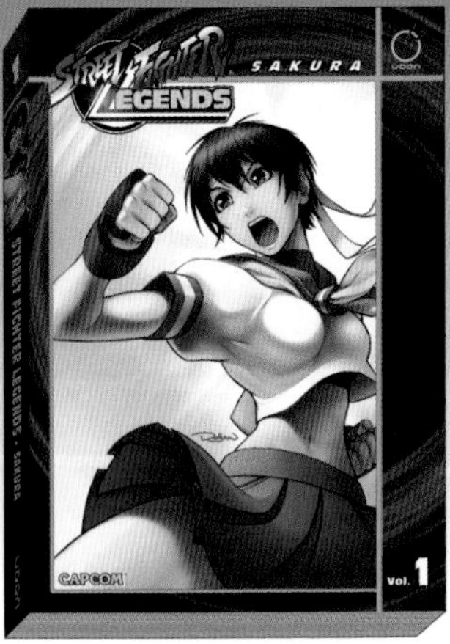
STREET FIGHTER LEGENDS
SAKURA
STREET FIGHTER LEGENDS - SAKURA
CAPCOM
vol. 1

STREET FIGHTER LEGENDS:
SAKURA VOL.1 TP
ISBN: 978-0-978138-64-6

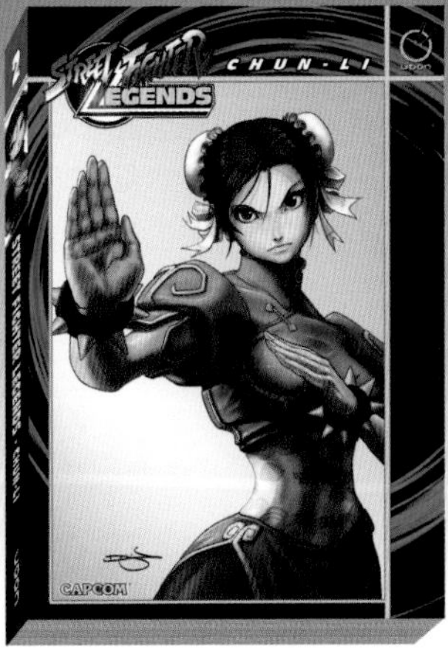
STREET FIGHTER LEGENDS
CHUN-LI
CAPCOM

STREET FIGHTER LEGENDS:
SAKURA VOL.2 TP
ISBN: 978-0-978138-65-3

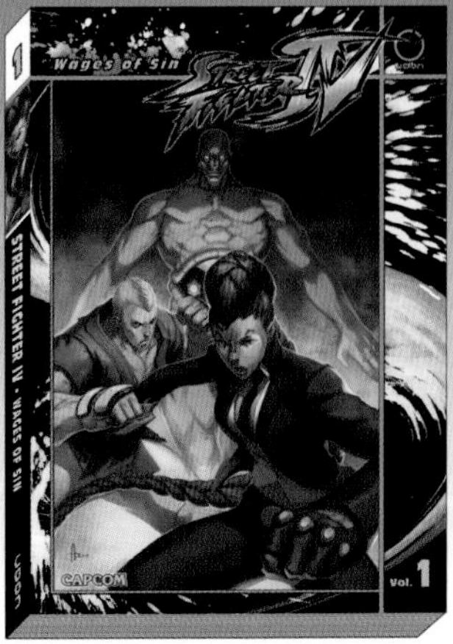
Wages of Sin
STREET FIGHTER IV
STREET FIGHTER IV - WAGES OF SIN
CAPCOM
vol. 1

STREET FIGHTER IV VOL.1
ISBN: 978-1-897376-59-1

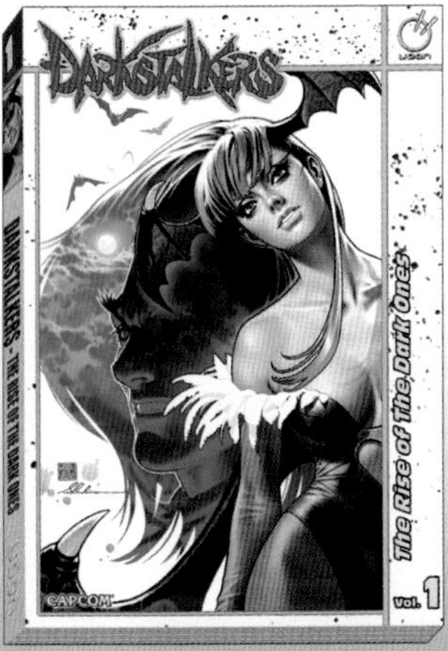
DARKSTALKERS
The Rise of the Dark Ones
CAPCOM
vol. 1

DARKSTALKERS VOL.1
ISBN: 978-0-973865-21-9

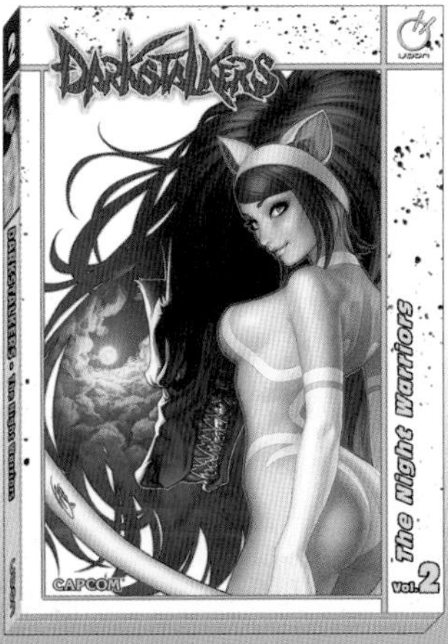
DARKSTALKERS
The Night Warriors
CAPCOM
vol. 2

DARKSTALKERS VOL.2
ISBN: 978-1-926778-02-0

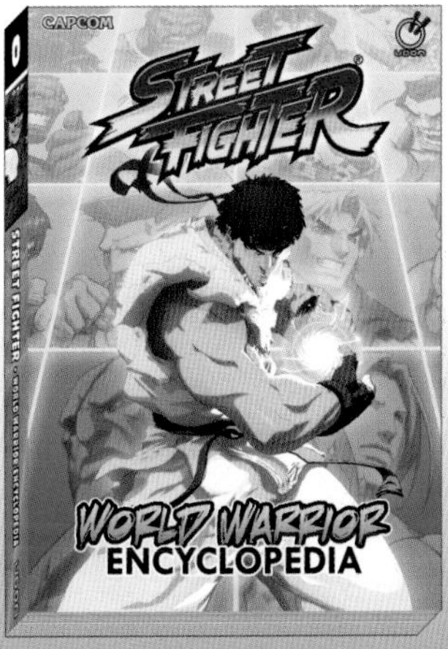
CAPCOM
STREET FIGHTER
WORLD WARRIOR
ENCYCLOPEDIA

STREET FIGHTER:
WORLD WARRIOR ENCYCLOPEDIA
ISBN: 978-1-926778-01-3

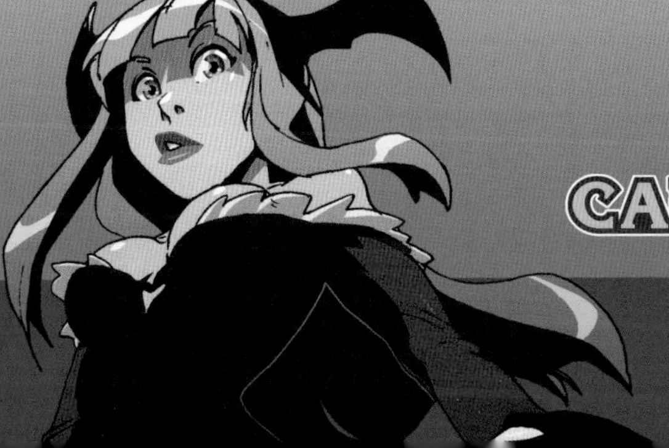

CAPCOM UDON

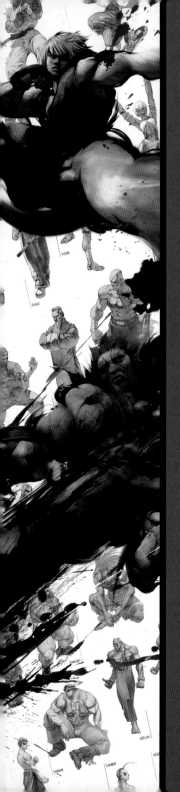
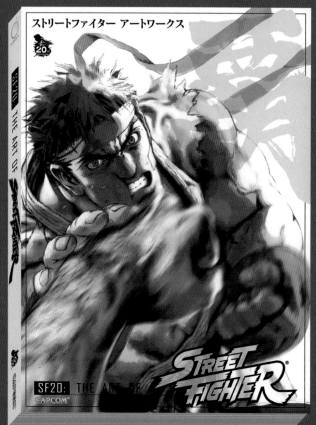